A Grievance Arbitration Guide For Educators

Kenneth H. Ostrander

University of Washington

ALLYN AND BACON, INC.
Boston London Sydney Toronto

To Joyce, Vin, and Vanessa

Library of Congress Cataloging in Publication Data

Ostrander, Kenneth H
    A grievance arbitration guide for educators.

    Bibliography: p.
    Includes index.
    1. Collective labor agreements — United States —
College teachers. 2. Grievance arbitration.
I. Title.
LB2335.885.U6O85   331.88'1137812'0973   80-39961
ISBN 0-205-07280-1

Printed in the United States of America.

Printing number and year (last digits):
10 9 8 7 6 5 4 3 2 1   86 85 84 83 82 81

Contents

Preface

This book is a guide to understanding arbitral interpretations as they are applied to the key issues arising in school grievances. The book's scope is broad, from both a historical and a geographical perspective, encompassing a thorough review of recorded grievance cases. It has been written to meet the needs of educators who want a comprehensive overview of arbitration decisions in schools.

Labor relations specialists, college instructors, union members, and administrators will all find the contents to be of value.

Administrators will be aided in

placing grievances in an appropriate administrative context

identifying significant administrative concerns in grievances

anticipating the possible outcomes of a given grievance.

College and university instructors will receive assistance in

identifying basic issues and procedures

identifying basic concepts

creating a framework for relating specific case examples to students' experiences.

Union members will find themselves

becoming more aware of individual rights under collective agreements

understanding how labor relations specialists think about grievance issues

learning what they need to know to assist labor relations specialists in their own cases.

Labor relations specialists will find valuable information on

interpreting existing contract language
considering new contract language
conducting inservice training programs.

The book will give the reader some useful assistance in understanding legal issues associated with grievance arbitration. Knowledge of the contents of this book will put the reader in a position to make effective use of expert legal counsel, should he or she choose to seek such counsel. However, the reader should not use the book as a substitute for legal counsel, as it is not intended as a source of legal advice.

In keeping with the distinction between this book and a legal treatise on grievance arbitration, the traditional style of footnoting arbitration cases has been modified. In instances where a case is cited more than once within a given chapter, the entire footnote is repeated on a second citing. This convention is used to save the reader the trouble of sorting through all the footnotes to find where a footnote of interest first appeared.

The arbitration reporting services of the Bureau of National Affairs (BNA) and the American Arbitration Association (AAA) were used to identify the cases cited in the footnotes. The reader who is interested in obtaining more information than is provided should consult these services. Using the case identification numbers provided in the footnotes, an interested reader will be able to obtain the complete case. University libraries, particularly law and business school libraries, frequently subscribe to the two arbitration services. In addition, labor relations specialists often subscribe to the services and can be approached for assistance in obtaining more information about a given case. Both BNA and AAA provide extensive indexes to the cases they report.

The treatment of footnoting and other organizational matters reflects the author's intention to make this book meet the needs of the several probable audiences within the education community. The needs of potential readers are quite diverse. For example, the college instructor's objectives in using this book with students will differ from those of a principal who is faced with an employee's grievance and a possible arbitration hearing. The attempt to write a single book that would meet a range of needs made a number of compromises necessary regarding the selection of issues covered, the detail provided, and the technical complexity of the presentation.

The book is organized by critical topics found in negotiated school agreements. Each topic is further subdivided into issues that have been dealt with in grievance arbitration. Chapter 1 places grievance arbitration in the context of collective bargaining activities. Chapter 2 covers pre-arbitration issues concerning disputes over procedures related to arbitration. Chapter 3 focuses on employee discipline and the standard of just cause. Chapter 4 addresses issues concerning the evaluation of teachers. Even though teacher evaluation is a separate topic, it is closely related to the topic in Chapter 5, the termination of nontenured teachers.

Chapter 6 surveys arbitration issues related to seniority. Seniority, in turn, is related to the topic of discrimination in school employment, which is covered in Chapter 7. In Chapter 8, a comprehensive analysis of arbitration cases dealing with working conditions is reported. Chapter 9 reports on arbitration cases that pertain to employee benefits.

CHAPTER

1

Grievance Arbitration in Perspective

Grievance arbitration is an activity that is part of a larger pattern of activities called collective bargaining. Some state legislatures have passed laws permitting public school employees to engage in collective bargaining with employers because they believed that collective bargaining was the most satisfactory way to resolve basic disputes over wages, hours, and conditions of work.[1] The belief in collective bargaining as a means of resolving labor-management disputes has been fostered by the relative success of the National Labor Relations Act (NLRA) in the private sector. The NLRA has been a persuasive model for state legislation and practices in the public sector.

To understand the purpose of grievance arbitration it is necessary to place it in the larger context of collective bargaining as a social mechanism for conflict resolution. In this chapter, the process of transforming conflict into resolutions is viewed from a general systems framework.

CONFLICT RESOLUTION WITHIN A SYSTEMS MODEL

A productive system has three major phases by which one state of affairs is transformed into another more desirable state of affairs.[2] Figure 1-1

1

INPUT ————————► THROUGHPUT ————————►OUTPUT

FIGURE 1-1. *Phases of a Productive System*

depicts the relationships among the three phases of a productive system. The phases are labeled input, throughput, and output.

The same model can be applied to conflict resolution. Figure 1-2 illustrates conflict resolution activities as a productive system. Conflict, the input, is transformed by dialogue, the throughput activity, into outcomes called conflict resolutions, the output.

Conflict between labor and management occurs under two circumstances. The first involves disputes that arise in conjunction with the initial negotiations of a contractual agreement. Such disputes are called interest disputes. The second circumstance involves disputes that are associated with the administration of a contractual agreement. These disputes are termed rights disputes.

In the public sector, three types of dialogue are used to resolve interest disputes: negotiation, mediation, and fact-finding. In negotiation, labor and management sit down as equals and exchange proposals which generally involve wages, hours, and conditions of work. If an impasse develops during negotiation, third parties are usually called upon to assist. Impasse procedures commonly used in the public sector include mediation and fact-finding. Mediation is a form of dialogue in which a third party confers with labor and management, either separately or together. By use of conference techniques, the mediator attempts to move the parties toward a mutually acceptable agreement. The dialogue in fact-finding is established by means of a hearing procedure. The fact-finder meets with labor and management and hears their evidence and arguments to support their particular contract proposals. After the hearing, the fact-finder issues a report containing his or her opinion on the outstanding issues. The fact-finder's findings and opinions are usually not binding.

The tangible manifestation of conflict resolution over interest disputes is a signed contractual agreement between labor and management. The contract is the output of a conflict resolution system involving negotiation and, as needed, third-party intervention.

The type of dialogue most commonly used to resolve rights disputes is grievance arbitration. Grievance arbitration uses a hearing procedure

CONFLICT ————————► DIALOGUE ————————► RESOLUTION
 (Input)   (Throughput)   (Output)

FIGURE 1-2. *Phases of Conflict Resolution*

similar to that found in fact-finding. In grievance arbitration, the issue on the table is usually the union's claim that management has violated one or more of the provisions of the contractual agreement. The output of the arbitration process is the arbitrator's award. The award resolves the conflict, since in most instances the principal parties have agreed to be bound by it.

CONTRACT ADMINISTRATION

The function of arbitration becomes more evident when contract administration activities are analyzed in detail. Like other collective bargaining activities, contract administration can be viewed as a productive system of activities. Figure 1-3 shows that the input phase of contract administration is the contractual agreement. The throughput phase involves a decision analysis, and the output phase is the implementation of a decision.

Figure 1-4 is a detailed illustration of the throughput phase of contract administration. The first two activities — articulating decision options and identifying applicable contract standards — are concurrent activities. That is, they take place roughly within the same time frame.

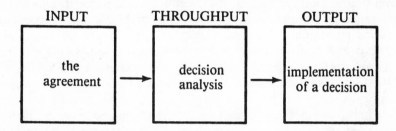

FIGURE 1-3. *Phases of Contract Administration*

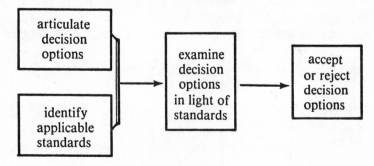

FIGURE 1-4. *Operational Activities Associated with Throughput Phase of Contract Administration*

For example, in a situation where an administrator contemplates taking disciplinary action against an employee, the administrator considers the various forms of discipline that might be used. In addition, the administrator reads the appropriate provisions of the contractual agreement covering disciplinary actions. The next activity is to examine decision options in light of contractual standards associated with employee discipline. An experienced administrator reviews his or her organization's experience in arbitration and the experience of other organizations in order to anticipate how an arbitrator might apply the contractual standard to the present situation. This review is followed by the next throughput activity — accepting or rejecting decision options. Finally, the administrator accepts a decision option that appears to be consistent with contractual standards.

AN ARBITRATOR'S ACTIVITIES

Once an administrator has implemented a decision, any employees affected by the decision are expected to comply with it, whether the effect is positive or negative.[3] After complying, however, an employee can usually grieve the decision if he or she believes that it is not consistent with one or more provisions of the contractual agreement. Should the grievance not be resolved in the early stages of the grievance procedure, binding arbitration is frequently the means selected to resolve an impasse over a rights dispute.[4] When the grievance comes before an arbitrator, it is the arbitrator's primary task to determine if the management's or the union's interpretation of the contractual agreement is appropriate.

In Figure 1-5, the arbitrator's activities are related to the productive system model. During the input phase of the arbitrator's activities, he or she hears the presentation of evidence by management and union representatives regarding their respective interpretations of the contractual agreement. The throughput phase consists of those activities in which the arbitrator exercises his or her judgment with regard to

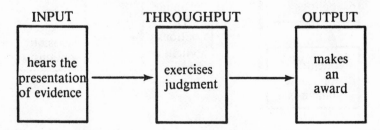

INPUT	THROUGHPUT	OUTPUT
hears the presentation of evidence	exercises judgment	makes an award

FIGURE 1-5. *The Arbitrator as a Productive Unit*

whether or not the grievance will be supported or denied in part or in whole, based upon the hearing record. The output phase involves activities associated with drafting an award and supporting opinion.

Seldom, if ever, is any contractual provision absolutely unambiguous.[5] Contract language usually can be interpreted in a number of ways. The purpose of the arbitrator's award and opinion is to reduce the ambiguity of contract language. The arbitrator must determine which meaning of the language in question best fits the intent of the parties at the time they signed the agreement.

The means by which an arbitrator reduces contractual ambiguity can be classified in five ways:

1. The arbitrator can base the award on the contract language as written, in light of the facts established at the hearing.
2. The arbitrator can draw on past practices, i.e., the actual behavior of the parties acting under the agreement.
3. The arbitrator can rely on good general practice, sometimes referred to as the "law of the shop."
4. The arbitrator can use precedents established by other arbitrators, the courts, and federal regulatory agencies.
5. The arbitrator can initiate a standard of his or her own.[6]

PRINCIPLES OF CONTRACT INTERPRETATION

The grievance arbitrator's first step in resolving contractual ambiguity is to try to base the award on the contractual language as written. In this effort the arbitrator is guided by the following general principles of contract interpretation:

1. The arbitrator should determine and give effect to the mutual intent of the parties.
2. If the arbitrator finds the language of the agreement to be clear and unequivocal, then he or she should not give it a meaning other than that expressed, even if the parties themselves find the language ambiguous.
3. When two interpretations are possible but one is lawful and the other is unlawful, the lawful interpretation should be used.
4. In the absence of anything indicating otherwise, the arbitrator should give words their ordinary and popularly accepted meanings and not some special or unusual meaning.
5. The meaning given to a particular word or phrase should be consistent with intentions expressed in other portions of the

document in order to maintain the integrity of the agreement as a whole.

6. The arbitrator should not make interpretations that would lead to harsh, absurd, or nonsensical results.

7. When the agreement specifically includes something, it is assumed that that which is left unstated is excluded.

8. Where general words follow a listing of specific terms, the general words should be so interpreted as to be consistent with the specific terms.

9. Where there is conflict between specific language and general language, the specific language should govern.

10. Given that there is no evidence to the contrary and the meaning of a term is unclear, the intentions of the parties should be viewed to be the same as those held during the negotiations leading up to the agreement.

11. In the interpretation of an ambiguous agreement, no consideration should be given to compromise offers or to concessions offered by one party and rejected by the other during exchanges that preceded arbitration.

12. The arbitrator should make interpretations that are reasonable and equitable to both parties.[7]

PAST PRACTICE

The current view of collective agreements is that the written contract by itself does not necessarily constitute the whole agreement. The whole agreement includes not only the written contract but also past practices. The phrase "past practice" refers to customs and practices that evolved as a normal reaction to a recurring situation.[8] For a past practice to be part of the whole contract it must be presumed that the parties involved have accepted the practice as a normal and proper response to a given underlying condition.

Whether or not arbitrators are willing to apply past practice when interpreting a contract depends on the relationship between the past practice and the written agreement. The most troublesome application of past practice occurs when the practice is clearly at variance with the contract. Some arbitrators stress that in such situations the written contract should rule. Other arbitrators claim that the past practice should rule when the parties are both fully aware that the past practice is at variance with the written contract. There is agreement among arbitrators that a consistent past practice should rule when the written agreement is silent or ambiguous. However, there also tends to be agreement that no weight should be given to an inconsistent past practice when the written agreement is silent or confusing.[9]

The following list of questions is useful in determining whether or not past practice is likely to be controlling:

1. Is the language of the contract plain and clear?
2. Is the contract silent? If so, is this because the matter has been strictly reserved for management's decision?
3. Does the contract, though not expressly embodying the practice, refer to it and contemplate its continuance?
4. Has the practice been consistently followed in the past?
5. How often has the practice been used?
6. How did it originate?
7. Has the contract been negotiated without repudiating or limiting the practice?
8. Has the practice been clearly enunciated and is it fully understood by both parties?
9. Was there any intention of giving new meaning to the contract through establishing the practice?
10. Does the practice deprive any of the parties of their rights under the law?[10]

SUMMARY

Grievance arbitration is part of an overall system of activities included in collective bargaining. The purpose of grievance arbitration is to resolve disputes between labor and management over the implementation of collective agreements. Disputes over contract administration are called rights disputes.

The grievance arbitrator resolves rights disputes by engaging in a series of activities analogous to a productive system. The input phase occurs when the arbitrator hears the evidence of the parties supporting their respective interpretations of the contract. The throughput phase occurs when the arbitrator exercises judgment in comparing the evidence presented in the hearing to his or her perception of the standard incorporated into the agreement. The output phase involves those activities associated with drafting an award and supporting opinion. In most instances the dispute is resolved when an award is issued, because the parties have contracted themselves to be bound by the arbitrator's decision.

The arbitrator's first effort in interpreting a contractual agreement is to give effect to the written words of the agreement. In accomplishing this task, the arbitrator is guided by standard principles of contract interpretation.

It is generally recognized by arbitrators that the written contract may not express the whole agreement. The whole agreement is usually perceived to include valid past practices. It is common for arbitrators to interpret an ambiguous contract by incorporating documented past practices into the agreement.

NOTES

1. A statement of the intention of state legislatures in passing collective bargaining legislation for educators is usually incorporated into such legislation. See *Government Employee Relations Report*, Reference File 51 (Washington: Bureau of National Affairs).
2. E. J. Miller and A. K. Rice, *Systems of Organization* (London: Tavistock Publications, 1967).
3. Frank Elkouri and Edna Asper Elkouri, *How Arbitration Works* (Washington: Bureau of National Affairs, 1973), p. 154.
4. Bureau of Labor Statistics, *Grievance and Arbitration Procedures in State and Local Agreements*, Bulletin No. 1833 (Washington: Government Printing Office, 1975), p. 4.
5. Paul Prasow and Edward Peters, *Arbitration and Collective Bargaining* (New York: McGraw-Hill Book Company, 1970), p. 50.
6. John W. Teele, "The Thought Processes of the Arbitrator," *The Arbitration Journal* 17:2 (1962): 85–96.
7. An expanded discussion of arbitration principles can be found in Frank Elkouri and Edna Asper Elkouri, *How Arbitration Works* (Washington: Bureau of National Affairs, 1973), pp. 296–320.
8. Richard P. McLaughlin, "Custom and Past Practice in Labor Arbitration," *The Arbitration Journal* 18:4 (1963): 206.
9. Charles T. Doyle, "Past Practice as a Standard in Arbitration," *Personnel* 39:3 (1962): 63–69.
10. Ibid., p. 68.

CHAPTER

2

Pre-arbitration Issues

Successful grievance administration requires that some issues be settled during the initial process of contract negotiations. For example, the question of what constitutes a grievance is usually answered before any given grievance develops. Similarly, the proper sequence of events for processing grievances is usually resolved before grievances occur. How are grievances filed? What time limits must be observed? What is the role of the representative organization? How is the arbitrator to be chosen? These too are issues usually resolved during initial contract negotiations.

CONTRACTUAL DEFINITIONS OF
GRIEVANCE

Contractual definitions of grievance vary in scope. Some definitions of grievance go beyond the usual mandatory negotiation topics of wages, hours, and working conditions. Although the scope of a grievance can differ from the scope of arbitration, frequently what is grievable is also arbitrable. A dispute over the arbitrability of a grievance is at times resolved by inspecting the contractual definition of a grievance.

SAMPLE DEFINITIONS

Some school board negotiators and teacher representatives restrict the definition of grievance to an alleged misinterpretation or misapplication of the terms of the collective bargaining agreement.[1] For example:

> Grievance. A grievance is a claim made by an employee that there has been a violation of a specific provision of this Agreement.
>
> *Des Moines, Iowa, Independent Community School District and the Des Moines Education Association.*[2]

Teachers and other school employees may have grievances in connection with the interpretation and administration of school board policies and directives. Policies and directives are not normally the product of bilateral communications in the same sense that a collective agreement is. Teachers may win consultation rights with regard to school board policies and administrative directives. However, consultation rights normally leave the teacher association or union in an advisory status with regard to the formulation of policies and directives. The basic process of policy making typically remains one of unilateral action on the part of management.

State collective bargaining laws have not generally imposed a duty to bargain all policies. Policies on topics that are not encompassed by the classifications of wages, hours, and conditions of work are within this exclusive purview of school boards. Nevertheless, some school boards have agreed to definitions of grievances which include disputes over the interpretation of policies and directives that are separate from the collective bargaining agreement. For example:

> A claim by a teacher that there has been a violation, misinterpretation or misapplication of any provision of this Agreement or any rule, order or regulation of the Board affecting matters covered by this Agreement may be processed as a grievance as hereinafter provided.
>
> *Board of School Commissioners of the City of Indianapolis, Indiana, and the Indianapolis Education Association.*[3]

Another source of grievances is past practice and custom from which teachers believe they derive some benefits. Should management attempt to alter or stop a desirable practice or custom, teachers or their representatives are likely to feel aggrieved and want the matter corrected. Some contractual definitions of grievance would include past practice and custom. For example:

Grievance means a claim based upon an event or condition which affects the conditions or circumstances under which an employee works, allegedly caused by misinterpretation or inequitable application of written District regulations, rules, and procedures, or District practices and/or the provisions of this Contract.

Seattle School District No. 1 and the Seattle Teachers Association.

Or:

A grievance is a complaint submitted as a grievance involving the work situation, or that there has been a violation, misinterpretation of a practice or policy; or that there has been a violation, misinterpretation, or misapplication of any provision of this Agreement.

Board of Education of Detroit School District and the Detroit Federation of Teachers.[4]

Aggrieved feelings on an employee's part need not be connected with a written document or established practice. Such feelings may grow out of day-to-day interactions among teachers and their supervisors. A teacher's sense of pride, self-respect, or personal standards of fairness may prompt aggrieved feelings given certain interactions with management representatives. Some specialists in labor relations believe that it is good policy to let employees "get things off their chests." Some observers of organizational behavior believe that unresolved aggrieved feelings only fester and cause problems at a later point in time.

The following definition would afford employees an opportunity to use the grievance procedure to air a broad range of grievances involving supervisors whom teachers might consider to be unfair or inequitable.

A grievance is a claim based upon an alleged violation of this Agreement, written District policies, regulations and rules adapted by the Board or unfair and inequitable treatment of an employee by an administrator.

Board of Directors, Tacoma, Washington, and the Tacoma Alliance of Educators.

In an attempt to achieve clarity on the issue of what constitutes a grievance, negotiators have devised definitions that state what is to be included and what is to be excluded. An example is the following definition:

A grievance shall mean a complaint by a member of the bargaining unit that (1) he has been treated unfairly or inequitably under the terms of this

Agreement or (2) there is a violation, misinterpretation, or misapplication of the provisions of this Agreement or of established policy or practice except the term "grievance" shall not apply to:

(1) Any matter for which a method of review is prescribed by law,

(2) Any rule or regulation of the State Board of Education,

(3) Any matter which, according to law, is either beyond the scope of Board authority or limited to action by the Board alone,

(4) A complaint of a non-tenured teacher which arises by reason of his not being re-employed, however such teacher may request a hearing before the Board, or

(5) A complaint by a teacher occasioned by appointment to or lack of appointment to, retention in or lack of retention in, any position for which tenure is either not possible or not required.

Board of Education of Wilmington, Delaware, and the Wilmington Federation of Teachers.[5]

"Arbitrability" is a term used to refer to a dispute over jurisdiction of an arbitrator. In such disputes, a school board typically takes the position that the collective bargaining agreement does not give an arbitrator jurisdiction over a dispute between the school board and the teacher association or union. The teachers typically assert that the arbitrator does have jurisdiction.

In the parlance of arbitration, an issue over the arbitrability of a grievance is a threshold issue. In other words, the issue of the arbitrability of a grievance is usually settled by the arbitrator before he or she addresses the merits of the issue.

In the private sector, it has become the customary practice to submit issues of arbitrability to an arbitrator at the same time as the grievance issue is submitted. The same practice is being adopted by the education sector.[6]

Contractual definitions of grievance have been used by school boards and teachers to support or refute the arbitrability of a grievance. Both parties have had varying success in convincing arbitrators that the contractual definition of grievance excluded or included the particular grievances brought to arbitration.[7]

GRIEVANCE PROCEDURES

When a teacher has a grievance, there are a number of issues involved in determining an acceptable procedure for seeking a remedy. Which administrator should the teacher approach? Does one administrative level speak for all? How long can a grievant take before seeking a remedy? How long must the grievant wait for administrative action?

What role shall the union or association play? Does the union or association have a stake in grievances separate from that of the grievant? The resolution of procedural issues is sought during the initial negotiation of the collective bargaining agreement.

A GENERAL GRIEVANCE PROCEDURE

Grievance procedures normally have two phases, an informal and a formal phase. The informal phase precedes the formal one. It usually consists of a meeting between the teacher and his or her immediate supervisor. If the grievance is not resolved to the teacher's satisfaction, he or she may initiate the formal phase by filing a grievance form. The formal phase consists of a number of appeal levels, which typically follow the progression of managerial authority in the school district. The number of possible appeal levels varies. Usually there are no fewer than three nor more than five. When binding arbitration is included in a grievance procedure, it is the last step in the formal phase.

The following is an example of a grievance procedure of the general type we have been describing. The informal phase procedure is outlined thus:

> Within thirty (30) school days of the time a violation arises, or when he could reasonably have known of the violation, the employee will present the grievance to the person alleged by the grievant to have violated, misinterpreted, or misapplied the provision(s) of this agreement. Within five (5) school days after presentation of the grievance, the supervisor shall give his answer orally to the employee.

The formal phase procedure is then defined:

> Step 1. Within five (5) school days of the oral answer, if the grievance is not resolved, it shall be reduced to writing, signed by the grievant, and presented to the same person referred to in the informal step. The "Statement of Grievance" shall name the employee involved, shall state the facts giving rise to the grievance, shall identify by appropriate reference the provisions of this Agreement alleged to be violated, shall state the contention of the employee (and of the Association) with respect to those provisions, and shall indicate the specific relief requested. If the grievant so desires, he shall have the right to have authorized representation of the Association present at any discussions of the formal grievance with the supervisor and at subsequent steps in the processing of the grievance. Within five (5) school days after receiving the grievance, the recipient of the grievance shall communicate his answer in writing to the grievant (and the Association).

Step 2. Within ten (10) school days of receipt of the written answer, if the grievance is not resolved, the grievant may file the same written grievance with the Superintendent of Schools or his designee. Within five (5) school days of the receipt of the written grievance, the Superintendent or his designee, and those he may further name, shall meet with the grievant (and the AASAS representative) for a full review of all of the facts and contentions involved, and render a written decision thereon within ten (10) school days of such meeting.

Proceeding to Step 3 requires approval of the AASAS Executive Board.

Step 3. If the employee and AASAS are dissatisfied with such decision, they may request arbitration of the dispute as follows:

(1) The request for arbitration must be made in writing, addressed to the Superintendent or his designee, and must be made within fifteen (15) school days after the rendering of the decision in Step 2.

(2) The question in the dispute shall then be referred to an arbitrator selected by the parties from a panel or panels submitted by the American Arbitration Association, in accordance with the rules of the American Arbitration Association provided that the parties may mutually agree on a different method of selecting an arbitrator than that herein set forth . . .

Arlington, Virginia, School Board and the Arlington Association of School Administrators and Supervisors.[8]

Figure 2-1 is a flowchart of the grievance procedure just described.

PROCEDURAL VARIATIONS

There are hundreds of school districts negotiating grievance procedures. It cannot be expected that any one set of procedures will satisfy all needs.

Some districts have a grievance committee composed of teacher representatives and administrative representatives. Recommendations of bipartisan committees are usually subjected to further review by managerial authority. Depending on the sequence of the committee's action in the grievance procedure, the reviewing authority may be the superintendent or the school board. Here is an example of provisions that specify the reviewing authority:

Fourth Step — If the grievance is not adjusted in a manner satisfactory to the MTEA or the teacher, within ten (10) working days of the written disposition of the Superintendent, it may be presented to the Rules and Complaints Committee for a hearing and decision within forty-five (45) working days, unless both parties mutually agree to extend or shorten the time limits. If the Rules and Complaints Committee declares against the

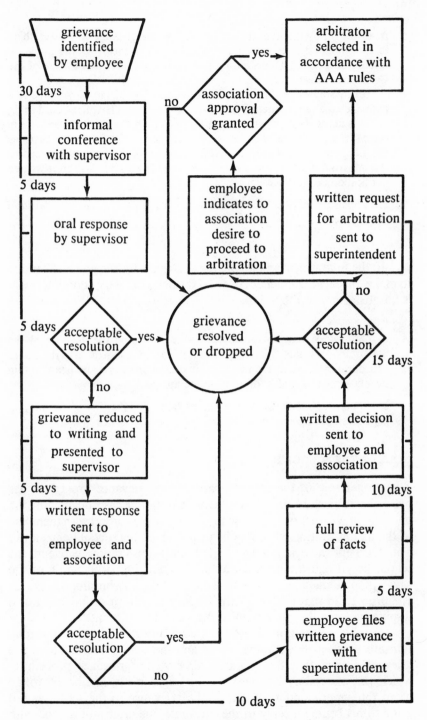

FIGURE 2-1. *Diagram of a General Grievance Procedure*

relief sought by the grievant or the MTEA, the grievant may be certified to the impartial referee by the MTEA in accordance with the impartial referee procedure, within ten (10) working days after notification of the Committee's decision.

Fifth Step — In the event the Rules and Complaints Committee recommends the relief sought by the grievant or the MTEA, the Board shall, at the next regularly scheduled meeting, pass upon the grievance and notify the MTEA in writing of its decision. In the event the full Board reverses the Committee's decision, the MTEA shall have the right to proceed to the impartial referee procedure within ten (10) working days after written notification of their decision.

Milwaukee Board of School Directors and the Milwaukee Teacher Education Association.[9]

In the following example, provision is made for the grievant's union to make appeals to the school board if the decision of the superintendent is unsatisfactory to the union.

Step 4. Within ten school days after receiving the decision of the Superintendent, the Union may appeal the decision in writing to the Board of Education, which shall give the Union opportunity to be heard within twenty school days after delivery of the appeal.

The Board of Education of the School District of the City of Detroit and the Detroit Federation of Teachers.[10]

ROLE OF THE SCHOOL BOARD

The proper role of the school board in the grievance procedure has been the subject of arbitration. One arbitration case dealt with the question of whether or not the school board could consult with members of the administration when a grievance reached the school board level. The teachers' association contended that consultation between the school board and the administration, without the participation of the association, denied the grievant a fair hearing. Arbitrator David G. Heilbrun ruled that it was not the board's role to sit in judgment of a dispute between its own administration and the grievant.[11]

Another arbitration case presented a different aspect of the relationship between the administration and the school board. There the grievant argued that the confidentiality of the grievance procedure, which was assured by a provision in the agreement, had been broken when the superintendent disclosed the grievance to the school board prior to his issuing a reply to the grievant. The arbitrator agreed with the grievant.[12,13]

FILING ACTION

Management does not know that an employee has a grievance until it is told. Most collective bargaining agreements provide for some standard means of informing management. The typical grievance is filed first with the grievant's immediate supervisor. However, some school boards and teacher representatives have negotiated procedures for "advanced step" filing.

Not all grievances are held by just a single individual. Whether or not group grievances can be filed is at times negotiated by the parties.

STANDARD GRIEVANCE FORMS

The formal phase of the grievance procedure is initiated by the grievant's filing a written statement. Many agreements merely indicate that a written statement will be filed without spelling out the details of the statement.[14] However, a number of other agreements are quite explicit about the contents of the grievant's written statement. The following exemplifies a general procedure:

> . . . the form for filing the grievance shall be designed by the Association and subject to the approval of the Employer, the written grievance shall state the nature of the grievance, shall note the specific clause or clauses of the Agreement, and shall state the remedy requested . . .
>
> *Des Moines, Iowa, Independent Community School District and the Des Moines Education Association.*[15]

The next example shows a more specific provision:

> . . . The "Statement of Grievance" shall name the employee involved, shall state the facts giving rise to the grievance, shall identify by appropriate reference the provisions of this Agreement alleged to be violated, shall state the contention of the employee (and of the Association) with respect to those provisions, and shall indicate the specific relief requested . . .
>
> *Arlington, Virginia, School Board and the Arlington Association of School Administrators and Supervisors.*[16]

Even though bargaining agreements call for a written statement, it is not always possible for the parties to agree on the issue that is being raised. Inability to agree on the issue probably contributes to a failure to find a resolution to the dispute. Frequently the problem of identifying the issue in explicit terms falls on the shoulders of the arbitrator.

Arbitrators have indicated that when the parties themselves are unable to agree to some explicit statement about the grievance being arbitrated, the grievance record itself is one of the arbitrator's guides to identifying the issue.[17]

GROUP GRIEVANCES

Grievance procedures are usually written as though the negotiating parties assumed the procedures applied to individual grievants exclusively. Some procedures attempt to provide more flexibility by permitting group grievances, sometimes referred to as class grievances or policy grievances. For example:

> If, in the judgment of the Association, a grievance affects a group or class of teachers, and teachers from two or more buildings petition the Association, the Association may submit such grievances in writing to the Superintendent or his designee directly and the processing of such grievances shall be commenced at Step Two of the formal grievance procedure.
>
> *Board of School Commissioners of the City of Indianapolis, Indiana, and the Indianapolis Education Association.*[18]

It is typical to use some modification of the basic grievance procedure for group grievances.[19] School boards have not successfully argued against the arbitrability of group grievances at a level normally used for individual grievances.[20] Arbitrators have tended to resolve any ambiguities regarding the use of group grievances in favor of their use. Favorable rulings have followed a showing that teacher representatives had cause to believe that conditions or actions being grieved affected a substantial number of teachers.[21] When persuasive evidence has been presented, arbitrators have expressed the opinion that failure to permit a group grievance would promote disharmony between the parties.[22]

In granting favorable rulings, arbitrators who have handled this issue in school settings have reasoned it is more costly and time-consuming to require each teacher to file a separate grievance. This passage illustrates the reasoning used:

> . . . it was not inappropriate for the Association to raise the issues herein in a grievance on behalf of the faculty generally. The Association has been presented with a number of complaints from a number of teachers, all involving basically the same issues. To grieve each of such complaints individually would have been burdensome, both in terms of time and money, on both the Board and Association. It would have been unnecessary and wasteful to have a number of individual meetings where the gist of each grievance and alleged contract violation was identical. By joining all such complaints into one grievance, on the other hand, similar or identical

issues can be decided in one hearing and proceeding, thus permitting the expeditious, efficient and inexpensive handling of the matter . . .[23]

ADVANCED STEP FILING

One intent of grievance procedures is to settle grievances at the lowest possible level. In keeping with this intent, most grievance procedures begin with an informal meeting between the grievant and his or her supervisor. To the extent that the supervisor has been involved in making some judgment which led to the grievance, the meeting between the two would seem to be useful to both. In those cases where some higher authority made a decision that precipitated the grievance, meetings between the grievant and the immediate supervisor are not necessarily productive in terms of resolving the grievance. In order to accommodate such situations, some agreements provide for filing the grievance at an advanced step in the procedure.[24]

TIME LIMITATIONS

Time limitations in grievance procedures most frequently become an issue in arbitration when management uses a grievant's allegedly untimely filing as a basis for challenging the arbitrability of the grievance. A study of arbitral rulings reveals that the direction a particular ruling takes often depends on the existence of certain critical conditions or circumstances.

Among the major factors entering into arbitrators' judgments are (1) the absence of contractual time limits, (2) the clarity of time limits, (3) the reasonableness of time limits in light of circumstances, (4) the existence of timely objections to the filing of a grievance, (5) the extent to which the grievant was aware that some action or condition existed which might have warranted a grievance, and (6) whether the action or condition being grieved constituted a continuing violation of the grievant's rights. The following sections discuss each of the six major factors in turn.

ABSENCE OF CONTRACTUAL TIME LIMITS

If the collective bargaining agreement does not specify any time limits for filing grievances, arbitrators have been willing to hear a grievance case on its merits. In some instances the delay in filing has been unusually long. For example, a teacher waited three years before grieving the fact that a salary given to a newly hired teacher was significantly higher than her own. The arbitrator noted that no time limits were specified in the contract nor would there be any prejudice to the school board in having the case heard.[25]

In another case, the contract specified a sixty-working-day time limit to the start of the informal procedure. The contract did not specify any time limits for initiating the formal phase of the grievance procedure. The school board argued that a sixty-working-day time limit for the start of the formal phase was implied by the contract. The arbitrator disagreed, stating that time limits would need to be in writing for him to observe them.[26]

In still another case, a group of teachers who served as chaperones waited several months before filing a grievance seeking compensation. The school board sought to bar the grievance, stating that the teachers had waited too long. The arbitrator disagreed with the school board because nowhere in the agreement was there a direct statement related to timeliness.[27]

The final example involves a case where the teachers' federation indicated to the superintendent that it was about to file a demand for arbitration, but did not do so until twenty-eight days later. The arbitrator held that the issue over a letter of reprimand was arbitrable despite management's objections about the timeliness of the filing. The arbitrator noted that the contract did not contain any time limits for filing a demand for arbitration. He also noted that the rights of management had not been prejudicially affected by the delayed filing.[28]

CLARITY OF TIME LIMITS

If an agreement does contain clear time limits for filing and prosecuting grievances, failure to observe them will generally result in the arbitrator's dismissal of the grievance if the failure is protested by management. An arbitrator dismissed a grievance over the placement of a new full-time teacher on the salary schedule and rejected the union's argument that the grievance was "continuous." Rejection of the grievance was based on the teacher's failure to file her grievance within the twenty-day time limit of discovery that her salary would be adjusted downward (because of her role in a strike during the previous year when she was a reserve teacher).[29]

Another arbitrator made a similar ruling when a teachers' union held that it had not exceeded the time limit for filing a grievance because of an understanding with the school board. The arbitrator held that the union had the burden of showing factual proof of an understanding waiving the time limit. Since the union was unable to do so, the grievance was dismissed.[30]

Another grievance was ruled to be untimely and unarbitrable because the grievant's contract specifically stated that an appeal of a level two decision had to be made at the next regularly scheduled board meeting. The grievant had waited until the second board meeting. In rejecting the arbitrability of the grievance, the arbitrator noted that the parties had historically placed great importance on observation of time limitations.[31,32]

REASONABLENESS OF TIME LIMITS

Even if the time limitations are clear, late filing will not always result in dismissal of a grievance. If the circumstances are such that the arbitrator finds it unreasonable to require strict compliance with the time limits, he or she may rule the grievance arbitrable. For example, in one school district the grievant was offered a principalship when his position of assistant to the superintendent was abolished. The grievant filed a claim for return of his position in Superior Court, instead of using the grievance procedure as a forum for his complaint. By the time the court directed him to use the grievance procedure, the contractual time limits for filing a complaint had been exceeded by more than a year. The arbitrator ruled that the grievant, who had thirty-eight years of service, should not be barred from protecting his employment rights through arbitration because of his initial error in selecting the court as a forum.[33]

In another school district, a school board did not renew the contract of a teacher. In the course of using the grievance procedure, the teacher failed to observe the time limits for notifying the school board of her appointment choice to the arbitration panel. The neutral member of the panel later ruled that the teacher's untimely notice did not create any evidence of harm or disadvantage to the board. The arbitrator thought it would be inequitable to bar the teacher from arbitration.[34]

In Waverly, Michigan, the collective bargaining agreement stated that application for salary adjustment had to be submitted before September 1. However, since the school was not open on September 1, a teacher seeking an advancement on the salary scale based upon recently completed college work was unable to meet the grievance time limitation, although she had informed school authorities about her new academic attainment by mail prior to September 1. The arbitrator ruled that it would be an unreasonable interpretation of the agreement to hold that time limits were operative while the school buildings were closed.[35,36]

EXISTENCE OF TIMELY OBJECTIONS TO FILING

Arbitrators may determine that time limitations have been waived by the parties if clear and timely objections were not made when time limits were violated. One arbitrator held that a grievance was arbitrable, despite the lack of compliance with the filing limit, in part because management had not raised objections to the timeliness of the grievance until the arbitration hearing.[37] Another arbitrator ruled that a board had waived timeliness by not making timeliness an issue during the first steps taken by the grievant.[38,39]

In apparent exception to the arbitration guide discussed here, one arbitrator supported management, stating that failure of management to raise the issue of timely grievance filing in the early steps did not prevent management from raising the issue for the first time at the arbitration hearing.[40]

EXTENT OF GRIEVANT'S AWARENESS

School boards have been unsuccessful in persuading arbitrators that a grievance should commence with oral notice of a grievable action,[41] written notice,[42] or the scheduling of a school board meeting during which a grievable action was decided.[43]

Arbitrators have tended to hold that a grievable action commences with the employee's first experiencing of the action.[44] Thus, in the instance of salary deductions, the occurrence of a grievable action took place when the teachers actually received their checks and noted the deductions.[45,46] Similarly, in the instance of a dismissal, for purposes of determining timeliness of filing the grievable action was the actual dismissal and not a verbal notice of intention to dismiss.[47]

In collective bargaining agreements where occurrence of a grievance is expressed in terms of employee's awareness of grievable action or circumstances,[48] awareness has been interpreted to include awareness of all circumstances associated with a grievable action[49] and awareness of all alternative courses of action available to the grievant.[50]

DETERMINATION OF CONTINUING VIOLATION OF
GRIEVANT'S RIGHTS

Arbitrators have held that continuing violations of an agreement provide a continuing basis for grievances. For example, an employee had been employed on a day-to-day basis for four years to instruct in a federally funded adult education program. The employee brought a grievance demanding that she be included in the bargaining unit. The school board contested the arbitrability of the grievance for lack of timely filing. The arbitrator ruled that the grievance was of a continuing nature, since the alleged violation, exclusion from the bargaining unit, occurred each day of employment.[51]

The following issues have been judged by arbitrators to be the basis for continuing grievances:

1. insurance coverage[52]
2. salary credit for a law degree[53]

3. reappointment of counselor to former counseling position[54]
4. issuance of regular teaching contract[55]
5. negotiation of change in evaluation form[56]
6. assignment of extra duties[57]
7. use of non-building personnel to evaluate teachers[58]
8. reinstatement of substitute teaching pool[59]
9. use of teacher aides for instructional purposes[60]
10. pay for noncontractual assignment.[61]

In some cases of continuing grievances, arbitrators have limited the extent of recoverable benefits or other compensations a grievant could claim.[62]

ROLE OF THE REPRESENTATIVE ORGANIZATION

Employee organizations have a stake in the use and outcomes of grievances. Approximately twenty-three percent of teacher-negotiated agreements specify that the teacher organization has a right to attend grievance meetings. The same number of agreements make reference to using teacher organization grievance committees. Twenty-three percent of negotiated agreements also state that the teacher organization may initiate grievances as an organization.[63,64]

As in the private sector, a significant issue in schools is what level of the grievance procedure is appropriate for the representative organization.[65] Management tends to take the position that members of the teacher organization should not be involved in the informal phase of the grievance procedure. It is thought that better relationships will develop between the supervisor and employee if the association or union representative is not present during the first meeting. Management spokespeople argue that the presence of association or union representatives escalates the seriousness of the grievance.

Employee organizations have claimed that early involvement is beneficial to the employee because of the moral support gained from the presence of the representative. Associations and unions contend that a timid employee will not push a grievance even though the grievance may have merit. Associations and union representatives have also claimed that their presence brings about a more uniform application of the agreement.[66] In addition, teacher organizations have sought to be present at meetings between individual teachers and management when they believed that the status of the individual teacher was jeopardized.[67]

Not only do teacher organizations seek to protect the interests of

their individual members through involvement of organization representatives, they also seek to protect and promote the interests of the
organization itself by filing separate grievances. Teacher organizations
have met with mixed success in pressing their perceived right to file
organizational grievances.[68]

SELECTION OF AN ARBITRATOR

Approximately ninety-three percent of grievance procedures in schools
utilizing arbitration involve the services of an outside agency. In fifty-
five percent of the cases, the American Arbitration Association has
been named. In thirty-eight percent, a state or local agency is used to
find an arbitrator.[69]

The following grievance provision illustrates how an outside agency
helps the parties in locating an acceptable arbitrator.

> Level Four — If TAAAC finds the Superintendent's decision not accept-
> able, it shall within ten school days notify the Board whether or not the
> grievance is to be submitted to advisory arbitration. If so, both parties shall
> promptly request the American Arbitration Association to submit to each
> party a list of persons skilled in arbitration in education matters. Within
> seven days each party shall cross off any names to which it objects, number
> the remaining names in order of preference and return the list to the
> American Arbitration Association. If a party does not return the list within
> the time specified, all persons named shall be deemed acceptable.
>
> From among the persons who have been approved on both lists, and
> in accordance with the designated order of mutual preference, the Amer-
> ican Arbitration Association shall invite the acceptance of an arbitrator.
> If either of the parties fails to accept any persons named, or if those named
> decline or are unable to act, or if for any other reason an appointment
> cannot be made from such a list of names, a second list of seven names
> shall be requested.
>
> The parties shall strike names alternately until only one name remains.
> That person shall be designated arbitrator . . .
>
> *Board of Education of Anne Arundel County, Maryland, and the Teachers
> Association of Anne Arundel County.*[70]

RULES OF THE AMERICAN ARBITRATION
ASSOCIATION

It is presumed that parties who elect to use the services of the American
Arbitration Association bind themselves by the rules of the Association.
The rules of the Association have been worked out over a period of
time since the Association's inception in 1928. The rules are intended

to serve as a guide to the parties and the administering official of the American Arbitration Association should disputes arise on the following issues.

What:

is to be arbitrated?
are the duties and obligations of each party?

How:

is arbitration initiated?
are arbitrators appointed and vacancies filled?
are time and place for hearings fixed?
are hearings opened? Closed? Reopened?
are costs controlled?

When:

are arbitrators appointed?
must hearings begin?
must award be rendered?

Where:

are notice, documents, and correspondence to be sent?
is the award to be delivered?
shall the hearing be held?

Who:

administers the arbitration?
keeps records and makes technical preparations?
appoints the arbitrator if the parties cannot agree?
fills vacancies on arbitration boards when necessary?
grants adjournments?

SUMMARY

Arbitration is normally used voluntarily at the option of the negotiating parties. On any given grievance, however, management may differ with the grievant over access to arbitration. One focus of dispute can be the definition of a grievance. A grievance is typically defined as an alleged misinterpretation and/or misapplication of the collective bargaining agreement. In some agreements, the definition is broadened to include the misinterpretation and/or misapplication of rules, regulations, policies and practices of school authorities. Management can at times take the position that the grievance does not fall within the contractual definition of a grievance and, therefore, is not arbitrable. Custom and practice within the private sector, which is being followed in the education sector, has left questions of arbitrability up to the arbitrator.

Another source of dispute over arbitration centers on the issue of the timeliness of grievance filing. Most grievance procedures include mention of time limits for the initial filing and progression of a grievance through the grievance procedure. Deviation from stated time limits can give management cause to contest the arbitrability of the grievance. Over the years, arbitrators have tended to handle the issue of timeliness in similar ways, given similar conditions and circumstances.

Other issues that arise at the time of negotiation are related to the role of the representative organization and the determination of how an arbitrator is to be chosen. Disputes over the role of the representative organization are of two major types. One is concerned with the appropriate level in the grievance procedure for association or union representatives to assist the grievant in meetings with school authorities. Management tends not to want representatives present during the initial informal meeting. However, associations and unions usually want to start the representation process as early as possible in the grievance procedure. The other type of major representation dispute is concerned with the right of an association or union to file a grievance as an organization. Closely associated with the right to file an organization grievance is the right to file group grievances. Disputes over organization and group grievances occur because most grievance procedures are written as though they were intended to be used by individual grievants. Thus, unless the negotiating parties make specific provision in their agreements, the initiation of organization and/or group grievances may generate a dispute over the arbitrability of these types of grievances.

Finally, the selection of an arbitrator can be the source of employee-management disputes. Most collective bargaining agreements tend to avert disputes in the area of arbitrator selection by utilizing the services of an outside agency. The American Arbitration Association and state public employment relations boards are the agencies most frequently used. The American Arbitration Association and some of the more experienced state agencies have developed rules which guide all parties in the selection and use of an arbitrator.

NOTES

1. Some school board consultants tend to stress the necessity of restricting grievances to misinterpretations and misapplications of the terms of the agreement. See Richard G. Neal, *Grievance and Grievance Arbitration in Public Education* ERIC ED 063 657 (Washington: Educational Service Bureau, 1971), p. 6. Teacher advocates seek broad definitions of grievance. See *Grievance Administration* (Washington: National Education Association, 1971), p. 15.
2. *Government Employee Relations Report,* No. 653 (Washington: Bureau of National Affairs, 1976), p. X-8.
3. *Government Employee Relations Report,* No. 631 (Washington: Bureau of National Affairs, 1975), p. X-4.
4. *Government Employee Relations Report,* Reference File 81, RF-116 (Washington: Bureau of National Affairs, 1976), p. 1022.
5. *Government Employee Relations Report,* No. 593 (Washington: Bureau of National Affairs, 1975), p. X-2.
6. For a discussion of the arbitrability issue in the schools, see W. Frank Masters, "The Arbitrability Issue in Michigan School Disputes," *The Arbitration Journal,* 28:2 (1973): 119–31. Also see Frank Elkouri and Edna Asper Elkouri, *How Arbitration Works* (Washington: Bureau of National Affairs, 1973), pp. 169–80.
7. See *Gresham (Oregon) Grade School District No. 4,* 80 AIS 11, Carlton J. Snow, Arbitrator; *Maine School Administrative District No. 1,* 80 AIS 6, Harry B. Purcell, Arbitrator; *San Francisco (California) Unified School District,* 72 AIS 18, Herman M. Levy, Arbitrator; *Yonkers (New York) Board of Education,* 69 AIS 7, Daniel G. Collins, Arbitrator; *Alpena (Michigan) Board of Education,* 68 AIS 19, James T. Dunne, Arbitrator; *New Carlisle-Bethel (Ohio) Board of Education,* 64 AIS 16, Richard I. Bloch, Arbitrator; *Gates Chili (New York) Central School District,* 61 AIS 15, Daniel C. Williams, Arbitrator; *Aberdeen (Washington) School District No. 5,* 58 AIS 9, J. B. Gillingham, Arbitrator; *Penfield (New York) Central School,* 55 AIS 8, Elizabeth B. Croft, Arbitrator.
8. *Government Employee Relations Report,* No. 657 (Washington: Bureau of National Affairs, 1976), p. X-6.
9. Ibid.
10. *Government Employee Relations Report,* Reference File 81, RF-116 (Washington: Bureau of National Affairs, 1976), p. 1001.
11. *Clawson (Michigan) Board of Education,* 17 AIS 3, David G. Heilbrun, Arbitrator.
12. *Belleville (New York) Board of Education,* 10 AIS 18, Henry Schuman, Arbitrator.
13. For a discussion of a management consultant view of school board involvement in the grievance procedure, see Richard G. Neal, *Grievance and Grievance Arbitration in Public Education* ERIC ED 063 657 (Washington: Educational Service Bureau, 1971), p. 23.
14. See *Government Employee Relations Report,* No. 574 (Washington: Bureau

of National Affairs, 1974), p. X-16; *Government Employee Relations Report*, No. 593 (Washington: Bureau of National Affairs, 1975), p. X-12; and *Government Employee Relations Report*, No. 622 (Washington: Bureau of National Affairs, 1975), p. X-2.

15. *Government Employee Relations Report*, No. 653 (Washington: Bureau of National Affairs, 1976), p. X-8.

16. *Government Employee Relations Report*, No. 657 (Washington: Bureau of National Affairs, 1976), p. X-6.

17. For a more detailed discussion of the importance of the grievance record to arbitration, see Benjamin Aaron, "Some Procedural Problems in Arbitration," *Vanderbilt Law Review* 10:4 (1957): 733–48; Byron R. Abernethy, "An Arbitrator Speaks to the Parties on Presentation of a Case," *The Arbitration Journal* 12:1 (1957): 3–13; Robert L. Howard, "Informing the Arbitrator," *Vanderbilt Law Review* 10:4 (1957): 771–87.

18. *Government Employee Relations Report*, No. 631 (Washington: Bureau of National Affairs, 1975), p. X-5.

19. See *Government Employee Relations Report*, No. 657 (Washington: Bureau of National Affairs, 1976), p. X-7; *Government Employee Relations Report*, No. 622 (Washington: Bureau of National Affairs, 1975), p. X-3; *Government Employee Relations Report*, No. 616 (Washington: Bureau of National Affairs, 1975), p. X-4.

20. *Rensselaer (New York) City School District*, 31 AIS 24, Irving R. Markowitz, Arbitrator.

21. *Gresham (Oregon) Grade School District No. 4*, 80 AIS 11, Carlton J. Snow, Arbitrator. Also see *Lake Shore Public Schools*, 58 LA 1135, James R. McCormick, Arbitrator.

22. *Columbus (Ohio) Board of Education*, 73 AIS 10, Clair V. Duff, Arbitrator.

23. *Fort Wayne Community Schools*, 61 LA 1159, 1163, Lawrence F. Doppelt, Arbitrator.

24. *Government Employee Relations Report*, No. 593 (Washington: Bureau of National Affairs, 1975), p. X-13; *Government Employee Relations Report*, Reference File 81, RF-116 (Washington: Bureau of National Affairs, 1976), p. 1023.

25. *Middlesex (New Jersey) County College*, 56 AIS 9, Jonas Aarons, Arbitrator.

26. *Kasson-Mantorville (Minnesota) Schools*, 60 AIS 11, James L. Hetland, Jr., Arbitrator.

27. *Niagara Falls (New York) Board of Education*, 55 AIS 9, Philip Ross, Arbitrator.

28. *Massapequa (New York) Board of Education*, 21 AIS 4, Daniel G. Collins, Arbitrator.

29. *Special School District No. 1 (Minnesota)*, 22 AIS 2, George Jacobs, Arbitrator.

30. *West Haven (Connecticut) Board of Education*, 23 AIS 13, Connecticut State Board of Mediation and Arbitration.

31. *Corunna (Michigan) Board of Education*, 63 AIS 9, Howard A. Cole, Arbitrator.

32. See also *Camden County (New Jersey) College*, 66 AIS 22, Jonas Aarons,

Arbitrator; *Braintree (Massachusetts) School Committee*, 49 AIS 17, Tim Bornstein, Arbitrator; *Board of Cooperative Educational Services (Putnam and Westchester Counties, New York)*, 49 AIS 11, Jonas Aarons, Arbitrator; *West Haven (Connecticut) Board of Education*, 31 AIS 13, Connecticut State Board of Mediation and Arbitration.

33. *New Haven (Connecticut) Board of Education*, 21 AIS 10, Joseph Brandschain, Arbitrator.

34. *River Falls (Wisconsin) Board of Education*, 26 AIS 8, Arlen C. Christenson, Arbitrator.

35. *Waverly (Michigan) Schools Board of Education*, 31 AIS 25, Robert G. Howlett, Arbitrator.

36. See also *Durand (Michigan) Area Schools Board of Education*, 72 AIS 16, Leon J. Herman, Arbitrator; *Temple University (Pennsylvania)*, 65 AIS 13, S. Herbert Unterberger, Arbitrator; *Central School District No. 2, Town of Bedford (New York)*, 24 AIS 10, Edward Levin, Arbitrator; *Carasiti v. Pilkington*, 80 LRRM 2577 (58 LA 964); *Board of Junior College No. 508 (Cook County, Illinois)*, 53 LA 530, John F. Sembower, Arbitrator.

37. *Washtenaw Community College Board of Trustees (Michigan)*, 34 AIS 9, Harry N. Casselman, Arbitrator.

38. *Freeport (New York) Board of Education*, 41 AIS 18, Jesse Simons, Arbitrator.

39. *Byron (Michigan) Area Schools*, 81 AIS 21, Richard L. Kanner, Arbitrator.

40. *Lakeland (New York) School District*, 29 AIS 9, Josef P. Sirefman, Arbitrator.

41. *Wayne County (Michigan) Community College Board of Trustees*, 49 AIS 4, Leon J. Herman, Arbitrator.

42. *Huntington (Ohio) Local Board of Education*, 64 AIS 12, Charles F. Ipavec, Arbitrator.

43. *Bethpage (New York) Board of Education*, 53 AIS 10, Allen Weisenfeld, Arbitrator.

44. *Yale (Michigan) Board of Education*, 57 LA 657, George T. Roumell, Jr., Arbitrator.

45. *Beecher (Michigan) Board of Education*, 73 AIS 1, James R. McCormick, Arbitrator.

46. See also *Monticello (New York) Board of Education*, 58 AIS 7, George Nicolau, Arbitrator; *Charlotte (Michigan) Board of Education*, 56 AIS 11, Howard A. Cole, Arbitrator.

47. *Wayne County (Michigan) Community College Board of Trustees*, 49 AIS 4, Leon J. Herman, Arbitrator.

48. See *Government Employee Relations Report*, No. 657 (Washington: Bureau of National Affairs, 1976), p. X-6; *Government Employee Relations Report*, No. 622 (Washington: Bureau of National Affairs, 1975), p. X-2; *Government Employee Relations Report*, Reference File 81, RF-58 (Washington: Bureau of National Affairs, 1976), p. 1073.

49. *Madison (Connecticut) Board of Education*, 55 AIS 5, Peter L. Adomeit, Arbitrator.

50. *Monroe (New York) Community College*, 63 AIS 18, John E. Drotning, Arbitrator.

51. *Montrose (Michigan) Community Schools,* 72 AIS 12, Richard L. Kanner, Arbitrator.
52. *Sweet Home Central School District (Amherst, New York),* 78 AIS 18, John W. McConnell, Arbitrator.
53. *School District of the City of Ferndale (Michigan),* 77 AIS 23, E. J. Forsythe, Arbitrator.
54. *Norwich (Connecticut) Board of Education,* 77 AIS 8, John W. McConnell, Arbitrator.
55. *Burlington (Vermont) Board of School Commissioners,* 77 AIS 6, Edward C. Pinkus, Arbitrator.
56. *Barnstable (Massachusetts) School Committee,* 76 AIS 15, Lawrence T. Holden, Arbitrator.
57. *Niagara-Wheatfield (New York) Central School District,* 67 AIS 18, James A. Gross, Arbitrator.
58. *Brentwood (New York) Board of Education, U.F.S.D. No. 12,* 51 AIS 13, Daniel G. Collins, Arbitrator.
59. *Woodbridge Township (New York) Board of Education,* 50 AIS 4, Allen Weisenfeld, Arbitrator.
60. *Monroe (Michigan) Board of Education,* 35 AIS 18, George T. Roumell, Jr., Arbitrator.
61. *Rock Falls (Illinois) High School Board of Education,* 22 AIS 11, Joel Seidman, Arbitrator.
62. See *Madison (Wisconsin) Joint School District No. 8,* 53 AIS 2, Reynolds C. Seitz, Arbitrator; *U.F.S.D. No. 12 (Islip, New York),* 45 AIS 11, Josef P. Sirefman, Arbitrator.
63. Bureau of Labor Statistics, *Grievance and Arbitration Procedures in State and Local Agreements,* Bulletin No. 1833 (Washington: Government Printing Office, 1975), p. 39.
64. See also Rule 22 of the American Arbitration Association, which would serve to clarify representation rights of employee organizations when the AAA has been chosen as the appointing agency.
65. For experience of the private sector on this issue, see Frank Elkouri and Edna Asper Elkouri, *How Arbitration Works* (Washington: Bureau of National Affairs, 1973), p. 127.
66. For a school arbitration case where the issue is one of employee representation at the informal meeting with the principal, see *Cranford (New Jersey) Board of Education,* 65 AIS 6, Jonas Aarons, Arbitrator.
67. See *Fox Chapel (Pennsylvania) Area School District,* 78 AIS 3, William C. Stonehouse, Jr., Arbitrator.
68. See *Commach (New York) Public Schools, U.F.S.D. No. 10,* 44 AIS 6, Max M. Doner, Arbitrator; *New Haven (Connecticut) Board of Education,* 39 AIS 9, Mark Santer, Arbitrator; *Elmira (New York) City School District,* 34 AIS 1, Milton R. Konvitz, Arbitrator; *Board of Education, U.F.S.D. No. 3 (Huntington, New York),* 31 AIS 40, Henry Schuman, Arbitrator.
69. Bureau of Labor Statistics, *Grievance and Arbitration Procedures in State and Local Agreements,* Bulletin No. 1833 (Washington: Government Printing Office, 1975), p. 42.
70. *Government Employee Relations Report,* No. 574 (Washington: Bureau of National Affairs, 1974), p. X-17.

3

Employee Discipline

Incorporated into the legal system of the United States is the belief that an individual should not suffer a loss of basic rights or privileges at the hands of his or her government for arbitrary, capricious, or discriminatory reasons. Each individual is assured by law that prior to experiencing a loss of basic rights or privileges brought about by governmental action he or she shall be afforded due process considerations.

The value of due process to the individual citizen has also found a place in employee-employer relationships. Just as a citizen expects to receive due process considerations when adversely affected by government action, an employee frequently expects to receive such consideration when adversely affected by managerial action.[1] When the employer is itself a unit of government, this provides even more impetus for raising questions regarding the presence of arbitrary, capricious, or discriminatory behavior.

Employee discipline by management is a major source of actions adversely affecting employees. One response of employees has been to use collective bargaining to obtain provisions in agreements with employers. Such provisions grant a degree of due process and protect employees from arbitrary, capricious, or discriminatory decisions.

Just cause is a standard of conduct that has been applied to management actions in cases of employee discipline. It is a concept that has both substantive and procedural features. In practice, if management's actions have met a standard of just cause, this means that the disciplinary actions were not arbitrary, capricious, or discriminatory.

The concept of just cause is found in many collective bargaining agreements. However, the way in which it has been written into agreements is not uniform. Just cause provisions vary particularly with regard to the scope of their coverage. In some instances, for example, they may cover employee discharge; in other instances they do not. In some agreements probationary teachers are covered; in other agreements they are excluded. Some provisions for just cause are careful to outline disciplinary procedures; others do not. This chapter identifies and provides examples of the various ways collective bargaining agreements include the concept of just cause.

What justification is there for disciplinary action against employees? What situations prompt management to take disciplinary action? This chapter offers a framework with which to classify situations in which management has taken disciplinary actions against school employees. In addition to identifying the types of situations likely to bring disciplinary action, the chapter isolates specific infractions associated with disciplinary situations.

Over the years, arbitrators have evolved criteria to apply to the term just cause. In general, whenever disciplinary action has been taken against an employee, for whatever reason, the arbitrator will employ one or more criteria of just cause to ascertain if the provisions for just cause have been met by management. This chapter includes the criteria generally used in school arbitration cases.

In most arbitration cases not related to discipline, it is the employee's obligation to show that management has deprived him or her of some right or privilege granted by the collective bargaining agreement. Not so in a case involving discipline. In a disciplinary case calling for a just cause standard of action, it is up to the management to show that it has met that standard. This chapter explains the essential issues involved in the presentation of evidence in a disciplinary case.

JUST CAUSE PROVISIONS

Just cause is a standard applied in arbitration when an employee claims to have been adversely affected by an official action. Such an action may occur when an employee is reprimanded, suspended, reduced in grade, rank, or compensation, dismissed, or involuntarily transferred. From the perspective of an employee, adverse action also occurs when he or she is denied some benefit or advantage provided by the collective bargaining agreement.

JUST CAUSE LIMITED TO ONE TYPE OF ADVERSE ACTION

An element of negotiations between employer and employees is the determination of which official actions shall be held to a just cause standard. It is possible to limit the standard to just one type of official action, as illustrated in the following collective bargaining agreement:

> No involuntary transfer shall be made except for just, fair, and equitable cause.
>
> *Newark Board of Education and Newark Teachers Union, Local 481.*[2]

ENUMERATION OF JUST CAUSE SITUATIONS

The negotiating parties may attempt a more comprehensive enumeration of adverse actions subject to a just cause standard. For example:

> No teacher shall be dismissed, terminated, reprimanded, disciplined, reduced in rank or compensation or deprived of any professional advantage without just cause.
>
> *Board of Directors MSAD, No. 5 (Rockland, Maine) and Teachers Association MSAD, No. 5.*[3]

INCLUSION OF PROCEDURES

In addition, some just cause provisions describe the procedures to be followed when an employee believes himself or herself to have been unjustly treated.

> . . . a teacher with tenure may only be dismissed for good cause and, if requested by the teacher concerned, after a hearing before the Arbitration Board created pursuant to Article XI of this agreement. . .
>
> *Leo High School, Chicago, Illinois and Catholic Lay Teachers Association, Local 1700.*[4]

DEFINITION OF ARBITRATOR'S AUTHORITY

Other agreements include language intended to delimit the authority of the arbitrator, as seen in the next example.

If any grievance alleging a violation of this Article should be taken to Arbitration, the arbitrator's authority shall be limited to the fact question of whether there was just cause and as follows:

1. If the arbitrator finds there was just cause, he may modify the disciplinary action taken only if it:

(a) was taken arbitrarily or
(b) was excessive;
    otherwise he must affirm it.

2. If he finds there was no just cause, he shall nullify the disciplinary action taken.

The Regents of the University of Michigan (Ann Arbor, Michigan) and American Federation of State, County and Municipal Employees, Local 1583.[5]

REASONS FOR DISCIPLINARY ACTION

Below is a discussion of reasons that frequently prompt school officials to take disciplinary action, and the common issues associated with alleged employee infractions.

FAILURE TO APPEAR FOR WORK

School principals and other school officials are concerned about the regularity with which employees show up for work. They consider tardiness and unauthorized absences as cause for disciplinary action. Some of the related issues are the following.

Did the employee fail to appear for work an "excessive" number of times? Absolute numbers are not a guide to determining whether or not absences are excessive. The contingencies in each situation contribute to an assessment of "excessive" absences. Assuming that a pattern of not showing up for work is evident from the employee's behavior, arbitrators appear to be most interested in evidence that employees have been given a warning that continued absences or tardiness would be followed by disciplinary action.[6] In a situation where a teacher had been late only one time and was disciplined without prior warning, the arbitrator thought it unjust to place a written reprimand in the teacher's personnel file.[7,8]

Did the employee fail to use appropriate procedures to notify management of the employee's anticipated tardiness or absence? Whenever an employee knows he or she will be absent or tardy, some school officials expect the employee to inform them so that adjustments can be made. In one case, a letter was placed in the personnel file of a teacher who had been warned about his tardiness. The letter stated that on the last occasion of tardiness the teacher failed to inform the principal even though he knew he would be late and gave an unsatisfactory answer when questioned by the principal about his tardiness. The presence of the letter in the teacher's file was upheld by the arbitrator in view of the teacher's previous record of tardiness and the accuracy of the contents of the letter.[9]

Had leave privileges been abused? Proof of abuse of leave privileges is not easy to obtain. One indication of abuse might be a pattern of absences, such as absences that regularly occur at the beginning or end of the week or the beginning or end of scheduled holidays.[10] Where absences are so frequent that the legitimate interests of management or students are jeopardized, absences may constitute a type of abuse to the organization and others involved.[11,12] Another way to determine the extent of abuse would be to compare an employee's attendance record against the norm for the organization, and see if there are extenuating circumstances accounting for the absences.

Were the reasons for the absences legitimately within the scope of the collective bargaining agreement? When employee absences occur concurrent with an event such as an illegal strike, management may inquire into the legitimacy of the employee's reasons for being absent when the employee attempts to claim pay for the absences. If it is found that absences were a form of work stoppage, management has been upheld in its refusal to grant payment to employees.[13] When a school official finds out that employees are about to be absent for reasons that may not be legitimate, it is important, if his or her later disciplinary actions are to be upheld, to warn the employees that disciplinary action may be taken against them.[14]

Teachers who are members of a union sometimes take leave to engage in activities in support of other union members. Such leaves may be legitimate if the collective bargaining agreement contains language permitting union members to be absent for union business. A close reading of the contract language may be necessary in such cases.[15] In some instances, the legitimacy of an absence is determined by whether or not the employee obtained prior permission to take the leave.[16,17]

NONCOMPLIANCE WITH WORK DIRECTIVES

There are times when employees and management differ over their respective rights and obligations under the collective bargaining agreement. Employees may refuse to do work assigned because they believe that they are protected from doing such work assignments under the agreement. At other times, employees' refusal to do work appears to reflect a deteriorating relationship between the employees and management.

Faced with refusals to do work, school authorities may believe that employees are being insubordinate. Insubordination presents a unique problem to management, since it tends to defy the existence of hierarchical authority. This hierarchy is a basic tenet of modern bureaucratic organizations. Insubordination, therefore, is a serious matter for managerial authorities. It involves issues such as the following:

What is the meaning of the term "voluntary" in the various contexts of a collective bargaining agreement? What discretion, if any, does an employee have when the term is used? An arbitrator determined that a group of teachers were unfairly given letters of reprimand when they were no longer willing to continue in their extracurricular activities. An examination of the collective bargaining agreement revealed that participation in extracurricular activities was to be on a voluntary basis. The teachers' association encouraged teachers to discontinue their extracurricular activities when negotiations on a new contract reached an impasse. In response to this encouragement, the grievants informed their principal that they would no longer be available for extracurricular activities. Management did not respond with any disciplinary warning. The lack of disciplinary warning, coupled with the reference to the voluntary language of the agreement, was the primary basis for the arbitrator's ruling to uphold the grievance.[18]

In another case, it was determined to be unjust for a principal to evaluate a teacher as needing improvement because the teacher refused to volunteer for extracurricular assignments.[19] In yet another case, teachers had given advance notice to their principal that they would not attend a "voluntary" open house. The arbitrator determined that the board of education had misused its powers to discipline by sending them letters of censure because it had not formed a policy and told the teachers of the consequences of not attending the open house. Prior warning is an element of due process that the arbitrator believed should have been part of management's actions.[20]

In the last case to be cited here, an arbitrator decided that a teacher was unjustly disciplined for refusing to chaperone a dance. The decision was based upon the inclusion of the word "voluntary" in the last agreement between teachers and the school board. Earlier agreements explicitly required the performance of duties beyond the normal school day. The controlling agreement stated that the expenditure of time beyond the normal school day was "voluntary."[21]

If an employee challenges the appropriateness of a supervisor's directive, is this insubordination? One agreement between a school board and teachers provided that when a teacher was unavailable to cover his or her scheduled assignment, an emergency situation existed. In such situations the agreement provided for the assignment of other teachers to the emergency situation on an interim basis. In one such situation, a teacher refused to cover the student lunchroom, claiming that a substitute teacher was available. Disciplinary action against the teacher was not upheld by the arbitrator when the principal was unsuccessful in persuading the arbitrator that the available substitute teacher was unqualified to handle the lunchroom.[22]

In another case, vandals had broken into a school, destroying and disarranging property in the classrooms. A group of teachers asserted that their classrooms were unfit to teach in, so they used hallways, the teachers' lounge, and the auditorium instead. When the teachers did not obey their principal's request to return to their regularly assigned classrooms, they were suspended. The arbitrator did not uphold the disciplinary action because he did not believe that the school board sustained its burden to prove that the discipline was reasonable under the circumstances.[23]

The following case involves a school board that had traditionally allowed teachers to challenge involuntary transfers. The arbitrator hearing the case did not uphold a principal's decision to transfer a teacher, for both procedural and substantive reasons. Procedurally, the teacher had not been given an opportunity to challenge the transfer, an opportunity established by past practice. From a substantive perspective, it was found that the reason for the transfer was related to the grievant's union activities during a recent strike and not to the teacher's insubordination, as was alleged by management.[24]

The next case concerns a school employee who lost his position as supervisor of busing when busing activities were administratively combined with other functions. The employee refused to accept the new assignment offered to him. Consequently, the school board placed him on "indefinite suspension" for insubordination. Following a hearing on the matter, the arbitrator concluded that the board had a right to abolish the position, but it acted unjustly in disciplining the grievant for insubordination. The grievant's refusal to accept the new position had apparently been based on advice of counsel — a misconception of his legal rights had occurred. The school board was directed to reinstate the grievant at his assigned grade in pay prior to suspension. However, the grievant did not receive any retroactive pay because he had refused to report for work.[25]

At issue in another case was a principal's right to request information regarding student grades and a teacher's obligation to supply the information. The school board suspended a teacher for two days when the teacher refused to supply the requested information. The arbitrator ruled that the school board had successfully proved its case by showing that the principal's request for information was reasonable, and that the two-day suspension was proper under the circumstances.[26]

The issue in another case was a teacher's refusal to accept a new student into her class unless background information on the student was provided. The teacher was given a five-day suspension for insubordination. The arbitrator was not persuaded that school officials were just in not providing the information requested by the teacher, since it was available and had been supplied in a subsequent reassignment of the student. In addition, the school board failed to convince the arbitrator that the teacher was insubordinate in refusing to accept the student without the background information. The arbitrator noted that there was a well-established practice with regard to placing a new student in a classroom, and, in the grievant's case, it was not followed.[27,28]

Under what circumstances does an employee's use of abusive language toward a supervisor warrant disciplinary action? In an incident at a local tavern, a school maintenance employee accosted his supervisor with profane language. The arbitrator reasoned that because the employee had attracted public attention, his action reflected upon his employers, and they were justified in disciplining the employee even though the incident took place off school grounds.[29]

Another case involved a teacher and a principal who got into an argument. During the course of the argument, the teacher uttered profane remarks directed at the principal. School officials took disciplinary action against the teacher. However, the arbitrator did not believe the discipline was justified when he learned that the principal had also used profanity during the argument with the teacher.[30]

Finally, a case occurred in which there was an exchange of abusive language between a supervisor and a school maintenance employee. The employee claimed that the supervisor accused him of being dirty, of being crooked, and of abusing sick leave privileges. The arbitrator ruled that even if the supervisor had used the alleged abusive language toward the employee, there was no reason for the employee to have become verbally abusive toward his supervisor. Thus, some disciplinary action was justified.[31]

CONCERTED ACTION TO PROMOTE WORK STOPPAGE

Except in a few states, concerted action such as a strike is illegal. One form of work stoppage that generates a number of arbitration cases is the sickout. Used to avoid the penalties that might be imposed in an outright strike, the sickout raises issues such as the following.

Does management have the right to demand medical evidence as proof of illness? When 163 out of 250 teachers called in sick the day after contract negotiations reached an impasse, school authorities required teachers to have a doctor verify that they were ill. If verification was not obtained, the employee claiming to have been sick was not paid for the day off. This departure from the usual procedure for claiming sick leave was deemed by the arbitrator to be justified in order to protect against the possible misuse of sick leave privileges under the circumstances.[32]

In another school district, school officials had received notice of an impending sickout to protest transfers to create racial balance in the district. The school officials in turn informed staff that any absence because of illness would have to be supported by a written medical excuse. Until then, written medical evidence had not been requested unless the absence was for three days or longer. Although the union contended that school officials could not require a medical excuse after only one day of leave, the arbitrator held that the school board had the right to deduct a day's pay from the checks of teachers who did not provide bona fide medical evidence of illness.[33]

In a third case, the arbitrator's findings differed from the two just cited. When eight teachers, the district's entire teaching staff, gave advance notice that they were taking personal leave at the same time, the reviewing arbitrator held that such an action was within the contractual rights of the teachers. The collective bargaining agreement provided that three days of leave for personal business could be taken without question and deducted from sick leave.[34,35]

If management closes schools due to mass sickout, can teachers' sick leave benefits be suspended? A school district found it necessary to close schools when 103 teachers called in sick on the same day. The grievant, one of the teachers who called in sick, claimed that he should not have had a day of sick leave charged against him, since the schools had been officially closed. The collective bargaining agreement allowed eleven days of sick leave, and he was unjustly being denied one of the days allowed. The arbitrator ruled, however, that if the grievant and others had actually been ill, then clear evidence should have been produced by the grievant at the hearing to confirm that the grievant and others were ill. Otherwise, it was reasonable to assume that he and others had participated in an illegal strike. The arbitrator stated that the action taken by the school official was a small loss to the grievant under the circumstances.[36]

Can sick leave be taken on days scheduled to make up time lost due to a strike? Following a seven-day teacher strike, a school board agreed to provide seven makeup days so that teachers could recoup their salaries. The provision for makeup days was part of a separate supplemental agreement. Evidence presented at the hearing indicated that teachers had been informed that they needed to be "present and performing" on the makeup days in order to be paid. Absences for any reasons would result in withheld pay. When three teachers were absent because of illness on a makeup day, the administration did not charge their absences against sick leave or their attendance record; the teachers simply were not paid.

The absent teachers filed a grievance for their pay. The arbitrator failed to uphold their grievance, noting that the provision for makeup days was a supplemental agreement and was not contained in the body of the collective bargaining contract in effect. The agreement providing for makeup days was one of the terms for terminating the seven-day strike. There was some evidence indicating that the parties had previously agreed that attendance on makeup days was necessary for pay. At any rate, in the arbitrator's opinion, school authorities had the right to unilaterally develop rules to administer the supplemental agreement.[37]

UNPROFESSIONAL CONDUCT

In arbitration cases, alleged unprofessional conduct usually refers to behavior of the employee which defies either the social conventions of the organization's environment or the social conventions and customs of the organization itself. Therefore, behavior of school employees which draws the public's attention to the schools in a negative way is apt to be labeled unprofessional.[38] A "negative attitude" toward one's work,[39] the use of or tolerance of obscenities,[40] racially inflammatory statements,[41] controversial topics used by speakers,[42] and mistreatment of students[43] have at one time or another been judged to be sufficiently detrimental to the interest of the schools to warrant disciplinary action.

The initial issue raised in professional misconduct cases is the question: Did the alleged misconduct actually take place? Second, if the conduct did take place, was the employee protected by contractual, statutory, or constitutional rights? Third, in balancing any rights of the employee against the interests of management, did the weight of management's interest warrant the action taken?

JUST CAUSE CRITERIA

Definitions of just cause do not generally appear in collective bargaining agreements. Faced with specific cases, arbitrators have developed a number of criteria regarding the meaning of just cause. Even though arbitrators are not bound by other arbitrators' decisions, they are influenced by one another. Arbitrator Clyde W. Summers has noted, "Although arbitrators often cite no other decisions in their opinions and never consider other cases as binding precedents, they usually are quite aware of the pattern of decisions by other arbitrators and are reluctant to deviate far from that pattern."[44]

The following criteria are frequently used to determine if management's actions meet a just cause standard: (1) Was the employee informed of management's rules and expectations? (2) Were management's rules and expectations reasonable? (3) Was adverse action necessary to maintain orderly, efficient procedures in the organization? (4) Was the employee's infraction investigated and were the procedures used fair? (5) Has management administered its rules equitably? (6) Was the employee given an opportunity to improve his or her conduct? (7) Was the imposed penalty reasonable?

A "no" answer to one or more of these questions would indicate that just cause might be lacking. The criteria are illustrated in the following examples.

WAS THE EMPLOYEE INFORMED OF MANAGEMENT'S RULES AND EXPECTATIONS?

Cases involving failure to inform employees of expectations are of three types. In the first type of case, failure to inform has been traced to the lack of a written policy. In the second type, management knew that the employee's behavior or performance was deficient but did not warn him or her before taking disciplinary action. The third type of case involves situations where management's expectations were unclear, ambiguous, or inconsistent.

Lack of written policy. Two teachers had initiated for high school seniors an elective class which covered contemporary issues. The selected issues, though controversial, were identified through consultation with community citizens, school administrators, and students. The topics included censorship, drugs, and crime. During a trip to a nearby prison, the topic of "victimless" crime was raised. Following through on the topic, the teachers invited a prostitute to talk to the class. The appearance of the prostitute caused concern on the part of parents of one of the students in the class. The complaining parents called on school officials for an explanation and informed the local media of the incident. When the incident came to the attention of school authorities, the teachers were reprimanded.

The arbitration hearing revealed that on earlier occasions the class had talked to drug addicts in a local rehabilitation program, and a few students had seen an X-rated movie as a part of a project on censorship. The arbitrator's opinion was that, in keeping with the nature of the class, authorities in the school had given the reprimanded teachers wide latitude in the selection of topics and speakers. Thus, the arbitrator concluded that the reprimand was not made for just cause, because no written statement of policy had been given to the teachers, and their experience previous to the appearance of the prostitute would not have caused them to think that they were acting contrary to the wishes of their superiors.[45]

In another situation, the lack of a written policy prompted an arbitrator to call for withdrawal of a reprimand after it had been issued by a teacher's principal. The teacher, who believed her room to be overcrowded, sent letters to the parents of her pupils, inviting them to visit her classroom to see the overcrowded conditions. Her principal issued her a letter of reprimand for interfering with the efficiency of the organization. Even though temporary overcrowding was not unusual and such situations were normally corrected within two weeks, the arbitrator ruled that the teacher could not be disciplined for sending the letter unless the rule was made known to her in a definite, precise, publishable form beforehand, and there was evidence that she knowingly or carelessly violated the rule.[46,47]

In the above cases, each arbitrator held that discipline could not be administered unless specific expectations had been made clear to the employee. However, in some instances arbitrators have held that teachers, as professional employees, could be expected to use sound judgment in applying general rules to their specific classroom situations. Thus, in two separate cases the disciplining of teachers who had used poor judgment in punishing students was upheld. In both cases, the teachers had been given general guidelines by their respective school boards.[48] In a different case, an arbitrator upheld discipline imposed on a teacher when it was shown that the teacher had failed to use his professional skill to analyze his students' learning problems and find means to correct their problems.[49,50,51]

Lack of prior warning. In a case involving the nonrenewal of a probationary teacher, deficiencies in employee behavior were not communicated to the employee prior to disciplinary action, even though the deficiencies were known beforehand. The arbitrator who heard the evidence did not uphold the school board. Instead, he determined that the teacher had been given "inadequate" warning prior to dismissal.[52]

Lack of clarity. Failure to inform was traced to unclear statements of expectation in a case in which a school board docked certain teachers a day's pay for not calling in to the answering service the night before their absences. The school board claimed that it was necessary for teachers to call in so that time was available to secure substitutes. A check of the faculty handbook revealed that specific expectations with regard to using the answering service the night before an unexpected absence had not been included. The arbitrator ruled in favor of the grievants, even though the school board claimed that detailed expectations had been given orally.[53]

In another situation, a teacher who advised the student newspaper was reprimanded by the principal for permitting certain articles to appear in the paper. The principal claimed that the appearance of the articles was in violation of written policy. Upon investigation, however, it was found that the written statements of policy referred to by the principal were both unclear and unknown to the grievant. The letter of reprimand was directed to be withdrawn from the teacher's file.[54,55]

Were management's rules and expectations reasonable?

Assessment of the reasonableness of a rule is probably more subjective than objective in nature. Therefore, most arbitrators' assessments of the reasonableness of a given rule have taken into consideration all of the factors that impinge upon the rule and its implementation in a given situation. Thus, failure on the part of an employee to follow a rule may not always result in denial of a grievance. If factors present in the situation would prompt others in the same situation to ignore the rule, then an arbitrator may uphold a grievance regarding the rule. However, an employee's refusal to follow rules is not taken lightly by arbitrators. Arbitrators understand that it may be onerous for an employee to follow a rule, but the burdensome nature of a rule is not in itself sufficient reason to disobey it.

The following examples illustrate the principle that employees are expected to follow a rule even though they may object to it on some grounds. Later, after compliance, they can seek redress through the grievance procedure.

In the first case, bad weather had caused a school to be closed, but the Assistant Superintendent for Curriculum requested that a clerical employee appear for work. The employee refused to appear, stating that her supervisor was the Assistant Superintendent for Personnel and only he could request her to show up for work when school was closed due to inclement weather. The arbitrator failed to support the grievant in her insistence that only her supervisor could give her a legal order to show up for work. Discipline of the grievant was justified, since she should not have sought her own remedy by refusing to appear for work.[56]

In the second case, a principal had told a teacher not to leave the school building at lunch time during examination days. The grievant teacher believed that the principal had exceeded his authority in setting this rule. When the teacher ignored the principal's rule, he was given a letter of reprimand for insubordination. The arbitrator upheld the principal's action, pointing out that the grievant had the obligation of first obeying and later filing a grievance on the issue.[57]

In the next three cases, the grievants involved in each case had refused to follow their superior's orders. In each case, the arbitrator's award supported the grievants.

The first case, mentioned earlier in this chapter, involved eight teachers who were suspended for refusing to return to classrooms that they claimed were unfit for instructional purposes. Instead, they chose to teach in the halls and lounges. The arbitrator held that management had not sustained the burden of showing the teacher's behavior to have been improper. To have expected them to use their rooms was unreasonable.[58]

In the second case, a teacher was suspended for refusing to chaperone a Saturday night dance. The arbitrator found the suspension to be unreasonable, since the collective bargaining agreement stated that such an assignment was to be voluntarily performed.[59]

In the third case, also mentioned previously, a teacher who refused to accept a new pupil unless given background information normally supplied was given a five-day suspension for insubordination. The arbitrator found the suspension to be unreasonable, since the information requested by the teacher had been given to the teacher to whom the pupil was subsequently assigned.[60]

These three cases demonstrate the close relationship between unreasonableness and insubordination. In each case, the arbitrator's determination that the rules were unreasonable meant that the employee's behavior was ruled not insubordinate.

WAS ADVERSE ACTION NECESSARY TO MAINTAIN
ORDERLY, EFFICIENT PROCEDURES IN THE
ORGANIZATION?

An adverse action may be considered just if an employee was knowingly unresponsive to management's legitimate interest in maintaining an orderly and efficient organization. In the next two examples, management was unable to sustain the burden of proof that its legitimate interests were disregarded by the grievant. In the third case, management's interests were recognized and upheld by the arbitrator.

As described earlier, a principal placed a written reprimand in a teacher's personnel file because the teacher refused to supervise the first lunch period during a supposed emergency situation. The existence of an emergency situation was crucial to proving that a vital management interest was at stake. The principal was unable to convince the arbitrator that a true emergency actually existed, since a qualified substitute teacher was available and could have been assigned to the lunchroom.[61]

In another case, a grievant's principal had filed a letter of reprimand because she was late to work. The principal contended that the safety of children in the school was in jeopardy when the teacher was late. The arbitrator did not believe that the facts sustained the principal's contention. In addition, the arbitrator was impressed by the fact that the grievant had only been late once and otherwise had an above average teaching record.[62]

The third example involves a situation in which a principal was refused information on students who had been failed by a teacher. The teacher claimed that the information could not be given in the time available and that the permission of the students' parents would be required before the information could be released to the principal. The arbitrator found the teacher's reply to be unresponsive to the principal's legitimate request and upheld the disciplinary measures imposed by the principal.[63]

WAS THE EMPLOYEE'S INFRACTION INVESTIGATED AND WERE THE PROCEDURES USED FAIR?

Notions about procedural fairness are in part derived from the concept of due process found in courts of law. In addition, elements of procedural fairness may be defined by the parties in their collective bargaining agreement. A fundamental concept of procedural fairness includes adequate warning. The importance of stating rules and expectations has been covered in the preceding portions of this section.

Procedural fairness also includes the granting of a hearing to the individual adversely affected. One arbitrator upheld a grievance because the school board had not held a fair hearing as required by the grievance procedure, before acting in support of a superintendent who had imposed a five-day suspension.[64,65]

Granting a hearing is not necessarily sufficient, however. For example, a counselor was given an immediate investigation of a parental complaint, as called for by the agreement, but was not given the opportunity to rebut the complaint. The parent's letter of complaint thus could not be placed in the teacher's personnel file or be considered as the basis for further disciplinary action against the counselor.[66]

During a fair hearing, it is the weight of evidence presented at the time of the hearing that contributes to the fairness of the proceeding. Where the evidence does not sustain the allegations against an employee, it would be unfair to discipline the employee. Not infrequently, the amount of evidence management had at the time disciplinary action was taken is assessed during the arbitration hearing. Should the arbitrator find that insufficient evidence was used by management to sustain the allegations against the teacher, the arbitrator may reverse management's actions.[67]

Arbitrators have given attention to other aspects of fair procedure. One aspect is the extent to which disciplinary procedures called for in the collective bargaining agreement were actually followed by management in imposing an adverse action on an employee. For example, in a situation where the agreement stated that disciplinary action must be preceded by written notification, the school board was held to be in violation of the agreement when notice was not given prior to withholding paychecks from the grievants.[68] Some collective bargaining agreements recognize that the union has certain rights in grievance proceedings. One commonly accepted provision is the right to be informed whenever disciplinary action is taken against a union member. When that is provided for in the agreement, failure to notify the union representative will weigh against management when the arbitrator makes his or her award.[69]

HAS MANAGEMENT ADMINISTERED ITS RULES EQUITABLY?

Arbitrator George T. Roumell, Jr., has pointed out that an employer need not penalize all employees guilty of a common offense in the same manner. However, the employer has the burden of explaining his or her reasons for penalizing some employees and not others.[70]

In a school district where some teachers had taken part in a parent picket line that sought the removal of the vice-principal, the school board took disciplinary action against the union building representative. Although she had not come in to work, she had neither encouraged nor discouraged the teachers and had not herself participated in the picket line. The school board justified its action by claiming that the building representative had greater knowledge of the contract and its no-strike provision. In addition, the school board believed the building representative was obligated to set an example for other teachers by returning to work. The arbitrator believed the discipline to be excessive. He faulted the reasoning of the school board on the grounds that the union president had been present in the picket line supporting the parents, and it would have been just as logical to expect him to have set an example for other teachers. No action had been taken against the union president.[71]

In another case, while school secretaries were on strike, some teachers had remained away from work in sympathy for the secretaries. The arbitrator felt that although management had the right to withhold pay from all teachers, it did not have the right to suspend some teachers who remained away and not others.[72,73]

Elsewhere, a principal had devised a rule that the teacher involved must report, in writing, all incidents involving student discipline. The principal was found in error when he disciplined one teacher for not writing the required reports but failed to enforce the same rule on other teachers who did not comply with it.[74]

WAS THE EMPLOYEE GIVEN AN OPPORTUNITY TO IMPROVE HIS OR HER CONDUCT?

It is expected that employees will be given an opportunity to correct any deficiencies in work habits and skills that are remediable in nature. When management can show there was opportunity to correct behavior, subsequent disciplinary actions are likely to be upheld. For example, two teachers had each established a record of excessive tardiness. Each was given a written warning that continued tardiness would lead to disciplinary action. When the pattern of tardiness did not improve, the teachers lost a day's work and pay. After noting that no evidence was presented to show that the tardiness was beyond the control of the teachers, the arbitrator upheld the disciplinary action.[75]

In a different case, upon return from a ten-day disciplinary suspension, an employee refused to accompany his supervisor to the supervisor's office to discuss the reasons for the disciplinary action and the supervisor's expectations of the employee for the future. The employee's refusal led to his discharge. Since the employee could not improve if he refused to know what was expected of him, and since he already had had a series of disciplinary actions taken against him, the discharge was upheld in arbitration.[76]

Another case involved an employee whose unscheduled absences usually preceded or followed scheduled days off. After repeated warnings for excessive absences, the employee was required to submit a medical certificate following each absence for claimed illness. When the pattern of repeated unauthorized absences continued, the employee was given a one-day disciplinary layoff. Since the employee was given ample opportunity to improve, the arbitrator upheld the disciplinary action.[77]

WAS THE IMPOSED PENALTY REASONABLE?

The following are situations in which arbitrators have been sensitive to excessive disciplinary penalties being imposed on the employee:

1. In situations where management has failed to establish just cause, arbitrators are likely to determine that such a failure should mitigate or eliminate the disciplinary penalty that was imposed.[78]

2. Where management has failed to follow the procedural features of the collective bargaining agreement, any penalties may be lessened or removed.[79]

3. Where the employee has a favorable past record, the arbitrator

may give the record enough weight to deem the imposed penalty excessive.[80]

4. Where it becomes apparent during an arbitration hearing that the grievant's supervisors widely differ in their assessment of the disciplinary action to impose, the arbitrator may question the appropriateness of the penalty.[81]

5. Where disciplinary action was taken for a single instance of poor judgment in the use of indecent language not associated with insubordination or racial slurs, the infrequency of the violation may cause the arbitrator to reassess the appropriateness of the penalty imposed.[82]

6. Where an employee has been disciplined for an infraction of rules that have been broken by other employees under similar circumstances, the arbitrator may consider the penalties imposed in previous situations in order to determine the appropriateness of the penalty in the case under consideration.[83]

PRESENTATION OF EVIDENCE

In cases where employees have been disciplined by management, management is obligated to show just cause for taking disciplinary measures. Usually management's obligation to show just cause is a consequence of having previously agreed to do so in the collective bargaining agreement. However, there have been instances where arbitrators have implied a just cause standard for discipline from the general language of a collective bargaining agreement.[84]

In discipline cases, it is customary for management to present its evidence first. At times, however, the order in which evidence is presented becomes a controversial issue. On the one hand, it may be argued that management proceeds first because it has the burden of proof in a disciplinary case, particularly in a case of discharge. There is also an expectation that management must establish its proof with evidence of such quantity and quality that a verdict favorable to management could be reached on the basis of its case alone. According to one school of thought, if management fails to produce the necessary standard of evidence, the grievant is not obligated to present its side of the case and may call for a favor judgment.

Some arbitrators use a different line of reasoning for having management proceed first with its evidence. Benjamin Aaron, for example, has claimed that the orderly unfolding of the evidence requires management to proceed first. He points out that management takes the initial action of disciplining the employee; hearing management's evidence first is an attempt to reconstruct the events in order to provide the arbitrator with a coherent picture of events from the participants' respective points of view. Aaron has argued that the adversarial model borrowed from criminal law, with its emphasis on the technicalities of burden of proof and the establishment of a prima facie case, is out of place in an arbitration hearing. Aaron suggests that this emphasis on adversarial models hinders reestablishment of normal working relationships after the hearing.[85]

Other reasons have been given to justify having management proceed first with the presentation of evidence:

1. Since disciplinary discharge is the most severe penalty that an employer is capable of imposing, the employer has the burden of justifying such a serious action.

2. If the grievant were required to present his or her case first, the grievant would need to prove that he or she was guilty of no offense of any kind, i.e., the universal negative.

3. By having management proceed first, the assumption is maintained that the grievant is innocent of wrongdoing until the evidence shows otherwise.

4. An organization that is scientifically managed weighs important decisions in an impersonal and objective manner. Management is called upon by stockholders, governmental agencies, and the public to justify decisions that have significant outcomes. Decisions on labor relations deserve the same quality of judgment that is applied to other areas of an organization's operations. Requiring management to justify its decisions in labor relations extends the expectation for rational behavior that exists in other areas.

5. The burden of proving the affirmative of an argument rests with the party who asserts it. For example, if an employee claims that some benefit created by the collective bargaining agreement has been wrongly withheld, the burden of proving the claim rests with the employee. Similarly, if management claims that an employee has engaged in some infraction of the rules requiring disciplinary measures to be taken, the burden of proving the existence of the infraction and appropriateness of the disciplinary action rests with management.[86]

THE GRIEVANT'S OBLIGATION

After management has presented its case, it is customary for the grievant's representatives to present the grievant's case. The grievant's case is often composed of three defensive arguments. First, the grievant may refute the fact that a violation or infraction that would warrant disciplinary action has taken place. Second, the grievant may claim that contractual procedures relevant to disciplinary cases were not followed, thus invalidating management's actions. Third, the grievant may claim that the disciplinary measures were excessive or in some other way unfair. Of course, any claim by the grievant must be accompanied by sufficient evidence to sustain the grievant's claims in view of what has already been asserted by management in the earlier phases of the hearing.

THE PROBLEM OF CONFLICTING EVIDENCE

Frequently, after each party has made its case, the arbitrator is faced with conflicting testimony. Did the grievant actually use profanity in responding to his superior or not? Had the grievant been warned on earlier occasions that she or he would be disciplined if certain behavior continued? When the parties take opposite positions on significant issues, whom is the arbitrator to believe? How is the arbitrator to weigh the merits of the opposing arguments and accompanying evidence?

Some indication of how an arbitrator sifts through the record established by the parties in the hearing has been outlined by arbitrator Samuel H. Jaffee:

> . . . resolution of the merits rests essentially on the credibility of the opposing testimony, often no easy task. Some preliminary comments should be noted. First, burden of proof in discipline cases is normally on the employer, and the more precise question, then, is whether the employer has sustained its burden of proof, including the requisite quantum of proof, to show cause for the discipline. Second, I need hardly say that no arbitrator (or judge for that matter) decides, strictly speaking, on the facts but, more accurately, on what he is *told* about the facts — that is, on the *evidence*. After all, I wasn't there when the incident in question occurred. This must take into account not only what the witnesses said, but the evaluation of what they said in light of the more likely probabilities and not unnatural biases, prejudices, and interests of the witnesses . . .[87]

Jaffee mentions that two aspects of the discipline hearing are particularly critical: one, the credibility of the witnesses, and two, the necessity for management to meet its burden of proof.

THE PROBLEM OF DETERMINING CREDIBILITY

Some guidelines do exist for arbitrators to use in determining the credibility of witnesses. The following have been suggested:

1. his [the witness's] demeanor while testifying and the manner in which he testifies

2. the character of his testimony
3. the extent of his capacity to perceive, to recollect, or to communicate any matter about which he testifies
4. the extent of his opportunity to perceive any matter about
   which he testifies
5. his character for honesty or veracity or their opposites
6. the existence or nonexistence of a bias, interest, or other motive
7. a statement previously made by him that is consistent with his
   statement at the hearing
8. a statement made by him that is inconsistent with any part of
   his testimony at the hearing
9. the existence or nonexistence of any fact testified to by him
10. his attitude toward the action in which he testifies or toward
    the giving of testimony
11. his admission of untruthfulness.[88,89]

According to arbitrator Paul Prasow, resolving issues of credibility
is an exercise in the use of the arbitrator's intuition. However, the
arbitrator who uses his intuition alone may be perceived to be saying
that one of the parties is telling the truth while the other party is lying.[90]
Prasow believes that it is preferable for an arbitrator to resort to the
traditional legal device of asserting presumptions. He states:

> Presumptions are analytic devices for determining what evidence will be
> given full weight and what evidence will be given little or no weight. A
> presumption puts the burden on one of the parties to produce evidence
> sufficient to avoid a ruling against the party on the issue . . . . How much
> less strained are the arbitrator's relationships with the parties when he can
> put the affirmative of the issue on Richard Roe and rule that Roe has not
> sustained the burden of proof instead of making a flat declaration that he
> does not believe Richard Roe.[91]

The burden of proof is placed on the party asserting the "affirmative
of an issue." For example, if an employer dismisses an employee for
physical abuse, the affirmative of the issue would be the employer's
claim that the employee had engaged in physical abuse of his supervisor.
To illustrate, the employer might claim that the employee struck his
supervisor with his fist. After making the charge, the employer must
present evidence to prove that it actually happened. Suppose, however,
that the employee does not dispute the fact that he struck his supervisor,
but makes the counterclaim that he was provoked into doing so by some
remark that the supervisor made to him. The affirmative of the em-

ployee's claim is that provocation existed, and the burden for presenting evidence rests with the employee.

QUANTUM OF PROOF

Another analytic technique arbitrators use to reach a decision is to presume that evidence of a certain quality and quantity is necessary to prove the affirmative of an issue. To illustrate, suppose a supervisor claims to have been struck by an employee, but there are no witnesses. However, to support management's contention that the supervisor was struck, management presents evidence that the supervisor had had difficulties with the employee over leaving work early and that the employee had received a formal reprimand for fighting with other employees. Further suppose that the employer is able to produce a witness who claims to have been told by the employee that he would like to "knock his supervisor's block off," and medical testimony that supports the possibility that the bruise on the supervisor's face had been made by a fist. Is such evidence of sufficient quality and quantity to support a disciplinary discharge of the employee for striking his supervisor?

In a case concerning the discharge of an employee or an accusation of moral turpitude against an employee, most arbitrators want to base their judgment on proof that is clear beyond a reasonable doubt.[92,93] Other discernible degrees of proof would be clear and convincing proof, and proof based on a preponderance of evidence.

Suppose that, in defense of the charge against him for striking his supervisor, the employee claims that the supervisor used a number of racial slurs which were demeaning in their intent; suppose that no witnesses could be found who heard the supervisor use the slurs that provoked the employee, but witnesses were presented who had frequently heard the supervisor use racial slurs on other occasions. Would the evidence presented by the employee sustain the affirmative of the issue that he had been provoked? Would an arbitrator deciding the case be faced with the problem of determining the credibility of the testimony presented?

An arbitrator's award in a discipline case results from the interaction of presumptions created by the arbitrator, the quality and quantity of evidence presented by the parties, and the credibility of key witnesses in asserting the affirmative of issues that would support an award for or against management's disciplinary action. The arbitrator is not a passive agent merely acting as a human scale which has evidence placed on one side or another of a given issue. The arbitrator accepts evidence given, but he or she also actively "weighs" the evidence. The weighing process is a logical process which involves both the arbitrator's reasoning ability and his or her intuition. In addition, some arbitrators attempt to keep in mind the impact the proceeding will have on the long-term relationships of the parties.

SUMMARY

School management has the right to discipline employees. However, in many school districts management has been willing to condition its right to discipline employees and to include these conditions in collective bargaining agreements. Just cause is the single most important concept of employee discipline that has been incorporated as a provision in collective bargaining agreements.

An analysis of arbitration cases in the education sector indicates that management tends to take disciplinary action under four major sets of circumstances. First, disciplinary actions have followed an employee's failure to appear for work. Some of the main issues concerned with employee attendance are the determination of "excessive" absences, the use of appropriate procedures to inform management of an absence, and an employee's adherence to leave policies.

Second, disciplinary actions have followed noncompliance with work directives. A number of arbitration cases have involved situations in which noncompliance was associated with interpretations of the term "voluntary." Other cases have arisen because employees have challenged management's authority to give directives.

Third, disciplinary actions have taken place when employees engaged in concerted action to promote a work stoppage. In cases involving employees' use of the "sickout," one of the major issues has been management's right to require medical evidence as proof of illness. Another issue has been management's right to suspend benefits to employees when schools are closed because of a "sickout."

Fourth, unprofessional conduct is a general category of cases referring to employee behavior that defies the customs and conventions of an organization or defies the dominant values of an organization's social environment. Negative attitudes, use or tolerance of obscenities, racially inflammatory statements, and abuse of students have prompted management to take disciplinary action for unprofessional conduct.

Also, disciplinary actions have been taken when an employee used abusive language toward a supervisor. Where abusive language was the issue, an important consideration has been to determine if provocation was present. It also has been important to determine the extent of damage done to the supervisor's authority if verbal abusiveness took place in front of other employees.

Over the years arbitrators have developed a number of criteria to assess whether or not a standard of just cause was adhered to by management when it took disciplinary action against an employee. The following criteria have often been used: (1) Was the employee informed of management's rules and expectations? (2) Were management's rules and expectations reasonable? (3) Was adverse action necessary to maintain orderly and efficient procedures in the organization? (4) Was the employee's infraction investigated and were the procedures used fair? (5) Has management administered its rule equitably? (6) Was the employee given an opportunity to improve his or her conduct? (7) Was the imposed penalty reasonable?

The presentation of evidence in cases of employee discipline is a topic of concern to all involved with arbitration. In general, arbitrators tend to avoid legal technicalities practiced in courts of law when it comes to the presentation of evidence by parties in arbitration. Most arbitrators are primarily interested in obtaining a coherent picture of the fact situation that bears upon the disciplinary action taken. For the sake of an orderly development of facts, management is usually expected to present its evidence first.

Not infrequently the parties give the arbitrator conflicting accounts of the fact situation. When the evidence presented is in conflict, arbitrators may resolve conflicting testimony by ascribing credibility to one account and not to another. In addition, arbitrators may weigh evidence by assigning a burden of proof to the party assuming the affirmative position on issues developed during the course of an arbitration hearing. In disciplinary cases, the initial burden of proof usually has been placed on management to show that it has met the just cause standard called for in the collective bargaining agreement. If the grievant employee asserts a counterclaim, then the burden of proof shifts to the employee to prove that procedural rights were denied. Finally, the weighing of evidence requires that the arbitrator determine what quality and quantity of evidence are necessary in order to overcome a burden of proof.

Various standards of proof have been adopted by arbitrators depending on the seriousness of the disciplinary action taken and the nature of the employee's infraction. Proof that is clear beyond a reasonable doubt, clear and convincing proof, and proof based on a preponderance of evidence have been three standards of proof commonly employed in discipline cases.

NOTES

1. The analogy between due process as a judicial procedure and due process as an element of organizational justice is intended to serve as an approximate analogy and not as an exact one. Some writers question whether or

not due process as seen in the courts can be duplicated by systems of organizational justice. See Mathew O. Tobriner, "An Appellate Judge's View of the Labor Arbitration Process: Due Process and the Arbitration Process," *The Arbitrator, the NLRB, and the Courts,* Proceedings of the Twentieth Annual Meeting, National Academy of Arbitrators (Washington: BNA Incorporated, 1967), p. 37. Also see Harry T. Edwards, "Due Process Considerations in Labor Arbitration," *The Arbitration Journal* 25:2, (1970): 141–69.

2. *Newark (New Jersey) Board of Education,* 14 AIS 13, Joseph F. Wildebush, Arbitrator, p. 2.
3. *Board of Directors MSAD, No. 5 (Rockland, Maine),* 39 AIS 19, John W. McConnell, Arbitrator, p. 2.
4. *Leo High School (Chicago, Illinois),* 1 AIS 25, Albert A. Epstein, Arbitrator, p. 2.
5. *The Regents of the University of Michigan (Ann Arbor, Michigan),* 23 AIS 14, Alan Walt, Arbitrator, p. 3.
6. *Smithfield (Rhode Island) School Committee,* 49 AIS 7, Craig E. Overton, Arbitrator.
7. *Framingham (Massachusetts) School Committee,* 62 AIS 7, Daniel G. Macleod, Arbitrator.
8. See also *Brick Township (New Jersey) Board of Education,* 39 AIS 17, Jonas Silver, Arbitrator.
9. *Rockville Centre (New York) Union Free School District,* 89 AIS 3, Tia Schneider Denenberg, Arbitrator.
10. *Hempstead (New York) Board of Education,* 68 AIS 11, Philip Harris, Arbitrator.
11. See *Grosse Pointe (Michigan) Board of Education,* 66 AIS 7, Harry N. Casselman, Arbitrator.
12. See *Macomb County (Michigan) Community College,* 64 AIS 1, Leon J. Herman, Arbitrator.
13. *Macomb County (Michigan) Community College,* 33 AIS 32, Leon J. Herman, Arbitrator.
14. *Montgomery County (Maryland) Public Schools,* 32 AIS 16, Howard G. Gamser, Arbitrator.
15. *Grosse Pointe (Michigan) Board of Education,* 29 AIS 15, David G. Heilbrun, Arbitrator.
16. *Carrollton (Michigan) Board of Education,* 29 AIS 6, George T. Roumell, Jr., Arbitrator.
17. See also *The Regents of the University of Michigan (Ann Arbor, Michigan),* 26 AIS 12, Alan Walt, Arbitrator.
18. *School Administrative District No. 33 (Maine),* 74 AIS 8, Edward C. Pinkus, Arbitrator.
19. *Carroll County (Maryland) Board of Education,* 62 AIS 2, Charles L. Mullin, Jr., Arbitrator.
20. *Manchester (Connecticut) Board of Education,* 41 AIS 2, William J. Fallon, Arbitrator.
21. *Groton Board of Education (Connecticut),* 2 AIS 13, William J. Fallon, Arbitrator.

22. *Board of Education of the District of Columbia,* 70 AIS 4, James M. Harkless, Arbitrator.
23. *Board of Education of the District of Columbia,* 32 AIS 11, Samuel H. Jaffee, Arbitrator.
24. *Board of Education, School District of Philadelphia (Pennsylvania),* 27 AIS 8, John Perry Horlacher, Arbitrator.
25. *New Haven (Connecticut) Board of Education,* 21 AIS 10, Joseph Brandschain, Arbitrator.
26. *Board of Education, Trenton (Michigan) Public Schools,* 12 AIS 19, Alan Walt, Arbitrator.
27. *Holliston (Massachusetts) School Committee,* 2 AIS 16, John W. Teele, Arbitrator.
28. See also the following two cases: *Crestwood (Michigan) Board of Education,* 1 AIS 1, M. David Keefe, Arbitrator; *School District of the City of Ferndale (Michigan),* 1 AIS 32, Leon J. Herman, Arbitrator.
29. *Jersey City (New Jersey) Board of Education,* 88 AIS 22, Samuel Ranhand, Arbitrator.
30. *State of Ohio, Ohio Youth Commission,* 55 AIS 6, Charles F. Ipavec, Arbitrator.
31. *Springfield (Ohio) Board of Education,* 49 AIS 13, Charles F. Ipavec, Arbitrator.
32. *Manalapan-Englishtown (New Jersey) Board of Education,* 72 AIS 9, Jonas Aarons, Arbitrator.
33. *Wilmington (Delaware) Board of Education,* 57 AIS 1, S. Harry Galfand, Arbitrator.
34. *Taylor School District (Michigan),* 1 AIS 23, Alan Walt, Arbitrator.
35. See also *The City of Detroit (Michigan) Board of Education,* 27 AIS 2, James R. McCormick, Arbitrator.
36. *Board of Education, South Stickney School District No. 220, Oak Lawn (Illinois),* 3 AIS 12, Pearce Davis, Arbitrator.
37. *Lakeland Board of Education (New York),* 32 AIS 17, Milton Rubin, Arbitrator.
38. See *South Colonie (New York) Central School District,* 92 AIS 4, William J. Fallon, Arbitrator; *Niagara-Wheatfield (New York) Board of Education,* 72 AIS 13, Lawrence I. Hammer, Arbitrator; *Highland Park (Michigan) School District,* 69 AIS 16, Leon J. Herman, Arbitrator.
39. See *Pontiac (Michigan) School District,* 44 AIS 11, C. Keith Groty, Arbitrator.
40. See *State of Ohio, Ohio Youth Commission,* 55 AIS 6, Charles F. Ipavec, Arbitrator; *Grand Blanc (Michigan) School District,* 35 AIS 10, Robert G. Howlett, Arbitrator.
41. See *Flint (Michigan) Board of Education,* 38 AIS 3, James R. McCormick, Arbitrator.
42. See *Cranston (Rhode Island) School Committee,* 34 AIS 2, Stanley M. Jacks, Arbitrator.
43. See *Warren Woods (Michigan) Public Schools,* 52 AIS 2, C. Keith Groty, Arbitrator; *Board of Education of the City of New York (New York),* 51 AIS 18, Benjamin H. Wolf, Arbitrator; *Parkland School District (Orefield, Pennsylvania),* 50 AIS 5, Clair V. Duff, Arbitrator.

44. Clyde W. Summers, "Arbitration of Unjust Dismissal: A Preliminary Proposal," in *The Future of Labor Arbitration in America,* ed. Joy Correge et al. (New York: American Arbitration Association, 1976), p. 162.
45. *Cranston (Rhode Island) School Committee,* 34 AIS 2, Stanley M. Jacks, Arbitrator.
46. *Highland Park (Michigan) School District,* 69 AIS 16, Leon J. Herman, Arbitrator.
47. See also *Massapequa (New York) Board of Education,* 21 AIS 4, Daniel G. Collins, Arbitrator.
48. *Upper St. Clair (Pennsylvania) School District,* 44 AIS 13, Clair V. Duff, Arbitrator; *Warren Woods (Michigan) Public Schools,* 52 AIS 2, C. Keith Groty, Arbitrator.
49. *Maynard (Massachusetts) School Committee,* 39 AIS 7, William J. Fallon, Arbitrator.
50. See also *Pontiac (Michigan) School District,* 44 AIS 11, C. Keith Groty, Arbitrator.
51. For a contrasting view, see *Odessa Montour (New York) Central School District,* 94 AIS 21, Rodney E. Dennis, Arbitrator.
52. *Niles Township (Illinois) Community High School,* 13 AIS 16, Aaron S. Wolff, Arbitrator.
53. *Black Horse Pike Board of Education (New Jersey),* 40 AIS 6, Margaret K. Chandler, Arbitrator.
54. *New Haven (Connecticut) Board of Education,* 14 AIS 2, Eric J. Schmertz, Arbitrator.
55. See also *Chelsea (Michigan) Board of Education,* 51 AIS 9, George T. Roumell, Jr., Arbitrator.
56. *Warwick (Rhode Island) School Committee,* 10 AIS 12, Mark Santer, Arbitrator.
57. *North Smithfield (Rhode Island) School Committee,* 68 AIS 3, Robert M. O'Brien, Arbitrator.
58. *Board of Education of the District of Columbia,* 32 AIS 11, Samuel H. Jaffee, Arbitrator.
59. *Groton Board of Education (Connecticut),* 2 AIS 13, William J. Fallon, Arbitrator.
60. *Holliston (Massachusetts) School Committee,* 2 AIS 16, John W. Teele, Arbitrator.
61. *Board of Education of the District of Columbia,* 70 AIS 4, James M. Harkless, Arbitrator.
62. *Framingham (Massachusetts) School Committee,* 62 AIS 7, Daniel G. Macleod, Arbitrator.
63. *Board of Education, Trenton (Michigan) Public Schools,* 12 AIS 19, Alan Walt, Arbitrator.
64. *Grand Blanc (Michigan) School District,* 35 AIS 10, Robert G. Howlett, Arbitrator.
65. See also *Cranston (Rhode Island) School Committee,* 34 AIS 2, Stanley M. Jacks, Arbitrator.
66. *South Brunswick (New Jersey) Board of Education,* 43 AIS 14, Jonas Aarons, Arbitrator.
67. *Board of Education of the District of Columbia,* 58 AIS 8, Warren L. Taylor,

Arbitrator; *Lansing (Michigan) School District,* 19 AIS 18, M. David Keefe, Arbitrator; *City of Chicago (Illinois) Board of Education,* 13 AIS 20, Arthur A. Malinowski, Arbitrator.

68. *Ann Arbor (Michigan) Board of Education,* 18 AIS 4, Harry N. Casselman, Arbitrator.
69. See *Morrice (Michigan) Board of Education,* 40 AIS 13, John H. Stamm, Arbitrator; *Crestwood (Michigan) Board of Education,* 1 AIS 1, M. David Keefe, Arbitrator.
70. *Genessee Community College Trustees (Michigan),* 21 AIS 14, George T. Roumell, Jr., Arbitrator.
71. *Board of Education of the District of Columbia,* 62 AIS 8, Bernard Dunau, Arbitrator.
72. *Macomb County (Michigan) Community College,* 33 AIS 32, Leon J. Herman, Arbitrator.
73. See also *Massapequa (New York) Board of Education,* 21 AIS 4, Daniel G. Collins, Arbitrator.
74. *State of Ohio, Ohio Youth Commission,* 55 AIS 6, Charles F. Ipavec, Arbitrator.
75. *Smithfield (Rhode Island) School Committee,* 49 AIS 7, Craig E. Overton, Arbitrator.
76. *The Regents of the University of Michigan (Ann Arbor, Michigan),* 23 AIS 14, Alan Walt, Arbitrator.
77. *The Regents of the University of Michigan (Ann Arbor, Michigan),* 26 AIS 12, Alan Walt, Arbitrator.
78. See *Grosse Pointe (Michigan) Board of Education,* 66 AIS 7, Harry N. Casselman, Arbitrator; *Gloversville (New York) Enlarged City School District,* 60 AIS 12, William A. Hazell, Arbitrator; *Independent School District No. 204, Kasson-Mantorville (Minnesota) Schools,* 60 AIS 11, James L. Hetland, Jr., Arbitrator.
79. See *Scappoose (Oregon) School District,* 82 AIS 10, Richard H. Jones, Arbitrator; *Paw Paw (Michigan) Public Schools,* 66 AIS 5, Harry T. Edwards, Arbitrator; *Montgomery County (Maryland) Public Schools,* 32 AIS 16, Howard G. Gamser, Arbitrator. Also see *Milwaukee Board of School Directors (Wisconsin),* 33 AIS 22, Abner Brodie, Arbitrator.
80. See *Quincy (Michigan) Board of Education,* 72 AIS 17, Richard L. Kanner, Arbitrator; *Reed City (Michigan) Board of Education,* 65 AIS 21, Richard I. Bloch, Arbitrator; *Flint (Michigan) Board of Education,* 38 AIS 3, James R. McCormick, Arbitrator.
81. See *Durand (Michigan) Area Schools,* 1 AIS 37, William P. Daniel, Arbitrator.
82. See *Harbor Beach (Michigan) Board of Education,* 73 AIS 23, George T. Roumell, Jr., Arbitrator.
83. See *Consolidated High School District 230 (Illinois),* 17 AIS 5, Albert A. Epstein, Arbitrator.
84. Frank Elkouri and Edna Asper Elkouri, *How Arbitration Works* (Washington: Bureau of National Affairs, 1973), p. 611.
85. Benjamin Aaron, "Some Procedural Problems in Arbitration," *Vanderbilt Law Review* 10:4 (1957): 733–48.

86. For further discussion, see Robert H. Gorske, "Burden of Proof in Grievance Arbitration" *Marquette Law Review* 43:2 (1959): 149–53.

87. *Board of Education of the District of Columbia,* 32 AIS 11, Samuel H. Jaffee, Arbitrator.

88. Committee Report, "Problems of Proof in the Arbitration Process: Report of West Coast Area," *Problems of Proof in Arbitration: Proceedings of the Nineteenth Annual Meeting, National Academy of Arbitrators* (Washington: Bureau of National Affairs, 1967), pp. 207–8.

89. See also Paul Prasow and Edward Peters, *Arbitration and Collective Bargaining: Conflict Resolution in Labor Relations* (New York: McGraw-Hill Book Company, 1970), p. 182.

90. Ibid., p. 183.

91. Ibid., p. 184.

92. Maurice C. Benewitz, "Discharge, Arbitration and the Quantum of Proof," *The Arbitration Journal* 28:2 (1973): 95–104.

93. Also see Owen Fairweather, *Practice and Procedure in Labor Arbitration* (Washington: Bureau of National Affairs, 1973), pp. 203–8.

CHAPTER

4

Evaluation of Teacher Performance

One arbitrator has asserted that a contractual provision for teacher evaluation was a "covenant of fair dealing."[1] Assurances of fair dealing are incorporated into evaluation provisions by means of certain procedural features. They obligate management to follow predetermined structural and/or process requirements when evaluating teachers. Structural requirements include a specification of the types of observations, the number of observations that should be undertaken, the designation of who can conduct observations, and the length of observations. Process requirements include the notification of teachers of impending observations, the use of supplemental evidence, and the identification of follow-up activities.

In addition to requirements that the parties themselves place in evaluation provisions, there is a requirement that the "common law" of arbitration places on management — the responsibility to deal fairly. Common law requires that authorities not behave in an arbitrary, capricious, or discriminatory manner. While arbitrators do apply these concepts, they may not always use the specific labels "arbitrary," "capricious," or "discriminatory" when describing managerial behavior. Frequently, criticism of managerial decisions will be muted by reference to such behavior as "an unreasonable application of evaluation criteria," without labeling the application as "capricious" or "arbitrary" *per se*.

60

STRUCTURAL REQUIREMENTS

This section presents illustrations of structural requirements that appear in contractual agreements on evaluation. Also reported are arbitration cases related to management's right to alter structural requirements.

TYPES OF OBSERVATIONS

Some contractual agreements distinguish between evaluation and rating activities. The distinction depends on management's purposes in conducting the activities. The following excerpt from a contractual agreement illustrates the distinction between evaluation and rating of teachers:

> Teacher assessment consists of two major components. Evaluation is that phase of the process by which administrative or supervisory personnel formally (scheduled) or informally (unscheduled) appraise a teacher's performance primarily for the purpose of providing direction and bringing about improvement; rating is that phase of the process by which administrative or supervisory personnel formally assess, according to a predetermined schedule and instrument, the attainment of previously identified goals for the teacher's assignment.[2]

NUMBER OF OBSERVATIONS

For the most part, probationary teachers are scheduled to receive more observations than are tenured teachers:

> . . . A minimum of two observations per semester shall be made for each probationary teacher. . . . All permanent teachers must be evaluated in writing at least once each five (5) years *or at the request of the teacher if said request is made before March 1 of any year.*[3] [Emphasis added.]

Not all provisions make it clear whether or not the number of observations mentioned in the agreement is a minimum or a maximum number of observations. However, the following contract is an example of one that does. It indicates that the administration can schedule more observations if needed:

> The teaching performance of non-tenure teachers will be observed and a written evaluation prepared at least three times each year. Two of such evaluations shall take place in the first semester and one in the second semester, each evaluation to be held in a different marking period. *This*

shall not prevent the principal from making additional observations for eval-
uation purposes as he deems necessary. . . . All tenure teachers will be
formally evaluated at least once every three years.[4] [Emphasis added.]

The primary purpose for evaluation is to discover and discuss the
teacher's weak areas so that proper remedial steps may be taken to
assist the teacher in improving. In view of the purpose for evaluation,
one arbitrator has held that the number of evaluations is a negotiated
right secured for the teacher's benefit.[5]

In another case, where the contract required that there be at least
four observations, an arbitrator determined that the agreement was
violated when a principal gave a teacher an unsatisfactory rating based
on one observation. The arbitrator contended that if the four observations had been completed and if the required counseling had taken
place, the grievant's rating might have been different.[6]

There have been similar arbitration rulings in other cases. In one
case, the observations of a teacher's performance in the classroom had
been erratic. Although the agreement called for three formal written
evaluations per year, the teacher had no evaluation during the first year,
two during the second, and four in the third year. The arbitrator found
additional reasons for upholding the grievance, but he listed a failure
to conduct the proper number of observations among his reasons.[7]

Even a slight deviation from the contracted number of observations
can cause an arbitrator to overturn a managerial decision based on
performance evaluations. For example, in a school district where the
agreement called for probationary teachers to receive two observations
per year, in the final year of probation the administration gave a teacher
only one observation. When the administration denied tenure, a grievance was filed. The arbitrator upheld the grievance based on the administration's failure to conduct all observations called for in the agreement.[8,9]

Another contract called for nine observations per year for probationary teachers. These were to include unwritten, informal observations as well as written observations. The administration conducted no
formal observations reported in writing. The decision not to grant tenure
was based exclusively on informal observations, such as looking through
the glass in the teacher's door while the class was in session. The arbitrator found the absence of formal written observations to be a fatal
flaw in the decision process. He could not comprehend how the teacher
could have improved without receiving any communication from the
administration.[10]

WHO CAN EVALUATE?

The question "Who can evaluate a teacher's performance?" presumes
the existence of two groups of individuals. One group is composed of

those individuals who have been identified by the collective bargaining agreement as evaluators, and the other group consists of individuals who have been excluded by the agreement.

The following contract provision carefully defines the group that *must* evaluate a teacher's performance:

> Before a teacher is rated unsatisfactory in instructional performance the following steps shall have been taken:
> a. The principal, assistant principal, or department head shall have observed the teacher's classroom performance at least twice.
> b. The teacher's supervisor shall have observed the teacher's classroom performance at least twice. . . .[11]

Even though the preceding provision identifies those individuals who *must* evaluate, the words of the provision do not convey the intention that the individuals named are the only ones who *may* evaluate teachers. Taken alone, the words would appear to leave room for the possibility of having supplemental evaluations done by individuals not specifically mentioned in the agreement as long as the supplemental evaluations were consistent with the established purposes for having evaluations.

In a district where principals were authorized by contract to write the evaluation report, a teacher grieved her evaluation because the principal had not actually observed her teaching performance. Instead, her teaching was observed by an elementary supervisor. The arbitrator denied the grievance and noted that the agreement did not state that the principal was the only one who should make observations.[12]

Some contract provisions appear to leave open the definition of those who can evaluate and those who cannot evaluate teacher performance. Consider the following contract provision:

> All monitoring or observation of the work performance of a teacher will be conducted openly and with full knowledge of the teacher. Teachers will be given a copy of any evaluation report prepared by the supervisors and will have the right to discuss such report with their supervisor.[13]

From the preceding provision it is clear that each teacher will receive a copy of an evaluation report. However, it is not clear who will prepare the report. The term "supervisor" could refer to a principal, vice-principal, department head, or central office supervisor. Furthermore, it is not clear from the words alone whether nonsupervisors, such as students and parents, can contribute to the evaluation of teacher performance as long as their assessment is "conducted openly and with full knowledge of the teacher." Taken alone, the provision cited above does not identify the sources of information that may be used by the "supervisor" to prepare the evaluation report.

One teacher brought a grievance claiming that a new reappointment process had been unilaterally created in violation of the collective bargaining agreement. After inspecting the collective bargaining language, the arbitrator determined that the agreement had not been violated. The board had the right to devise a form that served to gather information relevant to the teacher's reappointment. In addition, the arbitrator held that neither the contract nor past practice prevented the board from considering the teacher's entire academic record, including ability to teach.[14]

In another school district, a music teacher was evaluated by the music supervisor. The grievant argued that evaluations were to be performed by building personnel only, and the music supervisor was not included among building personnel. The arbitrator did not agree with the grievant's contention that only building personnel could evaluate performance. In an appendix of the agreement, the arbitrator found language which stated that, when competency was an issue, a supervisor from outside the building could participate in the evaluation process. When competency was not an issue, evaluations were intended to be undertaken by building personnel alone.[15]

The following contract provision does not specifically name the individuals who will evaluate teachers, but it does identify evaluators:

> The building principal or appropriate supervisor shall acquaint each new employee under his/her supervision with a formal evaluation procedure or other such formal procedures as may be used and advise each new employee as to the designated person or persons who will observe and evaluate his/her performance. No formal evaluation shall take place until such orientation has been completed.[16]

One conceivable advantage of the preceding provision is that it would appear to meet management's desire for flexibility in designating evaluators while at the same time meeting a teacher's need to know whom his or her evaluators are going to be. Implicit in the wording of the provision is the assumption that individuals who are not identified as evaluators cannot participate in the evaluation process. Thus, the provision provides a means for defining two groups, evaluators and nonevaluators.

The administration in one school district thought it had the flexibility to assign any supervisor to the evaluation of teacher performance. In a grievance contesting the administration's interpretation of its rights, the union showed that in past practice only the building supervisor had been assigned to evaluate teacher performance. The arbitrator supported the union's version of its agreement with the school board; he noted that it was the purpose of evaluation to help the teacher do the best possible job and that one could assume those most familiar with the teacher's work would be in the best position to assist the teacher.[17]

In another school district, the teacher evaluation form contained a category for teacher-parent relationships; management concluded that it could solicit evaluations from students' parents. The school district argued that, since management was unable to directly observe teacher-parent relationships, direct solicitations from parents were needed. An arbitrator failed to support management's actions and directed management to discontinue such solicitations. The arbitrator believed the contract was clear in designating administrators as the only evaluators.[18]

LENGTH OF OBSERVATIONS

Given that the general purpose for observations is to identify a teacher's strengths and weaknesses, it follows that the process takes some time. How much time is required is not always specified. However, some evaluation provisions do specify a minimum number of minutes to be spent in formal observations.[19]

PROCESS REQUIREMENTS

Observation is the basic method used to evaluate teacher performance. Since teachers may feel vulnerable regarding performance evaluations, some contractual provisions require that they be given prior notice. A question frequently raised in arbitration is whether or not an evaluator can supplement his or her judgment with performance evidence other than that which has been gathered through direct observation. Finally, there is a follow-up phase to evaluations during which evaluation information is conveyed to the teacher. In some instances where the evaluation was negative, management has had the duty to take steps to help the teacher to improve his or her performance. A teacher's right to union involvement during follow-up activities has been another issue disputed in arbitration.

NOTICE

Following is an illustration of a contractual provision regarding notice. It requires that teachers be given notice prior to evaluations on half of the occasions when evaluations are performed:

> Teachers shall be notified three (3) days in advance of one-half (1/2) of the occasions during which formal evaluations take place.[20]

The presence or absence of specific language in a contractual agreement has made a significant difference in arbitrators' opinions in regard to the right to notice in advance of evaluation. The presence of a clear contractual agreement on advance notice has been used by arbitrators to set aside an unfavorable evaluation when notice was not given.[21] However, when the contractual agreement has been silent on the issue, arbitrators have avoided interpreting the agreement to grant the right to advance notice.[22]

Not to be confused with the right to advance notice is the right to have observations performed in an open manner. The following contractual provision provides for openness:

> . . . All monitoring or observation of the work performance of a teacher shall be conducted openly and with full knowledge of the teacher. . . .[23]

In a case where a provision existed for openness but not for prior notice, an arbitrator refused to expand the meaning of the phrase "open observations with full knowledge" to include advance notice. The term "open" was interpreted to mean that the observation would not be conducted in secret.[24]

Closely related to the issue of advance notice is the use of pre-observation conferences. Pre-observation conferences are joint meetings between the teacher and his or her supervisor. Frequently, the purpose of the meeting is to agree on the focus of a forthcoming observation. If a pre-observation meeting is provided for in the contractual agreement, then it is a procedural right of the teacher to receive such a meeting. Failure to grant such a meeting has been cause for an arbitrator to set aside a teacher's contested performance evaluation.[25] Conversely, in a case where the contract did not call for pre-observation meetings, it was within a supervisor's right to institute such procedures.[26]

USE OF SUPPLEMENTAL EVIDENCE

Although direct observation of a teacher's classroom performance is the primary basis for an evaluation report, arbitrators have held that classroom observations need not be the sole basis for performance evaluations.[27] Arbitrators have permitted the use of rating forms other than those specified in the agreement, if the language of the agreement was permissive.[28] One arbitrator held that student evaluations were a reasonable administrative tool for improving course content and instructional performance.[29] In addition, an arbitrator has held that asking substitute teachers for any positive or negative comments was not an infringement on a teacher's evaluation rights.[30]

FOLLOW-UP

Arbitration disputes associated with follow-up activities have tended to be concerned with three issues. First, there has been the issue of management's duty to assist a teacher who has received an unsatisfactory evaluation to improve his or her performance. Second, there has been the issue of a teacher's duty to improve. Third, there has been the issue of a teacher's right to union representation and counsel following an unsatisfactory evaluation.

Management's duty to provide assistance. Arbitration disputes over management's duty to provide assistance have dealt with four major issues:

1. A teacher receiving an unsatisfactory evaluation should be informed of the specific inadequacies in his or her performance.[31]
2. An unsatisfactory evaluation should be accompanied by a warning regarding the consequences of a failure to improve.[32]
3. A teacher receiving an unsatisfactory evaluation should be given a detailed plan for improving his or her performance.[33,34]
4. A teacher should be given adequate time for making improvements in his or her performance.[35]

The teacher's duty to improve. Contractual agreements do not normally contain explicit language regarding a teacher's duty to improve his or her unsatisfactory performance. Nevertheless, in some instances arbitrators have held that such a duty does exist. Where it was shown that management had attended to procedural requirements, it was incumbent upon the teacher-grievant to show evidence of having tried to improve.[36] In one arbitration case it was held that a teacher cannot abdicate professional responsibility to make improvements in performance.[37]

Right to union representation. Arbitrators have regarded abridgment of union representation rights as a serious violation of procedural requirements. In one instance, an arbitrator set aside an unsatisfactory evaluation when management had failed to inform the union, even though the grievant was given copies of the evaluation report. The contract specifically called for a separate notification to the union in instances of negative evaluation.[38] Another arbitrator set aside an unsatisfactory evaluation when the grievant was denied the opportunity to explain and defend his position with the assistance of union representatives.[39]

COMMON LAW REQUIREMENTS

A survey of arbitration cases pertaining to evaluation reveals that arbitrators have set aside unsatisfactory employee evaluations when managerial authority was misused. The forms of misuse can be classified in three ways: unsatisfactory evaluations based on unsubstantiated allegations, unreasonable application of contractual provisions resulting in unsatisfactory evaluations, and unsatisfactory evaluations as a consequence of discrimination.

UNSUBSTANTIATED ALLEGATIONS

Managerial actions that adversely affect the status of teachers are at times precipitated by negative teacher evaluations. In some instances negative evaluations have not been based on direct observation of a teacher performance. Instead, the negative evaluation was based on information supplied by individuals other than the evaluator. When an evaluator uses information that contains allegations detrimental to a teacher's status without seeking support for the allegations, the evaluator runs the risk of having his or her negative evaluation set aside.

In one case, a teacher was denied tenure because of information contained in a letter alleging that she had failed in her performance as a teacher. Evidence obtained during the arbitration hearing indicated that the allegation of poor performance had been communicated to the teacher's principal by the assistant principal. The assistant principal had been the teacher's supervisor under a previous administrative organization. The evidence indicated that the assistant principal's allegations could have been a carry-over from his earlier association with the teacher. Also, there was some indication that the assistant principal was unfair in his evaluation of the teacher's performance. The principal had uncritically accepted the assistant principal's comments. Furthermore, the teacher had not been given an opportunity to defend herself against the allegations before being denied tenure. The arbitrator's reinstatement of the teacher was based on the lack of substantiation for allegations that had been used to deny tenure.[40]

In another case, a principal had made certain evaluations of a teacher based on hearsay from other teachers. The teacher was accused of being critical of school policies, which the principal interpreted as disloyal behavior. The principal indicated on the teacher's evaluation form that she needed improvement in her professional qualities, but did not confront the teacher with the allegations. The arbitrator took the position that it is often the most professional employee who raises questions. Since the principal had not determined the truth of the matter before evaluating the teacher negatively, the arbitrator directed management to remove the negative evaluation.[41]

UNREASONABLE APPLICATION OF CONTRACTUAL PROVISIONS

Most teacher evaluation procedures provide for teachers to be informed of the criteria by which their performance will be evaluated. These criteria usually include a reasonable time schedule for evaluations and performance improvements. Given these elemental features of evaluation provisions, arbitrators have held the following managerial actions to be unreasonable:

1. basing an evaluation solely on unfavorable information[42]
2. failing to consider evaluation data before taking actions having a negative effect on a teacher's status[43]
3. expecting too much improvement too soon[44]
4. basing a negative evaluation solely on parental complaints.[45]

DISCRIMINATION

With regard to performance evaluation, discrimination is pernicious because it undermines any attempt to base evaluations on merit. If employees believe that factors other than the merit of their performance account for the outcome of an evaluation, employee morale is likely to be seriously eroded. The few reported incidents of discrimination in employee evaluation can be classified in two ways. First, there has been discrimination based on personal animosity between the supervisor and the employee.[46] Second, there has been discrimination based on the employee's union activities.[47]

SUMMARY

Performance evaluations can have a negative effect on a teacher's status. A poor evaluation can prevent a teacher from obtaining tenure and can lead to dismissal. Given the possible adverse consequences of performance evaluations, arbitrators frequently interpret contractual agreements covering performance evaluations in such a way as to provide assurances of "fair dealing."

For example, when a specific number of observations is mentioned in an agreement, arbitrators have tended to insist that all these observations be undertaken. Management has not had the right to unilaterally reduce the number of observations mentioned in the agreement. The charge of limitations in performance is more credible if the limitations were evident on more than one occasion.

Because observation activities are complex, some parties have attempted to increase the reliability of evaluations by specifying in their contractual agreements the length of time for observation activities. In addition, parties have agreed on evaluation instruments and techniques for bringing certain features of the teaching act into clearer focus. Management has not been supported by arbitrators when it has failed to observe provisions of an agreement and thereby reduced the reliability of performance evaluations. However, there have been cases where arbitrators have sustained management's right to go beyond contractual provisions in order to increase the reliability of evaluations.

When a teacher has been given a poor evaluation, it has been incumbent upon management to inform the teacher of performance deficiencies and to take active steps to help remove the stated deficiencies before taking adverse action against him or her. Even if a contract has not specifically required management to inform teachers of deficiencies in evaluations and actively help teachers to remove deficiencies, the burden is likely to rest with management. At a minimum, arbitrators have been inclined to perceive teachers as having sufficient interest in their jobs and reputations that management has a significant burden to prove incompetency in performance.

In addition, arbitrators bring to their assignments the assumption that management should not use its authority in an arbitrary, capricious, or discriminatory way. The application of this "common law" assumption has meant that management has not been permitted to give negative evaluations based on unsubstantiated allegations, nor has management been permitted to make "unreasonable" interpretations of evaluation criteria. Finally, management has not been permitted to give a negative evaluation when personal animosity motivated the evaluator.

NOTES

1. *St. Vrain Valley School District (Longmont, Colorado)*, 93 AIS 8, John Phillip Linn, Arbitrator.
2. *Government Employee Relations Report,* No. 574 (Washington: Bureau of National Affairs, 1974), p. X-13.
3. *Government Employee Relations Report,* No. 631 (Washington: Bureau of National Affairs, 1975), p. X-9. See also *Government Employee Relations Report,* No. 653 (Washington: Bureau of National Affairs, 1976), p. X-4.
4. *Government Employee Relations Report,* No. 622 (Washington: Bureau of National Affairs, 1975), p. X-6.
5. *Niagara Falls (New York) Board of Education,* 45 AIS 15, W. Albert Rill, Arbitrator. See also *Pavilion (New York) Central School District,* 62 AIS 13, Thomas N. Rinaldo, Arbitrator.

6. *Penfield (New York) Board of Education,* 52 AIS 4, Rodney E. Dennis, Arbitrator.
7. *Penn Yan (New York) Central School District,* 93 AIS 6, Robert E. Stevens, Arbitrator.
8. *Pavilion Central (New York) School District,* 66 AIS 3, Robert J. Rabin, Arbitrator.
9. For a different view of slight deviations from an agreement, see also *Board of Higher Education of the City of New York (New York),* 45 AIS 3, Milton Rubin, Arbitrator.
10. *Carle Place (New York) U.F.S.D. No. 11,* 47 AIS 4, Jonas Silver, Arbitrator.
11. *Government Employee Relations Report,* Reference File 81, RF-116 (Washington: Bureau of National Affairs, 1976), p. 1014.
12. *Toms River (New Jersey) Board of Education,* 74 AIS 22, Jonas Aarons, Arbitrator.
13. *Government Employee Relations Report,* No. 622 (Washington: Bureau of National Affairs, 1975), p. X-6.
14. *Board of Higher Education (New York, New York),* 56 AIS 2, Mark L. Kahn, Arbitrator.
15. *Brentwood (New York) Board of Education, U.F.S.D. No. 12,* 51 AIS 13, Daniel G. Collins, Arbitrator.
16. *Government Employee Relations Report,* No. 653 (Washington: Bureau of National Affairs, 1976), p. X-4.
17. *North Colonie (New York) Central School District,* 66 AIS 6, Daniel House, Arbitrator.
18. *North Colonie (New York) Central School District,* 91 AIS 24, Jonas Aarons, Arbitrator.
19. *Government Employee Relations Report,* No. 622 (Washington: Bureau of National Affairs, 1975), p. X-6.
20. *Government Employee Relations Report,* No. 593 (Washington: Bureau of National Affairs, 1975), p. X-5.
21. See *Enlarged City School District of Troy (New York),* 91 AIS 13, James R. Markowitz, Arbitrator.
22. See *Onteora (New York) School District Board of Education,* 72 AIS 11, Louis Yagoda, Arbitrator.
23. *Government Employee Relations Report,* No. 631 (Washington: Bureau of National Affairs, 1975), p. X-9.
24. *Onteora (New York) School District Board of Education,* 72 AIS 11, Louis Yagoda, Arbitrator.
25. *Penn Yan (New York) Central School District Board of Education,* 82 AIS 9, Elizabeth R. Croft, Arbitrator.
26. *Pearl River (New York) Board of Education,* 83 AIS 14, Joseph F. Wildebush, Arbitrator.
27. *Hudson (New Hampshire) School District,* 94 AIS 20, Edward C. Pinkus, Arbitrator.
28. *Willingboro (New Jersey) Board of Education,* 53 AIS 16, John J. Saracino, Arbitrator.
29. *Niagara-Wheatfield (New York) Central School District,* 51 AIS 16, Margery Gootnick, Arbitrator.

30. *West Bloomfield (Michigan) Board of Education*, 45 AIS 10, Richard I. Bloch, Arbitrator.
31. See *Niles Township (Illinois) Community High School*, 13 AIS 16, Aaron S. Wolff, Arbitrator.
32. See *Board of Higher Education of the City of New York (New York)*, 32 AIS 5, Thomas G. S. Christensen, Arbitrator.
33. See *Boston School Committee (Massachusetts)*, 34 AIS 17, Daniel G. MacLeod, Arbitrator; *School District No. 1 (Denver, Colorado)*, 83 AIS 7, Clyde Emery, Arbitrator.
34. For illustrations of contractual language requiring a detailed plan for improvement, see *Government Employee Relations Report*, No. 574 (Washington: Bureau of National Affairs, 1974), p. X-13; *Government Employee Relations Report*, No. 631 (Washington: Bureau of National Affairs, 1975), p. X-9; *Government Employee Relations Report*, Reference File 81, RF-116 (Washington: Bureau of National Affairs, 1976), p. 1014.
35. See *City School of Gary (Indiana)*, 37 AIS 9, Jordan Jay Hillman, Arbitrator; *City School District of the City of New Rochelle (New York)*, 73 AIS 3, Alfred H. Brent, Arbitrator.
36. *City University of New York (New York)*, 32 AIS 8, Israel Ben Scheiber, Arbitrator.
37. *Maynard (Massachusetts) School Committee*, 39 AIS 7, William J. Fallon, Arbitrator. See also *Indianapolis (Indiana) Public Schools*, 12 AIS 15, Marlin M. Voltz, Arbitrator.
38. *Board of Education, Joint School Dstrict No. 8 (Madison, Wisconsin)*, 31 AIS 27, James L. Greenwald, Arbitrator.
39. *World Instruction and Translation, Inc.*, 19 AIS 13, James P. Whyte, Arbitrator. See also *Milwaukee (Wisconsin) Board of School Directors*, 61 AIS 1, Arlen C. Christenson, Arbitrator; *Fox Chapel (Pennsylvania) Area School District*, 78 AIS 3, William C. Stonehouse, Jr., Arbitrator.
40. *Penn Yan (New York) Central School District*, 93 AIS 6, Robert E. Stevens, Arbitrator.
41. *Fort Wayne (Indiana) Board of Trustees*, 53 AIS 15, Lawrence F. Doppelt, Arbitrator.
42. *Utica (New York) City School District*, 69 AIS 17, James A. Gross, Arbitrator.
43. *Board of Trustees of Schoolcraft College (Michigan)*, 1 AIS 30, Leon J. Herman, Arbitrator.
44. *Rockaway Township (New Jersey) Board of Education*, 13 AIS 6, Joseph F. Wildebush, Arbitrator. See also *Millis (Massachusetts) School Committee*, 70 AIS 19, Jerome S. Rubenstein, Arbitrator.
45. *Urbana (Illinois) School District No. 116*, 45 AIS 5, Reynolds C. Seitz, Arbitrator.
46. *Cranston (Rhode Island) School Committee*, 41 AIS 5, David R. Bloodsworth, Arbitrator. See also *Palmer (Massachusetts) School Committee*, 23 AIS 12, Stanley Young, Arbitrator.
47. *North Colonie (New York) Central Schools*, 79 AIS 7, Bernard D. Levy, Arbitrator.

Termination of Nontenured Teachers

The United States Supreme Court has established that under certain circumstances nontenured teachers do have constitutional "due process" protections against termination. The two leading cases, *Perry v. Sindermann* and *Board of Regents v. Roth,* are both described in this chapter.

In cases where terminated nontenured teachers have sought due process considerations, they have relied mainly on the concept of just cause. A few arbitrators have attempted to compare constitutional and collective bargaining provisions for due process, and such a comparison is included in this chapter. However, the primary purpose of the chapter is to present the issues that are raised when the concept of just cause is applied to terminated nontenured teachers.

CONSTITUTIONAL PROTECTIONS OF DUE PROCESS

The due process rights of nontenured teachers were considered in *Board of Regents v. Roth*[1] and *Perry v. Sindermann,*[2] cases heard by the Supreme Court in 1972. Before the *Roth* and *Sindermann* decisions, lower federal courts had failed to agree on the rights of nontenured teachers to a hearing before dismissal.[3] In *Roth* and *Sindermann* the Supreme Court determined that nontenured teachers had hearing rights prior to dismissal if the teachers could show that their constitutional rights to property or liberty were reduced by the actions of school authorities.

THE ROTH CASE

When David F. Roth accepted a position as assistant professor of political science at Wisconsin State University-Oshkosh, his employment notice specified that his appointment was for a fixed term of one academic year. At the end of the year, he was informed that he would not be rehired for the coming academic year. The rules of the University did not provide for a pre-dismissal hearing or a statement of reasons.

Roth first brought suit against the University in the United States District Court for the Western District of Wisconsin.[4] He asserted that the decision not to rehire him was an attempt to punish him for having made certain statements critical of the University's administration. He alleged that his dismissal violated his right to freedom of speech, and failure to give him reasons for his nonretention violated his right to procedural due process. The district court granted a motion supporting that portion of his case which called for due process procedures.

The University appealed the case to the United States Court of Appeals, Seventh Circuit.[5] The appeals court affirmed the opinion of the district court. The appeals court stated:

> The contest on this appeal is whether the state university, in deciding not to retain a non-tenure professor, must initially shoulder the burden of exposing to the limited test ordered by the district court the reasons on which its decision is predicated, and to that extent demonstrate that its reasons are not impermissible . . .

The appeals court resolved the issue in favor of Roth by balancing the respective interests of the parties; it found that Roth's interests in retaining his position were sufficient to warrant use of the due process procedures outlined by the lower district court. The appeals court added:

> The instant case arose after serious disturbance on that particular campus, and public expressions by plaintiff of his opinions, critical of the administrators. . . . An additional reason for sustaining application in the instant case, and others with a background of controversy and unwelcome expressions of opinion, is that it serves as a prophylactic against non-retention decisions improperly motivated by the exercise of protected rights.[6]

The case went to the United States Supreme Court. The only issue before the Supreme Court was whether Roth had a constitutional right to a statement of reasons and a hearing on the University's decision not to rehire him. The Supreme Court stated that Roth had not been deprived of any constitutional rights. This was the reasoning:

> The requirements of procedural due process apply only to the deprivation of interests encompassed by the Fourteenth Amendment's protection of liberty and property. When protected interests are implicated, the right to some kind of prior hearing is paramount (citation). But the range of interests protected by procedural due process is not infinite.[7]

THE SINDERMANN CASE

Robert P. Sindermann served as a professor in the Texas university system for ten years, the last four years at Odessa Junior College on successive one-year contracts. During his fourth year at Odessa, Sindermann became involved in a heated campus controversy. He aligned himself with a group that was critical of the college administration because it did not want to convert to a four-year college. When the governing board of the college voted not to offer him a new contract, Sindermann brought an action at the district court level. He alleged that he had not been rehired because of his criticisms of the governing board, and thus his right to free speech had been curtailed. He asserted that the board's failure to grant him a hearing violated the Fourteenth Amendment's due process clause.

The district court failed to uphold Sindermann's allegations. However, the appeals court reversed the lower court decision, stating that if the nonrenewal had been based on the teacher's exercise of his free speech right, the nonrenewal would have violated the Fourteenth Amendment. The appeals court also held that even though no formal tenure system existed, Sindermann could show that he had reason to expect employment.

The case eventually went to the Supreme Court and was heard on the same day as the Roth case.[8] However, in the case of Sindermann, the Supreme Court upheld the decision of the appeals court. In doing so, the Court affirmed the following:

> (1) the lack of a contractual or tenure right to re-employment, taken alone, did not defeat the teacher's claim, (2) the government may not deny a benefit to a person on a basis that infringes his constitutionally protected interest in free speech, (3) there is no requirement in the Constitution that a nontenure teacher be afforded a hearing or reasons for his nonretention unless it can be shown that the nonretention deprived the teacher of some interest in "liberty" or "property" protected by the Fourteenth Amend-

ment, (4) however, a teacher employed for a number of years at the same institution should be permitted to show that while no explicit tenure system existed, a *de facto* tenure system did exist at the institution, (5) proof that such a system existed would not entitle the teacher to reinstatement, but would entitle him to a hearing, (6) at the hearing, the teacher could be informed of the grounds for his nonretention and be given an opportunity to refute them, and (7) . . . [following] a hearing . . . the matter could then come before the courts for review . . . [9]

FOUR CONDITIONS THAT CREATE PROPERTY INTEREST

Unless a teacher can establish a legitimate claim to either a property or a liberty interest in continued employment, he or she may be dismissed without a hearing.[10] The Supreme Court has established four general conditions of employment that create a property interest.

First, a teacher has a property interest in continued employment if tenure status has been granted by the employing institution.[11] Second, a property interest can be established by possession of a contract of one or more years.[12] Thus, termination of a public employee in the middle of a contract, even a one-year contract, would entitle the employee to federal due process rights. Third, a property interest exists if a teacher can point to rules or mutually explicit understandings that support his or her anticipation of continued employment.[13,14] Fourth, a property interest exists if there is a clearly implied promise of continued employment.[15]

TWO CONDITIONS THAT CREATE LIBERTY INTEREST

The meaning of the right to liberty has been given a broad interpretation by the Supreme Court. In the *Roth* decision, it defined the right to liberty as follows:

. . . it denotes not merely freedom from bodily restraint but also the right of the individual to contract, to engage in any of the common occupations of life, to acquire useful knowledge, to marry, establish a home and bring up children, to worship God according to the dictates of his own conscience, and generally to enjoy those privileges long recognized . . . as essential to the orderly pursuit of happiness by free men.[16]

A nontenured teacher may acquire due process rights when termination jeopardizes his or her right to liberty. The Supreme Court has recognized a liberty interest in these circumstances:

1. A teacher is denied renewal for a reason that would damage his or her standing or association within a community, or would injure his or her reputation.[17]

2. The termination process imposes a stigma or other disability on a teacher's freedom to take advantage of future teaching opportunities.[18]

Under these conditions, a hearing is required as a due process right.

COMPARISONS OF CONSTITUTIONAL DUE PROCESS RIGHTS WITH THE ARBITRAL STANDARD OF JUST CAUSE

Arbitration standards and case law differ somewhat in their interpretation of due process rights. The difference is largely a matter of the degree of protection afforded.

A Wisconsin arbitration panel was presented with the issue of whether constitutional due process rights should provide a dismissed nontenured teacher with the same protection as received under a just cause standard of termination.[19] To resolve the issue, Chairman Arlen Christenson relied on court decisions in *Roth v. Board of Regents*[20] and *Gouge v. Joint School District.*[21]

Christenson noted that in *Gouge* the court ruled that a teacher in a public school is protected by the due process clause of the Fourteenth Amendment against a nonrenewal decision that is entirely without basis in fact or that denies the teacher some constitutional right, such as freedom of speech.[22] Christenson also cited the *Roth* ruling that a teacher must show that the reasons given for nonrenewal were wholly inappropriate. Only after such a demonstration would school authorities be obliged to defend their reasons.[23]

In briefs presented to Christenson by the school board and the union, the courts' remarks in the *Roth* and *Gouge* cases were given different interpretations. The union believed that the courts inferred a just cause standard; the school board contended that something less than just cause was required in the termination of nontenured teachers.

Christenson agreed with the school board, citing the court's decision in *Roth*. The court had stated that the due process standard was intended to be considerably less severe than the standard of "cause" as it was applied to professors with tenure. The court further stated that unless a substantial difference between the two standards were recognized in a case-by-case application of the constitutional doctrine as set forth in the *Roth* case, the rationale for the underlying doctrine would be impaired.

Being still more direct, the court added that in applying the constitutional doctrine, the court was bound to respect bases for nonretention "enjoying minimal factual support" and bases for nonretention supported by "subtle reason." Christenson concluded that the constitutional due process standard allowed a school board to terminate a nontenured teacher if the action was not wholly without basis in fact or wholly unreasoned or prompted by constitutionally impermissible grounds.[24]

In its review of *Roth v. Board of Regents,* the appeals court did not compare the due process standard and the just cause standard. Nor did the issue arise when the case was brought before the Supreme Court. The effect of the Supreme Court ruling was to spell out more precisely what constitutional rights (liberty and property) could not be abridged in the termination of nontenured teachers without invoking the Fourteenth Amendment due process clause.[25]

Arbitrator Christenson's comparison between an arbitral just cause standard and the due process standard remains one of the few such comparisons that apply to nontenured teachers. It is probably still valid; that is, the due process standard as applied to nontenured teachers provides fewer substantive or procedural rights than the just cause standard as applied to tenured teachers. In addition, it is clear that under due process procedures a terminated nontenured employee must initially carry the burden of showing substantial defect in the reasons, facts, or constitutional grounds of the employer's actions. It is only after proof of defective action that the employer is obligated to provide justification for terminating a nontenured employee.

The due process standard would appear to have features that weigh in favor of maintaining the initial action of school employers. However, a number of court cases have defined in more detail specific due process rights of public employees. For example, various federal courts have determined that under certain circumstances public employees have the right to advance notice of any charges against them,[26] the right to a hearing prior to any action taken against them,[27] the right to a hearing before an impartial decision maker,[28] the right to confront their accusers,[29] the right to cross-examine witnesses,[30] the right to a written decision,[31] the right to the use of legal rules of evidence,[32] and the right to representation by counsel.[33] The general thrust of the courts' opinions has been to increase the opportunities for showing some defect in the actions taken by public authorities.

Despite the willingness of the federal courts to expand on the procedural rights of public employees, it is doubtful that any single case would contain all the procedural rights that various court jurisdictions have permitted. However, the standard of just cause as developed in arbitration now encompasses a fairly coherent set of substantive and procedural rights. Just cause can be applied in each instance of termination or other adverse action if it has been incorporated into the collective bargaining agreement.[34]

An illustration of such an application is provided by a Colorado case arbitrated by William E. Rentfro. In this case the school board raised the issue of how to construe the term "just cause" in the context of nontenured teacher renewal. The board took the position that the just cause standard, when applied to nontenured teachers, could not be equated with the traditional concept of just cause. They claimed that the traditional concept of just cause grew out of an industrial experience and was foreign to situations involving teacher renewal. In regard to nontenured teachers, the board argued, the just cause requirement meant only that the board could not fail to reemploy a nontenured teacher for constitutionally or statutorily impermissible reasons, for no reason at all, or for a reason unrelated to the school system.

Arbitrator Rentfro agreed that just cause included the meanings ascribed to it by the school board; he did not agree that the just cause concept could not include more. For example, he thought that it was likely that just cause would include a consideration of the soundness and fairness of the evaluation system which led to the decision not to renew a nontenured teacher. In Rentfro's judgment, the meaning of just cause for nontenured teacher terminations would need to be worked out over a period of time:

> Concepts of "due process" and "just cause" as they relate to the school board's determinations of nonrenewal, and as they relate to other actions that affect tenure of employment, will be developed and refined as the parties to the process practice arbitration of "just cause" . . . . it [is] unwise to predetermine the limitations on the "just cause" concept. . . . The parameters will have to be developed on a case by case basis.[35]

It appears, then, that just cause implies something more in the context of an arbitration case than does a constitutional due process standard when applied to termination of nontenured teachers. However, there exists no final authoritative determination regarding how much more could be inferred; substantive and procedural rights must be determined in each application of the just cause standard to a specific case involving a nontenured teacher.

APPLICATION OF JUST CAUSE STANDARD TO THE TERMINATION OF NONTENURED TEACHERS

The termination of nontenured teachers can be viewed in terms of two broad issues: (1) are the standards for termination just? and (2) have termination standards been implemented fairly? Within each of the broad perspectives, specific cases have given rise to narrower issues.

With regard to the justness of standards, these issues have been raised in arbitration: (1) Is a school board obligated to keep a teacher who does not accept the school board's educational philosophy and methods? (2) Can a school board determine that "superior" teaching ability is necessary for tenure? (3) What obligation does a teacher have to show improvements in teaching performance when deficient performance is properly documented? (4) Does a school board have the responsibility to carefully consider the basis for a recommendation to dismiss a nontenured teacher?

With regard to fairness of implementation, these issues have been raised in arbitration: (1) What obligations does a school board have to communicate its expectation for improvement? (2) How important is it for school administrators to adhere to the number of classroom observations called for in the collective bargaining agreement? (3) How important is it for a school board to exclude information in arriving at a decision to terminate nontenured teachers? (4) Should a school board be held responsible for a "fair hearing" on a decision to terminate a nontenured teacher? (5) Should nontenured teachers be given an opportunity to rebut criticism? (6) Is a school board accountable for giving proper notification of a decision to terminate a nontenured teacher?

JUSTNESS OF STANDARDS

The following sections provide interpretation of the key issues in evaluating the justness of standards applied in the termination of nontenured teachers.

Is a school board obligated to keep a teacher who does not accept its educational philosophy and methods? As a result of an intensive self-study experience, one school board adopted an educational philosophy that stressed student involvement and minimized teacher direction in the learning process. In this case, evidence was presented which characterized the grievant as being capable of drilling students and raising their level of academic achievement by virtue of such drill. Evidence was not clear with respect to the grievant's willingness to adopt methods more in tune with the educational philosophy of the school board.

The arbitrator recognized that inherent in the problem of extending tenure to the grievant was the development of assumptions by the school board regarding the nature of a "good teacher." The arbitrator stated that:

> . . . views as to the qualities a good teacher must possess are widely disparate; different people emphasize different qualities. Obviously, a good

teacher must possess technical competence over the subject matter and the ability to transmit knowledge. More subtly, a good teacher must demonstrate an empathy with students and sympathy with an acceptance of a community's concept of educational goals. A good teacher must have the ability to stimulate intellectual curiosity in students and be able to motivate them to achieve academic competence independently.

In the arbitrator's opinion, a school board acting in good faith was "obligated to retain only such nontenured teachers as give full and unreserved acceptance of the educational methods and philosophy promulgated by the board on behalf of the community."[36]

Can a school board determine that "superior" teaching ability is necessary for tenure? A school board took the position that a candidate for tenure must possess "superior" teaching ability in order to be given tenure. The grievant was rated as "average" or "below average."

The grievant did not contest the right of the school board to establish the standard for retention. However, he did challenge the consistency with which the school board had pursued its requirement of "superior" teaching ability. The grievant claimed that the school board had a past policy of accepting teachers deemed to possess "satisfactory" teaching ability on the basis of "average" performance. The school board denied it had changed its standards and insisted it had always required "superior" or "above average" performance.

The arbitrator ruled that the grievant had not sustained the burden of showing that there had been a change in school board policy to the disadvantage of the grievant. The grievance was denied, and failure to renew the probationary teacher's contract was upheld.[37]

What obligation does a teacher have to show improvements in teaching performance when deficient performance is properly documented? A teacher had a long record of satisfactory teaching. However, during her last assignment as a teacher of junior high school drafting, the school administration became dissatisfied with her performance; the administration decided to discharge the teacher. Through the intervention of the union president, an *ad hoc* probationary period was arranged. The teacher was employed for an additional year in order to give her an opportunity to improve her teaching performance.

The administration identified specific areas of improvement and suggested means for making improvements. One of the suggestions was for the teacher to visit three classrooms in which teaching was taking place in the manner desired by the administration. The teacher, however, refused to make the visitations, claiming that it would have been inconvenient since she was not given sufficient notice. The teacher also failed to follow through in other areas of performance, such as improvement of her attitude toward students.

The arbitrator declared that the discharge of the teacher was justified. Both the administration and the teacher had had contractual obligations to work toward the improvement of the teacher's performance, and the teacher had not fulfilled her obligation.[38]

In more traditional probationary situations, nontenured teachers' failure to meet administrations' expectations for improvement has been cause for nonrenewal. When it can be shown through proper documentation that teaching performance is deficient, the teacher's failure to improve performance has been upheld as just cause for nonrenewal.[39,40]

Does a school board have the responsibility to carefully consider the basis for a recommendation to dismiss a nontenured teacher? When arbitrators rule that employers have acted arbitrarily or capriciously, it may be because employers have failed to carefully consider their actions. For example, after reviewing evidence regarding the release of one of two nontenured teachers, an arbitrator concluded that both teachers would have been retained if the evaluation policy and procedure had been applied objectively. The only apparent reason for retaining the one teacher over the other was the fact that the teacher who was retained could make a contribution to extracurricular activities that were of interest to the recommending principal. The arbitrator found the principal to have abused his power of recommendation. In addition, the arbitrator determined that no positive contribution was made by the director of instruction, who merely "rubber stamped" the principal's recommendation.[41]

FAIRNESS OF IMPLEMENTATION

The next sections report interpretations of key issues related to fairness in implementing just cause standards.

What obligation does a school board have to communicate its expectations for improvement? In the private sector, the concept of just cause has included the principle that discipline should not be punitive but corrective. The basic idea has been to save and improve the future usefulness of the employee. The seriousness of the employee's infractions has been used as a guide to the possibilities for improvement.[42,43]

The evaluation of nontenured employees is not necessarily a disciplinary matter.[44] However, certain aspects of the principle of corrective discipline have been considered in situations involving the retention of nontenured employees. Unless the collective bargaining agreement provides otherwise, it is normally expected that school management will make a conscientious attempt to assist nontenured employees in making improvements in their teaching performance when improvement is necessary for job retention.[45] The first step is communication to the employee of any defects in his or her performance which would contribute to nonretention if left uncorrected. Assistance also includes making available the resources of the organization, and giving specific suggestions for removing the performance defects.

Failure on the part of a school board to provide a nontenured teacher with help in overcoming deficiencies resulted in an arbitrator's deciding that the teacher should be reinstated. On the basis of evaluation reports submitted by various supervisors, the arbitrator determined that the deficiencies could have been remedied if adequate opportunity for improvement had been provided.[46]

A nontenured teacher cannot improve his or her performance if he or she is unaware or inadequately informed of deficiencies. An arbitrator ruled in favor of the reinstatement of a nontenured teacher who had not been informed of deficiencies in performance:

> What the Board did was to permit the first year conduct to continue into the second year without advising Mr. R. of the standard he was expected to meet and that he was not meeting that standard. In other words, Mr. R. was not given any opportunity to correct any standard deviation, if there was such a standard.[47]

In another situation, an arbitrator upheld the petition of a nontenured teacher for reinstatement when evidence showed that the supervisors' statements of deficiencies were so vague as to provide an inadequate guide to improvement. The grievant was alleged to have "poor judgment" and "poor relationships with students."[48]

Another type of ambiguity occurred when the supervisory evaluations were widely discrepant; it was judged that the nontenured teacher did not know what was expected of him and consequently was denied an opportunity to improve.[49]

To meet a just cause standard it is necessary to communicate adequate information to nontenured teachers about any deficiencies that may lead to their nonrenewal and to give sufficient time for them to take corrective action. However, timeliness is not always sufficient. In addition, some arbitrators have ruled that school management is responsible for providing the nontenured teacher with constructive criticism[50] and guidelines[51] that would assist the nontenured teacher in making the desired corrections.

How important is it for school administrators to adhere to the number of classroom observations called for in the collective bargaining agreement? Classroom observations provide an opportunity for school administrators to engage in constructive criticism and establish guidelines to help a teacher improve performance. Because classroom observations have the potential to assist a nontenured teacher in securing tenure, a failure on the part of supervisors to fulfill contractual obligations regarding observations is likely to be considered a serious infraction of the collective bargaining agreement.

One arbitrator conveyed his sense of the importance of classroom observations as follows:

> The bargained for times of evaluation were rights secured to a probationary teacher to take proper steps to make any required changes in order to qualify for tenure. Those provisions are not merely procedural steps, but substantive rights of the grievant.[52]

In another case, the language of the collective bargaining agreement provided the following conditions regarding the evaluation of nontenured teachers:

Teacher Evaluation

A. One of the responsibilities of the school administration is that of making periodic, ongoing evaluations of the performance of teachers for the purpose of assessing ability, effectiveness, and determining the need for any assistance necessary for improvement.

   1. Nontenure teachers shall receive a written evaluation at least two (2) times each year. This written evaluation shall be preceded by at least two (2) classroom observations. Observations shall be conducted openly and with knowledge of the teacher.

   2. The written evaluation shall be followed by an evaluator/teacher conference, in order that each teacher be aware of his strengths and weaknesses. Teachers needing improvement shall be given an opportunity to utilize professional help so that they may attempt to rectify difficulties. A written statement setting forth the problems, suggestions concerning ways to solve the problems, and the results which will occur if problems are not solved, shall be given the teacher.

   By the end of each nontenure year the teacher shall receive an Annual Formal Evaluation, a copy of which is to be placed in the Education Center Personnel File. This evaluation will be a composite of all evaluations for the year, and shall be discussed point-by-point with the teacher. The teacher shall sign one (1) copy which is to be returned to the administration. Such signature does not necessarily indicate agreement with the evaluation, and any teacher disagreeing may put objections in writing in the space provided.[53]

In one case, during the grievant's probationary term he was given one semester of teaching experience and one semester of nonteaching experience on a long-range planning committee. The administration rated his performance on the committee as below average. The low rating in the nonteaching area contributed to his termination. The arbitrator noted that the teacher's contract and the collective bargaining agreement provided for one full year of teaching, during which he would receive supervision and assistance. Since management had not fulfilled the terms of the teacher's contract or the collective bargaining agreement, the arbitrator recommended reinstatement.[54,55]

Arbitrators have made distinctions between the following two kinds of situations: (1) where management's failure to provide the required number of classroom observations may have contributed to the teacher's inability to improve teaching performance; and (2) where management's departure from contractual procedures had no clear negative impact on the decision on the teacher's retention. For example, in one situation not all members of the evaluation committee participated in making observations. The committee was composed equally of management and faculty representatives, and each committee member was responsible for making observations in the grievant's classroom. When one of the management representatives did not participate, this left the majority view in the hands of the faculty representatives. In the arbitrator's view, the absence of the management representative from the evaluation committee activities did not "fatally bypass" the procedures called for in the collective bargaining agreement.[56]

How important is it for a school board to include all pertinent information in arriving at a decision to terminate nontenured teachers? Usually arbitrators will not uphold a school board's decision to terminate a nontenured teacher in instances where the school board has excluded relevant information in reaching its decision. The relevance of the excluded information is, in part, determined by the collective bargaining agreement. Relevance is also determined by the arbitrator's assessment that there was a reasonable possibility that the excluded information would have changed the decision to terminate the nontenured teacher.

A number of collective bargaining agreements call for evaluation procedures. Some of the accepted procedures include specific criteria which evaluators are directed to use. Usually the criteria are contained in prescribed evaluation forms.[57] When evaluation results are excluded from consideration in reaching a decision to terminate, a school board in effect has substituted its own criteria for those which it had agreed to use. A school board is not necessarily restricted to using only those criteria it has agreed to use; however, it cannot exclude contractually agreed upon criteria.

For example, in making a recommendation to terminate a nontenured teacher, a superintendent admitted that he did not consider positive information which had been given to him by the teacher's supervisors. The evidence indicated that the decision to terminate had been based primarily on the administrator's concern about the teacher's involvement in two controversial incidents. In one incident the teacher had signed a poster being circulated by students which had "four-letter" words on it. In a second incident she had agreed to supervise students on an overnight ski trip. When the students' behavior became unruly, the teacher left the students, both girls and boys, with one male teacher. The administration did not support the teacher's decision to leave the students. Both incidents apparently caused the administration to overlook the positive evaluations the teacher had received regarding her teaching performance.

The arbitrator did not overlook the evaluation information, however. The arbitrator stated:

> There is no question that by contract a teacher's evaluation must be considered in determining his eligibility for reemployment. Dr. B. confessed that he did not consider the evaluation data at all, although the data were available to him and had been prepared by two members of the faculty, one of them the dean of the school. In failing to consider the evaluation, the employer has neglected the threshold requirement which determines reemployment of [the grievant]. It follows that this violation compels a reversal of the refusal to employ [the grievant] for the coming year and that, as a consequence, a permanent full status must be offered . . . . [58,59]

By excluding information, school authorities may have given too much weight to the factors that they did consider, in the judgment of arbitrators. The question in the arbitrators' minds appears to be whether or not school authorities attempt to weigh factors both for and against retention of the nontenured teacher. If factors favoring retention are excluded from consideration, then the decision to terminate may reflect a lack of balance.

For instance, when a school board did not take into consideration the adverse working conditions faced by a nontenured teacher who was terminated, the arbitrator failed to uphold the board's decision and suggested that the school board expectations were unrealistic.[60,61] In another case, the arbitrator upheld the grievant's case for reinstatement because the school board had failed to take into consideration improvements the grievant had made before the school board decided on termination.[62]

In one instance, an arbitrator reversed the judgment of the school board because the exclusion of favorable information was a clear transgression against the interests of a nontenured teacher in achieving tenure. The teacher had received a favorable letter of recommendation from a veteran principal in the school district. The teacher was not informed of the content of the letter, nor was it included in the teacher's personnel file; it was destroyed. When the former existence of the letter was discovered during the course of the arbitration hearing, the arbitrator ruled that destruction of the letter and failure to consider it in the final evaluation of the teacher violated the standard of just cause.[63]

Can a school board be held responsible for a "fair hearing" on a decision to terminate a nontenured teacher? Most arbitrators would agree that if nontenured teachers are covered by just cause provisions, a "fair hearing" is implied. Differences in arbitral perspective appear to depend on the final authority of the arbitrator's award. For example, in a case where arbitral authority was limited to an advisory opinion, the obligation for providing a "fair hearing" was placed on the school board. Arbitrator Aaron S. Wolff made this statement:

> We believe that what the agreement, as well as the Constitution, requires is a *fair* hearing: one that affords the teacher the right to present, confront and cross-examine witnesses. This concept of fair hearing has deep roots in this country. Ordinarily such hearing is best suited to develop the facts upon which action having serious consequences may be taken . . . . We agree with the School Board's position that under the contract the Arbitration Board functions essentially like a reviewing court without a "retrial" of the matters presented at the school board level [contract citation] . . . . This means the Arbitration Board must sustain the decision of the School Board on the merits if there is any substantial evidence to support it. Since the essential facts are to be adduced before the School Board it is crucial that the hearing at the School Board level be full and fair . . .[64]

The board of arbitrators determined that the school board had not conducted a "fair hearing." There were procedural inadequacies. Consequently, the arbitration board rendered an advisory opinion in favor of the grievant's reinstatement.

However, in a case where the arbitrator's award was final and binding, the arbitrator rendered a different opinion. His view of the school board's responsibility for providing a "fair hearing" reflected his perception of the school board's role as advocate. This was his judgment:

. . . The truth is that the Board hires and fires. To cast this body, at any stage of an individual's employment stint, in the role of an "impartial tribunal" is clearly wishful thinking and at odds with the primary responsibility which the Board serves: to protect and advance the interests of the institution. Only secondarily can the Board be concerned about the interests of its employees. It is not an arbitral body, standing neutrally between the institution and the work-force. It is in fact, the Employer, exerting controls and direction over the employees to the ends of promoting the school's interests . . . .[65]

Should nontenured teachers be given an opportunity to rebut criticism? In a number of collective bargaining agreements between school boards and teachers, there are provisions that restrict the placement of critical materials in a teacher's personnel file without first giving the teacher an opportunity to see and rebut any criticisms that may be in the materials.[66] The source of criticism may be comments by students, parents, fellow teachers, or supervisors. However, the major source of comments that reflect adversely on the work of a teacher are supervisors' written formal evaluation reports.

For example, a grievance dispute took place over the intent of the following collective bargaining provision:

1. Teacher Records File.

    a. Only one official Board file shall be kept for every teacher. If any other files contain material that relates to the teacher in any way, a copy of such material shall be placed in the official Board File.

        1) Every teacher may have access for examination purposes, at reasonable times, to all of the material in his official Board file except for confidential material such as recommendations by colleges or universities, or evaluations of a teacher by previous employers.

        2) Every teacher shall have the right:

            a) to add material to the Board's official file pertaining to such matters relevant to the teacher's service or his qualifications in general, and,

            b) to have dissenting or explanatory material attached to any document on file.

        3) A teacher shall be notified when any material is added to his file which in any way reflects adversely on the teacher or the conduct of his professional duties.

        4) Reasonable requests by teachers for copies of materials appearing in their files will be honored by the administration.

5) No teacher or school officer shall remove any material from the official teacher's file without notification to and acquiescence by both teacher and school officials.[67]

Although the grievant had been shown comments from two planned observations, he was not shown critical comments from reports following unplanned visitations. The school board took the view that failure to show the nontenured teacher all of the evaluations containing critical comments was a *de minimus* departure from the bargained evaluation procedures. That is, the departure was not significant enough to warrant an arbitral remedy.

The arbitrator attached importance to the teacher's opportunity to make written rebuttal prior to the decision to terminate his services:

> The Board concedes that there were deviations from the procedures contained in [the agreement] but claims that these were *de minimus* and that there was substantial compliance with the due process requirements of the contract. It is entirely possible, as the Board contends, that had the Board scrupulously observed all of the requirements . . . the action taken in this case would have been the same . . . . When [the agreement] is considered in its entirety, what is clearly contemplated is that a teacher be given copies of written evaluations so that he may have an opportunity to provide an explanatory response. If this right is to mean anything, it should precede in point of time transmittal to the teacher of a decision not to rehire. The parties certainly did not contemplate that explanatory material was to be placed in the file and not read or considered. The obvious purpose for giving a teacher the right to file dissenting or explanatory material is to make such material available to the school officials prior to their taking definitive action . . . .[68]

The arbitrator sustained the grievant's request for reinstatement.[69,70]

Not all detrimental material that a school board may take into consideration is of a written nature such that it can be placed in a teacher's personnel file. Verbal rumor, when taken into consideration by a school board, can also fall within the category of critical materials that must be brought to a teacher's attention before making a decision adversely affecting the teacher's welfare.

For example, when a teacher was denied tenure because of rumors of her involvement with a married male teacher, an arbitrator ruled that the school board had violated the collective bargaining agreement; it stated that a teacher shall have the right to know of any oral or written criticism and shall have the right of rebuttal.[71] The school board denied taking the rumors into consideration at the time they made the decision to terminate the nontenured teacher, but evidence produced during the arbitration hearing convinced the arbitrator that the rumors had been a factor.

Is a school board accountable for giving proper notification of a decision to terminate a nontenured teacher? State education codes and some collective bargaining agreements provide that proper notification should be given to nontenured teachers prior to their termination. Usually the state code or agreement specifies a date by which notification should take place. When school boards fail to meet notification dates, the issue of procedural adequacy and fairness may be raised.

Although it is difficult to generalize from one arbitration case to another, usually arbitrators do not equate a missed notification date with unfairness *per se*. Arbitrators tend to consider the circumstances that may have contributed to the school board's lapse in meeting the official notification date. If there is no finding of bad faith on the part of the school board, an arbitrator is unlikely to rule that a terminated nontenured teacher should be reinstated. For instance, in one situation the state law had changed regarding the notification of nontenured teachers, and a certain amount of confusion had accompanied the change. The school board thus notified a terminated nontenured teacher two months after the date called for in the new law. The arbitrator did not hold the school board accountable for the deviation and based his award on other factors in the case.[72,73] However, a procedural error may take on special significance in an arbitrator's judgment if the error is part of a pattern of inappropriate actions by a school board.[74]

SUMMARY

In the application of the just cause standard to arbitration cases involving the termination of nontenured teachers, two broad issues dominate. One, are the reasons for termination just? Two, are fair procedures used by school boards to arrive at a decision to terminate a nontenured teacher?

With regard to the first issue, the most obvious reason for terminating nontenured teachers is their failure to perform duties for which they are employed. As one moves away from competence as a reason for termination, the adequacy of the reason becomes more ambiguous. Nevertheless, it is apparent from a study of arbitral opinions that school boards have some latitude under the just cause standard for terminating a nontenured teacher. It has been determined through the arbitration process that under certain circumstances it is just to terminate a teacher who fails to accept a school board's educational philosophy and educational methods; it is just to set a standard of performance that calls for average or superior teaching; it is just to terminate a nontenured teacher for failure to improve performance after deficiencies have been pointed out.

With regard to the second major issue of fairness in implementing the just cause standard, arbitrators appear to agree that prior to termination the nontenured teacher must be given an opportunity to improve. The opportunity to improve is dependent upon a clear statement of specific expectations, accompanied by constructive criticism and specific guidelines for improvement.

The just cause standard of termination also includes a full and fair evaluation of all information prior to the decision to terminate a nontenured teacher. Thus, any school board decision based on an automatic acceptance of an administrative recommendation for termination is not likely to be supported as a "full and fair" evaluation. Similarly, an active exclusion of information, particularly information that would favor the granting of tenure, would most likely result in a decision that would fall short of the just cause standard.

Classroom observations are generally accepted as an important source of information for assisting nontenured teachers to achieve tenure. Failure on the part of school administrators to perform classroom observations is thus weighed unfavorably by arbitrators when considering if the just cause standard has been met.

A complete record of information for and against retention of a nontenured teacher includes proof that the teacher was given an opportunity to become aware of any criticisms and an opportunity to rebut them. Usually the right to such opportunities is provided for in collective bargaining agreements. Under some circumstances, arbitrators have held school boards accountable for not informing the nontenured teachers of verbal rumors when they were considered by the school board in making the decision on termination.

When nontenured teachers are to be terminated, fairness requires that they be informed in advance so that they can take advantage of any due process rights they may have or seek alternative employment. Nevertheless, should a school board miss an official notification date through some procedural error on the school board's part, such an error alone is not likely to bring about the reinstatement of a nontenured teacher unless it can be shown that the error was part of a pattern of bad faith actions committed by school management.

Taken as a whole, the arbitral interpretation associated with the concept of just cause tends to give a nontenured teacher greater due process protection than does the Constitution, based on court interpretations in the *Roth* and *Sindermann* cases. One of the more obvious differences lies in the fact that in an arbitration case the school board has the burden of persuading an arbitrator that the reasons for terminating a nontenured teacher were for just cause. However, in a court of law, before a nontenured teacher can begin to question the merits of the school board action, he or she must first show the court that a constitutionally protected property interest or liberty is at stake.

NOTES

1. *Board of Regents v. Roth,* 408 U.S. 564 (1972), 92 S. Ct. 2701, 33 L. Ed. 2d 548.
2. *Charles R. Perry v. Robert P. Sindermann,* 408 U.S. 593 (1972), 92 S. Ct. 2694, 33 L. Ed. 2d 570.
3. See *Orr v. Trinter,* 444 F. 2d 128 (CA 6); *Jones v. Hopper,* 410 F. 2d 1323 (CA 10); *Freeman v. Gould Special School District,* 405 F. 2nd 1153 (CA 8); *Drown v. Portsmouth School District,* 435 F. 2d 1182 (CA 1); and, *Ferguson v. Thomas,* 430 F. 2d 852 (CA 5).
4. *Roth v. Board of Regents,* 310 F. Supp. 972 (W.D. Wis. 1970).
5. 446 F. 2d 806 (7th Cir. 1971).
6. 446 F. 2d 810 (7th Cir. 1971).
7. *Regents v. Roth* at 570.
8. Argued January 18, 1972; decided June 29, 1972.
9. 33 L. Ed. 2d 570, 571.
10. *Regents v. Roth* at 567.
11. *Regents v. Roth* at 577.
12. *Regents v. Roth* at 577.
13. *Sindermann* at 600.
14. See also Gordon Morris Bakken, "Campus Common Law," *Journal of Law and Education* 5:2 (1976): 201–8.
15. *Sindermann* at 602.
16. *Regents v. Roth* at 572.
17. *Regents v. Roth* at 573.
18. *Regents v. Roth* at 573.
19. *River Falls (Wisconsin) Board of Education,* 26 AIS 8, Arlen C. Christenson, Arbitrator.
20. *Roth v. Board of Regents,* 310 F. Supp. 972 (W.D. Wis. 1970).
21. *Gouge v. Joint School District No. 1.,* 310 F. Supp. 984 (W.D. Wis. 1970).
22. *River Falls* at 8.
23. *River Falls* at 8.
24. *River Falls* at 7.
25. *Regents v. Roth.*
26. See *Collins v. Wolfson,* 498 F. 2d 1100 (5th Cir. 1974); *Horton v. Orange City Board of Educ.,* 464 F 2d 536 (4th Cir. 1972); *Olson v. Regents of the University of Minnesota,* 310 F. Supp. 1356 (D. Minn. 1969).
27. See *Muscare v. Quinn,* 520 F. 2d 1212 (7th Cir. 1975); *Skehan v. Board of Trustees of Bloomsburg State College,* 501 F. 2d 31 (3rd Cir. 1974); *Arnett*

v. Kennedy, 416 U.S. 134 (1974); *Davis v. Vandiver,* 494 F. 2d 830 (5th Cir. 1974); *Vance v. Chester City Board of Sch. Trustees,* 504 F. 2d 820 (4th Cir. 1974); *Brubaker v. Board of Educ. Sch. Dist. 149,* 502 F. 2d 973 (7 Cir. 1974).

28. See *Hortonville Educ. Ass'n v. Hortonville Board of Educ.,* 225 N. W. 2d 658 (Wis. 1975), *Cert. Granted,* 44 USLW 3180 (Oct. 6, 1975); *Hostrop v. Board of Junior College District No. 575,* 471 F. 2d 488 (7th Cir. 1972), *cert. denied,* 411 U.S. 967 (1973); *Burnley v. Thompson,* 524 F. 2d 1233 (5th Cir. 1975); *Nelson v. Kleepe,* 494 F 2d 514 (5th Cir. 1974); *Davis v. Vandiver,* 494 F. 2d 830 (5th Cir. 1974); *Simard v. Board of Educ. of Town of Groton,* 473 F. 2d 988 (2nd Cir. 1973).

29. *Arnett v. Kennedy,* 416 U.S. 134, 94 S. Ct. 1633, 1651; *Kelley v. Herak,* 252 F. Supp. 289 (D. Mont. 1966).

30. *Kelley v. Herak,* 252 F. Supp. 289 (D. Mont. 1966); *Buggs v. City of Minneapolis,* 358 F. Supp. 1340 (D. Minn. 1973).

31. *Antinore v. State of New York,* 371 N.Y. S. 2d 213, 216 (App. Div. 1975).

32. *Jaeger v. Stevens,* 346 F. Supp. 1217 (D. Colo. 1971).

33. *Olshock v. Village of Skokie,* 401 F. Supp. 1219 (N. D. Ill. 1975); *Vance v. Chester City Board of Sch. Trustees,* 504 F. 2d 820 (4th Cir. 1974).

34. See Clyde W. Summers, "Arbitration of Unjust Dismissal: A Preliminary Proposal," in *The Future of Labor Arbitration in America* ed. Joy Correge et al. (New York: American Arbitration Association, 1976), pp. 159–95.

35. *Jefferson County School Dist. (Lakewood, Colorado),* 32 AIS 22, William E. Rentfro, Arbitrator, p. 18.

36. *Board of Education, Edison (New Jersey),* 29 AIS 11, Allen Weisenfeld, Arbitrator, p. 6.

37. *Union Free School District (East Rochester, New York),*58 AIS 1, Alice B. Grant, Arbitrator.

38. *Public Schools of the District of Columbia,* 61 AIS 22, James M. Harkless, Arbitrator.

39. *Toms River (New Jersey) Board of Education,* 74 AIS 22, Jonas Aarons, Arbitrator.

40. See also *Billerica (Massachusetts) School Committee,* 94 AIS 8, Joseph P. O'Donnell, Arbitrator.

41. *St. Vrain Valley School District (Longmont, Colorado)* 93 AIS 8, John Phillip Linn, Arbitrator.

42. Clyde W. Summers, "Arbitration of Unjust Dismissal: A Preliminary Proposal," in *The Future of Labor Arbitration in America,* ed. Joy Correge et al. (New York: American Arbitration Association, 1976), p. 165.

43. See also *The Board of Cooperative Educational Services (Yorktown, New York),* 3 AIS 2, James V. Altieri, Arbitrator.

44. See *Indianapolis (Indiana) Public Schools,* 12 AIS 15, Marlin M. Volz, Arbitrator.

45. See *Downsville (New York) Central School District,* 72 AIS 3, Rodney E. Dennis, Arbitrator.

46. *City School of Gary (Indiana),* 37 AIS 9, Jordan Jay Hillman, Arbitrator.

47. *Owendale-Gagetown (Michigan) Board of Education,* 39 AIS 18, George T. Roumell, Jr., Arbitrator.

48. *Marion (Indiana) Community Schools,* 85 AIS 8, Sol M. Elkin, Arbitrator.
49. *Enlarged City School District of Troy (New York),* 91 AIS 13, James R. Markowitz, Arbitrator.
50. *Boston (Massachusetts) School Committee,* 34 AIS 17, Daniel G. MacLeod, Arbitrator.
51. *Marion (Indiana) Community Schools,* 85 AIS 8, Sol M. Elkin, Arbitrator.
52. *Niagara Falls (New York) Board of Education,* 45 AIS 15, W. Albert Rill, Arbitrator.
53. *Indianapolis (Indiana) Board of School Commissioners,* 27 AIS 14, Robert G. Howlett, Arbitrator.
54. *Indianapolis (Indiana) Board of School Commissioners.*
55. See also *Pavilion Central (New York) School District,* 66 AIS 3, Robert J. Rabin, Arbitrator; *Plainedge (New York) Public Schools,* 62 AIS 12, Nathan Cohen, Arbitrator.
56. *St. Clair County (Michigan) Community College,* 28 AIS 4, M. David Keefe, Arbitrator.
57. See *Government Employee Relations Report,* Reference File 81, RF-157 (Washington: Bureau of National Affairs, 1978), p. 1014; *Government Employee Relations Report,* No. 653 (Washington: Bureau of National Affairs, 1976), p. x-4; *Government Employee Relations Report,* No. 622 (Washington: Bureau of National Affairs, 1975), p. x-6.
58. *Board of Trustees of Schoolcraft College (Michigan),* 1 AIS 30, Leon J. Herman, Arbitrator.
59. See also *Utica (New York) City School District,* 69 AIS 17, James A. Gross, Arbitrator.
60. *Millis (Massachusetts) School Committee,* 70 AIS 19, Jerome S. Rubenstein, Arbitrator.
61. See also *The School Board of Lake County (Florida),* 85 AIS 18, Julius G. Serot, Arbitrator.
62. *Westwood Heights (Michigan) Board of Education,* 64 AIS 4, C. Keith Groty, Arbitrator.
63. *Pine Valley (New York) Central School District,* 92 AIS 9, Fred L. Denson, Arbitrator.
64. *Niles Township (Illinois) Community High School,* 13 AIS 16, Aaron S. Wolff, Arbitrator.
65. *St. Clair County (Michigan) Community College,* 28 AIS 4, M. David Keefe, Arbitrator.
66. See *Government Employee Relations Report,* Reference File 81, RF-157 (Washington: Bureau of National Affairs, 1978), p. 1014; *Government Employee Relations Report,* Reference File 81, RF-150 (Washington: Bureau of National Affairs, 1977), p. 1607; *Government Employee Relations Report,* No. 631 (Washington: Bureau of National Affairs, 1975), p. x-10; *Government Employee Relations Report,* No. 593 (Washington: Bureau of National Affairs, 1975), p. x-10.
67. *Board of Education, South Stickney School District No. 200 (Oak Lawn, Illinois),* 10 AIS 10, Alex Elson, Arbitrator, p. 11.
68. *South Stickney* at 20.

69. For examples of arbitration opinions that engaged in similar reasoning, see *Providence (Rhode Island) School Committee,* 16 AIS 9, George F. McInerny, Arbitrator; *Yale (Michigan) Board of Education,* 28 AIS 14, George T. Roumell, Jr., Arbitrator; and *Penn Yan (New York) Central School District,* 93 AIS 6, Robert E. Stevens, Arbitrator.
70. For an opinion that employed different reasoning, see *Paradise Valley (Arizona) School District,* 68 AIS 10, Donald Daughton, Arbitrator.
71. *Olean (New York) City School District,* 76 AIS 19, Jean T. McKelvey, Arbitrator.
72. *York (New York) Central Board of Education,* 41 AIS 13, Matthew A. Kelly, Arbitrator.
73. See also *Harrison Central District No. 1 (New York),* 32 AIS 24, Josef P. Sirefman, Arbitrator; *Levittown (New York) Public School System,* 9 AIS 22, Benjamin H. Wolf, Arbitrator.
74. See *Rockford (Illinois) Board of Education,* 27 AIS 7, M. David Keefe, Arbitrator.

CHAPTER
6

Seniority

Events that take place in organizations affect the fate of employees as individuals. Employees are promoted, granted leaves of absence, given changes in assignments, laid off, and recalled. The events affect the organization unequally in the sense that all employees are not involved. For example, not all employees are promoted at a given time, nor are all employees granted sabbatical leave, and if there is a reduction in force, not all employees get laid off.

For the well-being of employees as individuals and for the good of the organization, it is important that decisions having different effects on employees are perceived to be just. Morale can be lowered if there is a general perception among employees that management decisions have been made in an arbitrary, capricious, or discriminatory manner.

The concept of seniority, which is utilized by both union and non-union organizations, is pervasive as a standard for the making of management decisions that affect the fate of an individual employee. Seniority has been embraced by unions as an equitable standard in situations in which all employees do not participate.

In its simplest form, the concept of seniority places a positive value on length of service in an organization. Generally, unions regard it as just that employees who have worked the longest should be the first to receive the benefits of employment and the last to experience any deprivations.

A review of arbitration cases[1] reveals that, in the cases involving the use of seniority to determine who shall receive benefits, promotion[2] and job preference[3] are the two most common topics. Less frequently mentioned are seniority cases involving summer school assignments,[4] sabbatical leaves,[5] overtime,[6] vacation time,[7] and voluntary transfer.[8] Among arbitration cases in which seniority is used to protect a senior employee from adverse action, the topics most frequently reported on are layoff[9] and involuntary transfer.[10]

The major issues that appear most frequently in cases involving seniority are as follows:

1. To what extent is management obligated by the collective bargaining agreement to use seniority as the sole factor for determining which individuals will gain some benefit or suffer some adversity? In a number of arbitration cases, management has included in its decisions consideration of factors such as educational qualifications, ability, or the need to meet the requirements of state or federal regulations. At issue in arbitration was whether or not the seniority provision of the collective bargaining agreement prevented management from considering any factors other than seniority.

2. In making distinctions between individual employees, whether for an employee's benefit or not, is management required to develop objective criteria? For example, a number of collective bargaining agreements have required that in instances where qualifications are equal the person with the most seniority shall be chosen to receive the benefit being granted. Such an agreement assumes that comparison will be made between individuals. What is not always clear is the degree to which management is restrained in the use of subjective criteria.

SENIORITY PROVISIONS

Usually an employee does not have any seniority rights unless provision for seniority appears in the collective bargaining agreement. Seniority provisions are of two basic types, strict and modified. Given a strict seniority provision, management must restrict consideration solely to seniority when making a decision in which seniority applies. With a modified seniority provision, it is understood that management may take into consideration factors other than seniority.

STRICT SENIORITY PROVISION

A strict seniority provision states, or can be interpreted to mean, that seniority is the sole criterion to be used by management. An illustration of a strict seniority provision occurred in a case involving the selection of teachers for sabbatical leave. The collective bargaining agreement contained the following statement:

> No more than six percent (6%) of the certified staff shall be on sabbatical leaves at any one time. If more than six percent (6%) of the certified staff apply for sabbatical leave at any one time, the Superintendent shall select the applicants on the basis of years of service in [the school system].[11]

At issue in the case was the meaning of the term "shall select." The school board argued that the clause referring to the selection of applicants had to be interpreted in light of other statements that had been made about sabbatical leave. When that was done, the school board claimed, it could be seen that there never was any intention to have seniority be the exclusive criterion for selection of individuals granted sabbatical leave. The teachers' association argued that the word "shall" was used to mean "must select" on the basis of seniority.

The arbitrator noted that a number of separate sections in the provision for sabbatical leave contained the word "shall" or the word "may." The arbitrator engaged in an analysis of the words "shall" and "may" as they had been used elsewhere in the leave provision. He concluded that the word "shall" had consistently been used to convey the meaning "must."

Since the grievance had been brought by a teacher whose request for sabbatical leave met all the stated criteria and yet was declined in favor of the request of another teacher with less seniority, the arbitrator concluded that the school board had erred is not granting the grievant sabbatical leave. His remedy required that sabbatical leave be granted as requested by the grievant.[12]

MODIFIED SENIORITY PROVISION

With a modified provision, management is not limited to an exclusive consideration of seniority but can consider other factors as well. Ability is a common modifying factor included in seniority provisions. The two standard ways in which ability is used as a modifying factor involve "sufficient ability" and "relative ability."

Sufficient ability. A seniority provision may require the senior employee to have sufficient ability before some preferred action can be taken. If the employee with the most seniority lacks sufficient ability, then employees junior in rank may be considered until one is found who has both sufficient ability and greater seniority than others who might have been chosen.

A Michigan case involved a full-time custodian who applied for a vacant position as a paraprofessional teacher's aide. He had had two years' seniority in a similar position, but he was denied the new vacancy. The apparent reason for the denial was an incident in which a principal had alleged that the grievant had walked away from her when she questioned him regarding his work. He maintained that the way in which she questioned him was demeaning, so, rather than risk an exchange of words he might later regret, he had walked away. He had reported the incident to his supervisor and submitted a written statement of his perception of the incident for his personnel record. The incident was the only negative factor in his record. All other aspects of his record indicated that he had the qualifications to fill the vacancy as a paraprofessional.[13]

The arbitrator agreed with the grievant that he should have been offered the position. In reversing the school board's decision, the arbitrator took note of the following contract provision:

Promotions within the bargaining unit shall be made on the basis of seniority and qualifications. Job vacancies will be posted for a period of seven (7) calendar days, in a conspicuous place in each building setting forth the minimum requirements for the position. Employees interested shall apply within the seven (7) day posting period. The senior employee applying for the promotion who meets the minimum requirements as posted shall be granted a four (4) week trial period to determine:

(a) His desire to remain on the job.

(b) His ability to perform the job.[14]

In his written opinion the arbitrator pointed out that the critical feature of the promotion clause came in the last sentence. The last sentence clearly indicates the relative weight to be given to seniority and qualifications, since it states that a senior employee need meet only the "minimum" qualifications.

With an analysis of the contract as background for his remarks, the arbitrator proceeded to review the school board's decision:

The Board has the discretion to pick candidates and to determine qualifications, if contract standards are observed, without having that discretion substituted for by that of an Arbitrator. Nevertheless, the exercise by the

Board, or its agent, of that discretion is reviewable in the grievance procedure to determine whether it is arbitrary, capricious, discriminatory, or based on an improper standard.

A review of this case clearly shows that despite contrary protestations, grievant was disqualified on the basis of the single incident: Mrs. P's testimony was not available to show aggravated circumstances, nor to account for her *alleged* [emphasis supplied by arbitrator] excessively caustic and unfairly critical review of the grievant's work. In brief, there was a basis for the grievant's walking away to avoid exacerbating the difference of opinion . . . . It seems apparent that it was arbitrary and unwarranted to have disqualified grievant on the basis of this single isolated incident . . . . It further appears that O. was selected, not because grievant did not have the *minimum* [emphasis supplied by arbitrator] qualifications . . . but because a comparison was made and O. was preferred . . . . I fully appreciate the Board's desire to obtain the best possible candidate, but this cannot be done in derogation of the rights of the senior qualified candidate.[15]

Relative ability. A seniority provision may specify that when relative ability is equal, the individual with the most seniority shall be the recipient of the preferred action. If management determines that a junior employee has more ability than a senior employee, management has the right to disregard the greater seniority of the senior employee. For example, the relative ability clause in one agreement was as follows:

Selection and/or promotion and/or transfer to a more desirable position within the school system shall be made on the basis of overall qualifications for the particular job. If qualifications are determined to be equal by the Assistant Superintendent of Personnel in consultation with the appropriate department head, seniority with the school department shall be the deciding factor.[16]

A grievance was brought by a senior employee who claimed that management did not follow an equal ability provision of the agreement. One of the specific issues in the case was whether there were any limitations on the criteria that management had considered in comparing abilities. The posted vacancy contained a list of job specifications. The grievant claimed that in the past she had successfully performed many of the job tasks listed. Management took the position that the tasks listed made up a part of the statement of qualifications, and it was not limited to a consideration of the job description alone. The arbitrator supported management's basic position. Additionally, the arbitrator found that the grievant was not equal to the successful candidate on several of management's criteria.[17]

In another case, the criteria to be considered in selecting an individual for a vacant position had been incorporated into the collective bargaining agreement. Even when criteria are specific and limited, the burden of proving equal ability is difficult if there is evidence in the hearing record that raises doubts in the arbitrator's mind.[18]

Where the determination of relative ability is an issue, the union must show that a grievant with more seniority is at least equal in ability to the successful candidate with less seniority. Certainly the grievant cannot prove equal ability unless criteria for the position are known. The burden of proof probably increases in difficulty when the collective bargaining agreement contains a provision cautioning the arbitrator not to substitute his or her own judgment for that of management.[19]

Multiple factor clause. Another type of modified seniority provision is a seniority provision that lists a number of other factors in addition to length of service and ability. A distinguishing characteristic of such multiple factor provisions is the lack of any indication of how much weight to accord each factor. In cases involving multiple factors, arbitrators tend to assume that management should consider all factors listed.[20]

When it is apparent that some factors were given more weight than others, arbitrators will review the reasonableness of the weight given to the factors by management in light of the circumstances faced by management. For example, one arbitrator supported management's position when it gave most weight to program needs and minimized reassignment priorities, when faced with the necessity of making involuntary transfers following a reduction in force.[21,22]

However, in situations where management's staffing needs are less discernible, arbitrators are not easily persuaded that the seniority rights of an employee should be given little or no weight. In a case involving a school board's failure to promote an employee to the position of bus driver, an arbitrator was not persuaded to give as much weight to the employee's past performance record as the school board had.

The collective bargaining agreement stated that promotions would be based on seniority, ability, and past performance. The school board had rejected the employee's requested assignment on the basis of a prior conviction for reckless driving and two traffic violations. The reckless driving conviction had occurred a number of years prior to the employee's employment by the school board. His record while with the school district contained no detrimental entries. In fact, he met minimum qualification standards. The arbitrator concluded that the employee should be given an opportunity to qualify for the position of bus driver and should not be permanently barred from such a position because of a single incident in the distant past. In the arbitrator's words, "There comes a time when the slate should be wiped clean and a man be given a chance to redeem himself."[23]

AFFIRMATIVE ACTION PROGRAMS

Many school districts have agreed to implement affirmative action programs. Such programs are an attempt to employ and retain persons who are representative of minority groups in the vicinity of the school district. Affirmative action programs have caused school authorities to modify the seniority rights of nonminority employees.

In one situation, a nonminority teacher brought a grievance when she was unable to return to her old position following an involuntary transfer. Her seniority gave her the right to return to her former position. However, to meet certain conditions of its affirmative action program, the school district had placed a minority teacher in the position rather than returning the senior teacher to her former position. The arbitrator recognized the seniority rights of the nonminority teacher, but he denied the grievance because he agreed with the school district's position that it was bound by its agreement with the state's Human Rights Commission. The arbitrator saw the action of school authorities as being consistent with the school district's affirmative action plan.[24]

In another case, a physical education teacher was involuntarily transferred while a minority teacher with less seniority was retained. The action was taken to stay within HEW guidelines for a proper ratio of minority faculty. The arbitrator was persuaded that the district had been motivated by a genuine concern to maintain federal funds, which she interpreted to be a legitimate need. Consequently the involuntary transfer of the senior employee was proper.[25,26]

ARBITRAL REVIEW OF COMPARATIVE CRITERIA

A relative ability clause usually states that, when ability is equal, management will decide in favor of the employee with the most seniority. The relative ability clause presumes that a comparison of abilities takes place before seniority is considered.

The act of comparing two employees for their relative abilities has been subject to examination by arbitrators. Of concern to some arbitrators is the possibility that management may avoid a rigorous comparison of employees' abilities. If management favors a junior employee when the junior employee is in fact less capable than a senior employee, the seniority system is weakened, and the "relative ability" agreement is violated.

Two tests have been used by arbitrators to ensure that a true comparison of abilities has taken place. One test is to examine the objectivity of the standards of comparison used. Objective standards are more readily verified than are subjective standards. For example, in a situation where a senior applicant for the position of chairperson of a science department was denied on the basis of a count of courses in under-graduate and graduate studies, the arbitrator held that the denial was improper because the school district had failed to develop more "tangible evidence" of ability.[27] In another case related to hiring a department chairperson, the arbitrator did not feel the decision of the district superintendent complied with the agreement because the superintendent did not use "objective criteria" to support his conclusions.[28]

The second strategy used to ensure a true comparison of abilities is proof of superiority. In instances where a junior employee is favored over a senior employee, the abilities of the junior employee must be shown to be more than marginally superior. The junior employee must be far superior to any senior employee not favored.[29]

Not all arbitrators would agree that they have the authority to adopt strategies to ensure that a true comparison of relative ability has taken place. For example, in a case where it was clear that management had used subjective standards to compare the relative abilities of teachers, the arbitrator declared that, unless the collective bargaining agreement provided a basis for reviewing management's subjective judgments, or unless management's judgments were clearly arbitrary, he had no authority to challenge the judgments.[30] Other arbitrators have taken the position that unless objective criteria or tests are called for in the collective bargaining agreement, management is free to develop its own standards as part of its managerial function.[31]

Another reason given by arbitrators for permitting management to use subjective standards is the apparent absence of any objective means of assessing a relevant variable. In a situation where management subjectively assessed the responses of applicants for a leadership position, the arbitrator perceived the interview as a nonobjective format but concluded that no objective standard existed to measure leadership potential in that school district. Therefore, the interview procedure was appropriate for the purpose it was intended to fulfill.[32]

SENIORITY STANDING

Seniority is a means of protecting an employee's rights based on his or her length of service in a designated seniority unit. Seniority does not assure an employee of a job, but depending upon the language of a collective bargaining agreement, it usually gives some protection to senior employees in instances of layoff or involuntary transfer. In addition, a seniority system usually assures senior employees of consideration in the event of promotion or some other potential improvement in job status. Seniority is a means of ordering the relationship between employees with regard to certain designated decisions that management might make. The rank held by an employee in comparison with other employees is his or her seniority standing.

An employee has a right to seniority standing when provision for seniority is negotiated into the collective bargaining agreement. Some issues encountered in the administration of a seniority provision that may affect an employee's seniority standing have been the definition of the seniority unit, interruption in employment, service outside the seniority unit, and the granting of superseniority to union officers.

DEFINITION OF THE SENIORITY UNIT

The term "seniority unit" refers to the group to which individual employees have been assigned for seniority purposes. The seniority unit may consist of all employees in the bargaining unit. Typically, a school district will have more than one seniority unit. For example, a school district may have one seniority unit for its elementary teachers and another seniority unit for its secondary teachers.

Other possibilities include basing the definition of seniority on experience in different localities of the school district. In some collective bargaining agreements, seniority has been based on length of service in a single school building rather than on experience in the district as a whole. Under such a definition it is possible for a teacher with more total years of school district experience to be laid off before another teacher who has less total years in the district but greater time in a particular building.[33]

Definitions of the seniority unit may be modified to reflect the abilities of teachers who compose the unit. For example, the collective bargaining agreement may specify that a seniority unit be composed of certificated secondary teachers who have specific subject endorsements.[34] The implications of such a bargaining unit are that in the event of a layoff, an elementary teacher who was laid off could not automatically transfer into a vacancy at the secondary level unless he or she had proper state certification and subject endorsement.[35] If layoffs were being made within the secondary level, it would be possible to lay off teachers by subject matter specialization.[36]

Another option followed in designating seniority units is to have different units for different purposes. For example, the seniority unit for the purpose of a layoff could be different from the seniority unit for the purpose of determining sabbatical leave or summer school assignments.[37]

Although definitions of seniority units usually are incorporated into the collective bargaining agreement, in the absence of a clear definition, management has proceeded to define the seniority unit as a function of its managerial rights. In one situation where management was faced with the need to lay off teachers because of a declining student enrollment, management considered teachers in grades kindergarten through sixth as constituting a seniority unit, since the decline was being experienced in the elementary grades.[38]

INTERRUPTION OF EMPLOYMENT

Seniority is normally calculated in terms of continuous service within the seniority units. Therefore, when an employee's service is interrupted, questions are likely to occur. How shall interruptions in employment affect the calculation of seniority? Will the time spent away from work count toward seniority?

Arbitrator George T. Roumell, Jr., has noted that seniority provisions in the education sector provide far less detail than do agreements in the private sector.[39] Nevertheless, the first place to look for answers to questions concerning the effect of interruptions in employment on seniority is in the collective agreement. Some school districts have included statements that differentiate between those forms of interrupted employment which continue to contribute to seniority and those forms of interruption which reduce seniority. The following are illustrations:

> Seniority in the Detroit Public School System means total accumulated contract service and/or other permanent assignment service in this bargaining unit in any of the Detroit Public Schools since the most recent date of appointment. *Seniority also accrues while the employee is on sabbatical leave, professional service leave, and approved military service leave. Seniotiry does not accrue while on any other kind of leave.* [Emphasis added.]
>
> *The Board of Education of the School District of the City of Detroit and the Detroit Federation of Teachers, Local 231, AFT, AFL-CIO.*[40]

And:

> Where applicable herein for purposes of rotation, "seniority in the school" shall be determined by the number of years of continuous service in the school as a regularly appointed teacher and as a regular substitute teacher. In the case of teachers who were excessed into the school, continuous service in the school shall include in addition the number of years of continuous regular and regular substitute service in the previous school. *Continuity of service shall not be deemed to be interrupted by absence determined to be due to illness, accident or injury suffered in line of duty or by time spent in military service, the Peace Corps or VISTA, or by layoff or leave without pay of one year or less. Teachers on layoff or leave without pay for*

more than one year up to four years shall regain the school seniority they had at the commencement of their leave after they serve in the school for one school year following their return. [Emphasis added.]

The Board of Education of the City School District of the City of New York and United Federation of Teachers, Local 2, AFT, AFL-CIO.[41]

If a collective bargaining agreement is silent or unclear regarding the effect of an interruption in employment, an arbitrator may be able to make a determination based on previous practices in the school district. For example, a female bus driver went on maternity leave. Upon her return from leave, she was classified as a substitute driver, and her seniority was reduced. Evidence presented at the arbitration hearing showed that in the past supervisors had granted extended leaves without altering the employee's seniority standing. In addition, the arbitrator noted that the seniority provision in the collective bargaining agreement made no distinction between regular and substitute employees.[42,43]

Traditionally, when an employee has been drafted into military service, seniority continues to accrue. Provision for continuous seniority during military service has been a feature of draft laws passed by Congress. This fact demonstrates the importance attached to seniority, since Congress has taken it into consideration by seeking to ease the sacrifice made by persons drafted.

Historically, such provisions as those Congress makes for seniority of draftees reflects the cyclical pattern of employment and unemployment often experienced in the private sector. An employee with seniority can feel more secure in his or her job. Although public employees have historically had greater job security, in recent years school teachers have grown more concerned about it.[44] The outcome of such concern may be that more attention will be given to seniority provisions in teacher-negotiated agreements and more arbitration cases will be brought by teachers attempting to protect their seniority.

SERVICE OUTSIDE THE SENIORITY UNIT

In the education sector, issues concerning service outside the seniority unit are likely to come up during a reduction in force involving principals. For purposes of determining seniority in the event of a layoff, should principals be included in the same seniority unit as teachers? Should principals be given seniority credit for the time they have served outside the seniority unit containing teachers? Should principals be given seniority credit for time spent as teachers prior to becoming principals?

In one arbitration case, an arbitrator held that school authorities violated the collective bargaining when administrators such as principals and assistant principals were placed on the teachers' seniority list. The arbitrator noted that principals were not in the same bargaining unit as teachers. The fact that principals held teaching certificates was not relevant. Furthermore, given the fact that a layoff was pending, placement of the principals on the teachers' seniority list would tend to place teachers in the lower seniority categories. However, it was the arbitrator's view that placement of administrators on a teachers' seniority list was a topic more properly resolved in negotiations and not in arbitration.[45,46]

In a different situation, an arbitrator upheld a school board's decision to return a principal to the position of an elementary teacher, a position in which the principal had fifteen years' experience. The teachers' association unsuccessfully argued that the position should have gone to a laid-off teacher who had fifteen years of seniority as an elementary teacher.[47]

In a related case, an arbitrator held that the seniority of a custodian had been frozen when he was involuntarily transferred out of the custodians' seniority unit. Upon return to the unit three years later, he automatically acquired the seniority he had previously earned in the unit.[48]

SUPERSENIORITY

Superseniority is a special status that is sometimes negotiated for union officers in recognition of their responsibilities for administering the collective bargaining agreement. Superseniority is an exception to the usual procedure of determining seniority on the basis of service within some designated seniority unit. Under a negotiated provision, in the event of a layoff a union officer with fewer years of actual service will be retained over an employee with more seniority. The justification for superseniority is that it contributes to the stability of labor-management relationships.[49]

ACCOMMODATION OF SENIORITY RIGHTS

Given the existence of a seniority system, a basic issue in the administration of such a system is the degree of accommodation that employees may expect by virtue of having seniority. Accommodation, as used in this section, means a deferral of managerial interests or a deferral of the interests of junior employees in order that the interests of senior employees may predominate. A review of arbitration cases in schools indicates that accommodation by management is often an issue when senior employees file grievances for a revision of work schedules or a revision in work assignments. Accommodation by junior employees takes place when bumping is permitted. Latent in the meaning of the term "accommodation," as used here, is the suggestion that it involves a conflict of rights of two groups.

REVISION OF WORK SCHEDULES

Unless this right is taken away by negotiation, school management has the right to direct the work force of the school district. The term "to direct the work force" includes establishing work schedules. A grievance challenging an action taken by management to direct the work force is likely to highlight the fundamental rights of both employees and management. The two cases to be described illustrate the issues that arise when individual employees put their seniority rights against management's right to direct an organization by devising work schedules.

A case of reduced classes. Four days after summer school started, because of low enrollment a teacher lost one of three classes he had been teaching. The administration offered to prorate his summer school salary on the basis of the two classes he continued to teach. In addition, the administration offered to make payment for the days that he had met with the class that was canceled.

The teacher, however, took the position that the cancellation of one of the classes was the same as a layoff. He argued that under provisions of the collective bargaining agreement, summer school classes should have been rescheduled so that he would have a full load. The administration refused to reschedule summer school classes and pointed out that none of the teachers received assurances of having a full teaching load before management saw what the actual enrollment figures were. In addition, the administration recalled that the union had tried in the past to introduce language into the collective bargaining agreement that would have based summer school assignments on seniority, but had failed to obtain school board agreement.

The arbitrator's view of the case was that the grievant had misused the term layoff, since the provision for layoff did not apply to the cancellation of a summer school class. The arbitrator also found it to be reasonable that the administration would make summer school contracts contingent upon actual enrollment figures. The arbitrator believed it would be absurd to interpret the negotiated agreement as requiring a rescheduling of summer school classes because one teacher had his teaching load reduced because of a low enrollment. Nowhere in the agreement was there any indication that seniority was intended to be the controlling variable in the assignment of summer school classes.[50]

A case of second thoughts. A school district, faced with student overcrowding, instituted an extended teaching day. Two teachers accepted late-hour teaching schedules, on the assumption that they would receive additional compensation with an overload. When they discovered that no overload would be necessary and consequently no additional compensation would be forthcoming, they attempted to compel the school administration to revise their work schedules. They used as authority for their request a provision in the negotiated agreement which stated that length of service would be recognized for scheduling and assignment purposes.

The administration refused to reschedule the teachers' classes. The case turned on the arbitrator's interpretation of the following negotiated provision:

> Whenever reasonable and practicable, the Principal and Department Chairman shall work out a schedule which will give senior teachers their choice of early or late shifts.[51]

The arbitrator distinguished between the terms "scheduling" and "rescheduling." He regarded the former term as referring to a pre-school year activity, at which time management could consider length of service and scheduling preferences. He did not believe the same could be said for rescheduling. The arbitrator did not think that the agreement prevented the administration from rescheduling once the school year had begun. However, the phrase "whenever reasonable and practicable" gives management the choice of determining whether it is possible to reschedule or not.[52]

REVISION OF WORK ASSIGNMENTS

Another way in which management directs the work force is through the assignment of individual employees to specific positions. Compared to their firmness in exercising the right to develop work schedules, school authorities appear to be more willing to restrict this right. Limitations of this right take the form of seniority systems that give senior employees certain rights to express their preference for specific positions and to have their preferences considered. An employee's preference for a position need not be regarded as an inviolable claim to the position, yet under certain circumstances the preference of a senior employee can cause management to modify its efforts to direct the organization. A number of arbitration cases have occurred in connection with employee transfers, the recall of an employee from a layoff, and the return of an employee from a leave of absence.

Unheeded preferences. The following cases describe situations in which school authorities violated the seniority rights of employees. In the first case, a teacher of instrumental music was laid off. At the time of the teacher's layoff, a vacancy existed for a choral music instructor. In the arbitration hearing, evidence was presented which persuaded the arbitrator that the laid-off teacher was fully qualified to instruct choral music. Therefore, when the teacher claimed his right to the choral position by virtue of both his qualifications and his seniority, the arbitrator upheld the teacher's right to the position over the interests of the individual who had been chosen by the administration to fill the vacant position.[53]

In another case, following the reorganization of a school district, a senior teacher was not placed in one of two positions she had requested. Instead, two teachers with less seniority were placed in the positions. The senior teacher was given a position working with children who had special education problems. Notwithstanding the fact that the senior teacher had the required training and skills to work with special education classes, the arbitrator directed the school board to give the grievant her preference. School authorities had treated the situation as though they were administering a modified seniority system with regard to transfers when in fact they were not.[54]

Finally, in a case where a number of part-time employees had been laid off, a preferential rehiring list was created on the basis of straight seniority. An arbitrator held that the school authorities erred when they failed to reemploy individuals from the preferential list and instead hired teachers who were junior to those on the list.[55]

Noncontrolling preferences. In the following cases, school authorities were upheld in not placing employees in positions that they requested. In Michigan, an occupational education coordinator was laid off. When he was rehired, there were no occupational education positions open so he accepted an assignment as a regular teacher. Two weeks later, an occupational education position opened. He requested a transfer to the position, but the request was denied. When the grievant brought his case before an arbitrator, the arbitrator upheld the school board, pointing out that the grievant's right to be placed in his former position ended when he accepted the position of a regular teacher.[56]

In a situation where the collective bargaining agreement contained a modified seniority provision, school authorities were within their rights when they assigned a high school English teacher to a junior high school upon her return from a one-year leave of absence. In earlier negotiation sessions, the union had attempted to make years of experience the main consideration in determining assignments and transfers, but had failed to get the school board to agree to this limitation.[57]

In the last example, an arbitrator upheld the right of the New York Board of Education to assign a first-grade teacher to the fifth grade, even though the teacher was senior to all but one of the five first-grade teachers who remained in the position. The teacher's principal persuaded the arbitrator that she had been neither arbitrary nor capricious, as alleged by the grievant. The principal had based her decision to transfer the grievant on evidence that the grievant could successfully teach older children. In addition, teachers who had been assigned to kindergarten and first grades held early childhood education licenses, while the grievant had no similar license.[58]

BUMPING

A seniority system is a means of establishing an ordered relationship among employees in a given seniority unit based on length of service in the unit. The purpose of establishing an ordered relationship is to have an impartial system based on length of service that will determine who will "lose" and who will "gain" from decisions of management associated with such events as promotions or layoffs. "Bumping" is a term used when a senior employee claims the position held by a junior employee. Issues concerning bumping include the existence of the right to bump and limitations on the right to bump.

The right to bump. If the right to bump is clearly stated in the collective bargaining agreement, there is usually no issue with regard to its use by senior employees. However, when the collective bargaining agreement is unclear or silent, the right to bump may become an issue for arbitration. In the private sector, when a contract is silent on the right to bump, arbitrators have tended to hold that the right to bump is implied, especially when the contract provides for the application of seniority in a plant-wide layoff situation.[59] In the education sector, no definite trend has been established by arbitral decisions; indeed, very few cases have been reported in the education sector. In one case, the arbitrator did hold that the grievant had no bumping rights because bumping was not granted in the collective bargaining agreement.[60]

Limitations. In two other cases, the issues pertained to the application of the right to bump. In one case, the arbitrator held that bumping rights existed, but they did not apply to a summer school appointment which the grievant had unsuccessfully tried to secure by means of bumping.[61] In another case, the arbitrator held that bumping rights were restricted to job classifications which were equal to or lower than the classification held by the grievant. In the same case, however, the arbitrator determined that union officers could bump into higher job classifications as well as equal and lower classifications.[62]

SUMMARY

A seniority system is created for the purpose of protecting employees from such vagaries of employment as layoffs and involuntary transfers. The protection afforded through seniority systems benefits those who have the most years of service in a designated seniority unit. Another reason for instituting a seniority system is to provide a union-sponsored basis for influencing management decisions which may aid an individual.

The decision to lay off employees, make involuntary transfers, or promote individuals lies within a domain called management rights. However, seniority systems do influence or modify management's decisions in areas covered by seniority. The extent to which management's decisions are influenced depends on the nature of the seniority provisions negotiated.

There are essentially two types of provisions, one based on strict seniority rights and the other based on modified seniority rights. The terms "strict" and "modified" are descriptive of the influence that the two types of provisions have on management decisions. Under a strict seniority system, length of service in the seniority unit is the sole criterion for making a decision to which the seniority provision applies.

With a modified seniority system, other factors may be considered in addition to length of service. Ability is a common modifying factor. A "sufficient ability" feature allows management to determine if an employee has the minimum requirements to perform in a position before his seniority is taken into consideration. A "relative ability" feature allows management to compare employees to see who has the most ability. If a junior employee is significantly superior in ability to a senior employee, the junior employee can be chosen over the senior employee. Another type of modified seniority provision exists wherein a number of variables are considered to be relevant criteria in making a decision. Management is expected to take into account each variable listed, but it is usually unrestrained in unilaterally weighing each variable, including length of service, as it sees fit.

Of the different types of modified seniority provisions used, the relative ability provision has generated the greatest number of disputes over its administration. By its nature, a relative ability provision leaves scope for interpretation. For one thing, comparing the abilities of two individuals can involve either objective or subjective criteria. At times, parties to an agreement will designate the appropriate criteria to be used. Not infrequently, however, a grievance will be brought on the issue of management's use of subjective criteria. Some arbitrators have supported the notion that a true comparison of abilities requires the development and use of objective criteria. Other arbitrators are reluctant to interpret an agreement as requiring objective criteria if the agreement is silent on the matter. As long as management is not shown to be arbitrary or capricious in its use of subjective criteria, some arbitrators will uphold management's right to use them.

An essential administrative task with most seniority systems is to develop a seniority list. The list shows the relative rank of each employee in the seniority unit based on length of service. Arbitration cases tend to arise over management's ranking of an employee following circumstances such as an interruption in employment. The question becomes, Shall the time spent on leave be added to or held from the computation of an employee's length of service? Arbitration cases also occur when an employee — for example, a principal — performs services outside the seniority unit and later returns to the unit. How shall his or her service outside the unit be counted? Do employees lose their accumulated seniority by leaving one seniority unit and entering another?

Finally, a special seniority standing called "superseniority" is at times negotiated into seniority agreements. Typically, superseniority is a negotiated right of union officers to be placed at the top of the seniority list. The rationale for providing superseniority is that it provides stability within the ranks of union leadership.

Grievances based on a senior employee's claim to preferred status have been placed into three classifications. One class of grievances pertains to a senior employee's claim that a revision should be made in his or her work schedule. A second class of grievances pertains to a senior employee's demand for revision in work assignments. The third class of cases involves the use of bumping by senior employees. Bumping is a right that is at times negotiated into an agreement. When a senior employee has bumping rights, it means that he or she can take the position of an employee who is junior in rank under certain situations as agreed upon in the contract.

NOTES

1. See *Arbitration in the Schools,* Vols. 1–96.
2. See *Woonsocket (Rhode Island) School Committee,* 2 AIS 14, William J. Fallon, Arbitrator; *Ohio University,* 2 AIS 23, Robert C. McIntosh, Arbitrator; *Warwick (Rhode Island) School Committee,* 2 AIS 35, John W. Teele, Arbitrator; *Board of Education, Union Free School District No. 12 (Brentwood, New York),* 3 AIS 18, Henry Schuman, Arbitrator; *Passaic County (New Jersey) Board of Education,* 6 AIS 12, Joseph F. Wildebush, Arbitrator; *Ohio University,* 9 AIS 6, James J. Willingham, Arbitrator; *School District of the City of East Detroit (Michigan),* 17 AIS 13, Leon J.

Herman, Arbitrator; *Harvard University (Massachusetts)*, 17 AIS 20, Charles O. Gregory, Arbitrator; *The University of Delaware (Newark)*, 31 AIS 7, Laurence E. Seibel, Arbitrator; *School Committee of the City of Warwick (Rhode Island)*, 33 AIS 28, Mark Santer, Arbitrator; *Southwestern Central School District (Jamestown, New York)*, 59 AIS 3, Irving R. Markowitz, Arbitrator; *Mt. Morris (Michigan) Board of Education*, 68 AIS 2, Richard L. Kanner, Arbitrator; *Willingboro (New Jersey) Board of Education*, 80 AIS 22, William B. Post, Arbitrator; *Warwick (Rhode Island) School Committee*, 87 AIS 6, William J. Fallon, Arbitrator.

3. See *Dracut (Massachusetts) School Committee*, 4 AIS 2, John W. Teele, Arbitrator; *Warwick (Rhode Island) School Committee*, 9 AIS 20, Arnold Zack, Arbitrator; *Inkster (Michigan) Board of Education*, 12 AIS 4, Harry N. Casselman, Arbitrator; *Suffolk County (New York) Community College*, 14 AIS 9, J. Ozias Kaufman, Arbitrator; *Lincoln Park (Michigan) Board of Education*, 19 AIS 14, George T. Roumell, Jr., Arbitrator; *Bay City (Michigan) Board of Education*, 22 AIS 13, Richard I. Bloch, Arbitrator; *Birmingham (Michigan) Board of Education*, 24 AIS 5, James R. McCormick, Arbitrator; *North Providence (Rhode Island) School Committee*, 26 AIS 15, Kenneth L. Glynn, Arbitrator; *Menominee (Michigan) Area Public Schools*, 33 AIS 36, James R. McCormick, Arbitrator; *Board of Education of the City of New York (New York)*, 36 AIS 19, Benjamin H. Wolf, Arbitrator; *Southwestern Central School District (New York)*, 39 AIS 11, James A. Healy, Arbitrator; *Area Board of Vocational, Technical and Adult Education, District 1 (Eau Claire, Wisconsin)*, 39 AIS 12, Donald B. Lee, Arbitrator; *Ann Arbor (Michigan) Public Schools*, 41 AIS 10, William P. Daniel, Arbitrator; *Wethersfield (Connecticut) Board of Education*, 54 AIS 10, Stanley L. Aiges, Arbitrator; *New York (New York) Board of Education*, 58 AIS 3, I. Robert Feinberg, Arbitrator; *Arlington (Virginia) Public Schools*, 60 AIS 2, Samuel H. Jaffee, Arbitrator; *San Francisco (California) Unified School District*, 67 AIS 7, Joseph R. Grodin, Arbitrator; *Alexis I. Du Pont School District (Delaware)*, 71 AIS 14, Louis E. Seltzer, Arbitrator; *Oscoda (Michigan) School District Board of Education*, 90 AIS 1, Robert G. Howlett, Arbitrator; *Gloversville (New York) Central School District*, 92 AIS 15, Daniel C. Williams, Arbitrator.

4. See *Board of Education, Union Free District No. 23 (Massapequa, New York)*, 5 AIS 15, Louis Yagoda, Arbitrator; *Sachem (New York) Board of Education*, 53 AIS 12, Edwin Levin, Arbitrator; *Poughkeepsie (New York) Board of Education*, 65 AIS 20, Lawrence I. Hammer, Arbitrator.

5. See *Mahwah (New Jersey) Board of Education*, 29 AIS 2, Lawrence I. Hammer, Arbitrator; *Central Islip (New York) Board of Education*, 86 AIS 20, Philip J. Ruffo, Arbitrator.

6. See *Medford (Massachusetts) School Committee*, 51 AIS 10, Peter B. Deringer, Arbitrator.

7. See *Board of Education Riverview (Michigan) Community School District*, 13 AIS 2, George T. Roumell, Jr., Arbitrator.

8. See *Boston (Massachusetts) School Committee*, 28 AIS 2, Thomas Kennedy, Arbitrator; *Pinellas County (Florida) School Board*, 37 AIS 16, James J. Sherman, Arbitrator.

9. See *Bloomfield Hills (Michigan) School District, Board of Education*, 14

AIS 1, George T. Roumell, Jr., Arbitrator; *Board of Education, School District of Detroit (Michigan)*, 31 AIS 1, Leon J. Herman, Arbitrator; *Jackson (Michigan) Public Schools*, 31 AIS 18, Jerome Gross, Arbitrator; *Kent (Ohio) State University*, 35 AIS 19, Merton C. Berstein, Arbitrator; *Kimberly (Wisconsin) Joint School District No. 6*, 39 AIS 14, John T. Coughlin, Arbitrator; *Ann Arbor (Michigan) Board of Education*, 46 AIS 13, Richard I. Bloch, Arbitrator; *Rumford (Maine) School Committee*, 52 AIS 9, Lawrence T. Holden, Jr., Arbitrator; *South Redford (Michigan) School District*, 53 AIS 17, Harry N. Casselman, Arbitrator; *Trenton (Michigan) Board of Education*, 59 AIS 17, Geroge T. Roumell, Jr., Arbitrator; *Indianapolis (Indiana) Board of Education*, 62 AIS 17, Charles F. Ipavec, Arbitrator; *Independent School District No. 621 (Mounds View, Minnesota)*, 66 AIS 9, George Jacobs, Arbitrator; *Providence (Rhode Island) School Committee*, 75 AIS 17, Peter R. Blum, Arbitrator; *Warren Woods (Michigan) Public School*, 77 AIS 21, Theodore J. St. Antoine, Arbitrator; *Camden County (New Jersey) College*, 80 AIS 7, Jonas Aarons, Arbitrator; *Westbury (New York) Union Free School District*, 81 AIS 18, Joseph P. Doyle, Arbitrator; *Clover Park (Washington) School District*, 83 AIS 8, Michael H. Beck, Arbitrator; *Centennial (Pennsylvania) School District*, 87 AIS 11, Walter J. Gershenfeld, Arbitrator; *Board of Education of City of Flint (Michigan)*, 87 AIS 18, Dallas L. Jones, Arbitrator; *Buffalo (New York) Board of Education*, 88 AIS 2, Fred L. Denson, Arbitrator; *Board of Education of City School District of City of New York*, 68 LA 271, George Nicolau, Arbitrator.

10. See *Beecher (Michigan) School District*, 11 AIS 19, E. J. Forsythe, Arbitrator; *Board of Education, School District of Detroit (Michigan)*, 31 AIS 1, Leon J. Herman, Arbitrator; *School District No. 1, City and County of Denver (Colorado)*, 36 AIS 3, William E. Rentfro, Arbitrator; *Rochester (New York) Board of Education*, 43 AIS 18, Irving R. Markowitz, Arbitrator; *Centennial (Pennsylvania) School District*, 52 AIS 6, J. Charles Short, Arbitrator; *Newport (Rhode Island) School Department*, 53 AIS 6, John W. McConnell, Arbitrator; *New York (New York) Board of Education*, 58 AIS 3, Robert Feinberg, Arbitrator; *Arapahoe County (Colorado) School District*, 59 AIS 6, Peter Florey, Arbitrator; *School District of Philadelphia (Pennsylvania)*, 67 AIS 15, Jay Kramer, Arbitrator; *San Francisco (California) Unified School District*, 70 AIS 10, La Verda O. Allen, Arbitrator; *The Levittown (New York) Union Free School District*, 74 AIS 19, Lawrence I. Hammer, Arbitrator; *The Board of Education, School District No. 11 (Colorado Springs, Colorado)*, 80 AIS 18, Thomas T. Roberts, Arbitrator; *Polk County (Florida) School Board*, 92 AIS 23, John J. Managan, Arbitrator.

11. *Mahwah (New Jersey) Board of Education*, 29 AIS 2, Lawrence I. Hammer, Arbitrator.

12. *Medford (Massachusetts) School Committee*, 51 AIS 10, Peter B. Deringer, Arbitrator.

13. *Inkster (Michigan) Board of Education*, 12 AIS 4, Harry N. Casselman, Arbitrator.

14. *Inkster Board of Education* at 2.

15. *Inkster Board of Education* at 15, 16.

16. *Warwick (Rhode Island) School Committee,* 9 AIS 20, Arnold Zack, Arbitrator.

17. *Warwick School Committee.*

18. For a related case example, see *Ohio University,* 9 AIS 6, James J. Willingham, Arbitrator.

19. For a related case example, see *Warwick (Rhode Island) School Committee,* 33 AIS 28, Mark Santer, Arbitrator.

20. For a related case example, see *Board of Education, Union Free School District No. 12 (Brentwood, New York),* 3 AIS 18, Henry Schuman, Arbitrator.

21. *Board of Education, School District No. 11 (Colorado Springs, Colorado),* 80 AIS 18, Thomas T. Roberts, Arbitrator.

22. See also *Centennial (Pennsylvania) School District,* 52 AIS 6, Charles Short, Arbitrator.

23. *School District of the City of East Detroit (Michigan),* 17 AIS 13, Leon J. Herman, Arbitrator.

24. *Seattle (Washington) School District,* 70 AIS 5, J. B. Gillingham, Arbitrator.

25. *San Francisco (California) Unified School District,* 70 AIS 10, La Verda O. Allen, Arbitrator.

26. See also *Ann Arbor (Michigan) Board of Education,* 46 AIS 13, Richard I. Bloch, Arbitrator.

27. *Warwick (Rhode Island) School Committee,* 2 AIS 35, John W. Teele, Arbitrator.

28. *Woonsocket (Rhode Island) School Committee,* 2 AIS 14, William J. Fallon, Arbitrator.

29. See *The University of Delaware (Newark),* 31 AIS 7, Laurence E. Seibel, Arbitrator.

30. *School District No. 1, City and County of Denver (Colorado),* 36 AIS 3, William E. Rentfro, Arbitrator.

31. For a related case example, see *Harvard University (Massachusetts),* 17 AIS 20, Charles O. Gregory, Arbitrator.

32. *School Committee of the City of Warwick (Rhode Island),* 33 AIS 28, Mark Santer, Arbitrator.

33. See *Kimberly (Wisconsin) Joint School District No. 6,* 39 AIS 14, John T. Coughlin, Arbitrator.

34. See *Roseville (Michigan) Board of Education,* 31 AIS 10, George T. Roumell, Jr., Arbitrator.

35. See *Warren Woods (Michigan) Public Schools,* 77 AIS 21, Theodore J. St. Antoine, Arbitrator.

36. See *Roseville (Michigan) Board of Education,* 31 AIS 10, George T. Roumell, Jr., Arbitrator.

37. *Government Employee Relations Report,* Reference File 81, RF-116 (Washington: Bureau of National Affairs, 1976), p. 1010.

38. *Rumford (Maine) School Committee,* 52 AIS 9, Lawrence T. Holden, Arbitrator.

39. *Roseville (Michigan) Board of Education,* 31 AIS 10, George T. Roumell, Jr., Arbitrator, pp. 8–10.

40. *Government Employee Relations Report*, Reference File 81, RF-116 (Washington: Bureau of National Affairs, 1976), p. 1010.
41. *Government Employee Relations Report*, Reference File 81, RF-150 (Washington: Bureau of National Affairs, 1977) p. 1594.
42. *Southwestern Central School District (New York)*, 39 AIS 11, James A. Healy, Arbitrator.
43. See also *Lincoln Park (Michigan) Board of Education*, 19 AIS 14, George T. Roumell, Jr., Arbitrator.
44. W. Frank Masters, "Teacher Job Security Under Collective Bargaining Contracts," *Phi Delta Kappan* 7:56 (1975): 455–58.
45. *Independent School District No. 621 (Mounds View, Minnesota)*, 66 AIS 9, George Jacobs, Arbitrator.
46. See also *Clover Park (Washington) School District*, 83 AIS 8, Michael H. Beck, Arbitrator.
47. *Westbury (New York) Union Free School District*, 81 AIS 18, Joseph P. Doyle, Arbitrator.
48. *Alexis I. Du Pont School District (Delaware)*, 71 AIS 14, Louis E. Seltzer, Arbitrator.
49. *Jackson (Michigan) Public Schools*, 31 AIS 18, Jerome Gross, Arbitrator.
50. *Area Board of Vocational, Technical and Adult Education, District 1 (Eau Claire, Wisconsin)*, 39 AIS 12, Donald B. Lee, Arbitrator.
51. *Bay City (Michigan) Board of Education*, 22 AIS 13, Richard I. Bloch, Arbitrator, p. 4.
52. *Bay City Board of Education.*
53. *Bloomfield Hills (Michigan) School District, Board of Education*, 14 AIS 1, George T. Roumell, Jr., Arbitrator.
54. *Newport (Rhode Island) School Department*, 53 AIS 6, John W. McConnell, Arbitrator.
55. *New York City (New York) Board of Higher Education*, 62 AIS 14, Walter E. Oberer, Arbitrator.
56. *Ann Arbor (Michigan) Public Schools*, 41 AIS 10, William P. Daniel, Arbitrator.
57. *Wethersfield (Connecticut) Board of Education*, 54 AIS 10, Stanley L. Aiges, Arbitrator.
58. *New York (New York) Board of Education*, 58 AIS 3, I. Robert Feinberg, Arbitrator.
59. Editorial staff, *Grievance Guide* (Washington: Bureau of National Affairs, 1972), p. 98.
60. *Camden County (New Jersey) College*, 80 AIS 7, Jonas Aarons, Arbitrator.
61. *Birmingham (Michigan) Board of Education*, 24 AIS 5, James R. McCormick, Arbitrator.
62. *Jackson (Michigan) Public Schools*, 31 AIS 18, Jerome Gross, Arbitrator.

CHAPTER

7

Discrimination Issues in School Employment

Arbitration is sometimes referred to as a system of private law. The private law of arbitration is based on interpretations of collective bargaining agreements between employees and employer. In contrast to private law, public law consists primarily of federal and state constitutions, statutes, and judicial interpretations. Public law is also termed "external law," as opposed to the internal law that is based on locally derived values and expectations of labor and management.

The distinction between public and private law has been easier to maintain in theory than in practice, particularly in public sector labor relations. Arbitration cases involving discrimination issues are especially inclined to include aspects of both public and private law. The particular public discrimination laws that have been applied most frequently in one way or another to labor-management relationships are the Civil Rights Act of 1964 and the Equal Opportunity Act of 1972. Key elements of these acts will be identified in this chapter.

The traditional view of the grievance and the arbitrator's role in that process has been to view the arbitrator's authority as coming exclusively from the written agreement between labor and management.

The social upheavals associated with civil rights over the past two decades have resulted in federal legislation, administrative directives, state statutes, and local ordinances to remove sources of discrimination based on race, sex, religion, age, color, or national origin. Professional arbitrators differ in their views of the impact that external law should have on the traditional role of arbitration. This chapter summarizes the positions that influential arbitrators have taken.

A review of discrimination cases occurring in the schools indicates that the two most frequently reported forms of discrimination are racial discrimination and discrimination against women. The substantive issues in racial discrimination cases have been as follows:

1. staff balance as a contractual obligation
2. impact of affirmative action goals
3. staff balance as an administrative goal.

In the area of sex discrimination, the substantive issues have been the following:

1. sex discrimination in job qualifications
2. equity in compensation
3. mandatory maternity leave
4. sick leave pay for pregnant teachers.

Illustrations of each issue are examined in this chapter.

EXTERNAL LAW

The Civil Rights Act and the Equal Opportunity Act were passed by Congress with the intention of protecting employees from discrimination due to race, sex, color, religion, or national origin. The Civil Rights Act of 1964 did not provide directly for the protection of employees in educational institutions. However, the 1964 Act did apply to contractors with the federal government. Employees of educational institutions that held contracts with the federal government were thus covered. Employee coverage was expanded in the 1972 Act to include all educational institutions with 15 or more employees. Approximately 120,000 educational institutions were brought directly under the provisions of the Act.[1]

UNFAIR EMPLOYMENT PRACTICES

Title VII of both the 1964 Act and the 1972 Act defined unfair employment practices by employers as the following:

Section 703. (a) It shall be an unlawful employment practice for an employer:

(1) to fail or refuse to hire or to discharge any individual, or otherwise to discriminate against any individual with respect to his compensation, terms, conditions, or privileges of employment, because of such individual's race, color, religion, sex, or national origin; or

(2) to limit, segregate, or classify his employees or applicants for employment in any way which would deprive or tend to deprive any individual of employment opportunities or otherwise adversely affect his status as an employee, because of such individual's race, color, religion, sex, or national origin.

The 1972 Act amended the 1964 Act so as to provide for a definition of unlawful practices which would apply to unions.

Section 703. (c) It shall be an unlawful employment practice for a labor organization:

(1) to exclude or to expel from its membership, or otherwise to discriminate against, any individual because of his race, color, religion, sex, or national origin;

(2) to limit, segregate, or classify its membership or to classify or fail or refuse to refer for employment any individual, in any way which would deprive or tend to deprive any individual of employment opportunities, or would limit such employment opportunities or otherwise adversely affect his status as an employee or as an applicant for employment, because of such individual's race, color, religion, sex, or national origin; or

(3) to cause or attempt to cause an employer to discriminate against an individual in violation of this section.

ENFORCEMENT

At the time of the passage of the 1972 Act, an amendment was offered which would have given the Equal Employment Opportunity Commission (EEOC) sole jurisdiction over enforcement of the Act. The amendment was not passed. Consequently, responsibility for protecting against discrimination is shared. In those instances in which state and local regulations provide the same or greater protection, EEOC will defer action until the state or local agency has had an opportunity to address the case brought to it by an employee. If the case is not disposed of in the required period of time or if it is not handled in a manner suitable to the employee, the case may be brought to EEOC; the commission in turn may investigate and, if necessary, bring an action against the employer to court. If the employer is a state or local government unit, the Attorney General is authorized to bring civil action. Under certain circumstances the employee may bring his own case to court.[2,3]

Under the provisions of the 1964 Act, EEOC was unable to initiate court action. Its methods of enforcement were limited to negotiation and mediation. Among the strategies used by EEOC was one of persuading employers to adopt affirmative action plans. Affirmative action plans were not required by law. Section 703(j) specifically states the following:

> Nothing contained in this title shall be interpreted to require any employer, employment agency, labor organization, or joint labor-management committee subject to this title to grant preferential treatment to any individual or to any group because of race, color, religion, sex, or national origin of such individual or group on account of imbalance which may exist with respect to the total number or percentage of persons of any race, color, religion, sex, or national origin employed by any employer, referred or classified for employment by any employment agency or labor organization, admitted to membership or classified by any labor organization, or admitted to, or employed in, any apprenticeship or other training program, in comparison with the total number or percentage of persons of such race, color, religion, sex, or national origin in any community, State, section, or other area, or in the available work force in any community, section, or other area.

However, where there has been evidence of a pattern or practice of discrimination, EEOC often has been able to prod employers who were government contractors into adoption of affirmative action plans under threat of loss of funds.[4] In addition, the courts have tended to support EEOC's affirmative action strategies by taking the position that Section 703(j) must be interpreted in light of the broader purpose of the Act.[5]

EXEMPTIONS

Two broad exemptions in the 1972 Act are of potential interest to educational institutions. First, sections 703(e) and 704(b) permit an exemption if religion, sex, or national origin is a *bona fide* occupational qualification reasonably necessary to the normal operation of a particular business or enterprise. A *bona fide* occupational qualification cannot include race or color. Second, a religious organization may discriminate with regard to an employee's religion. Under the 1964 Act, exempted religious discrimination was limited to the religious aspects of the employing organization. However, the 1972 Act expanded the religious exemption to include not only religious activities but all the activities of a religious organization. Religious organizations cannot discriminate on the basis of race, color, sex, or national origin.

ANTI-DISCRIMINATION PROVISIONS IN AGREEMENTS

Some collective bargaining agreements contain provisions prohibiting discrimination. The following is an illustration:

Affirmative Action

1. It is the policy of the Seattle School Board to select employees as needed on the basis of merit, training, and experience and that there shall be no discrimination against any employee or applicant because of race, creed, color, national origin, sex or age, except as may be permitted to meet a bona fide occupational qualification and the District shall comply with state or national laws as may pertain thereto. This policy also shall be extended to apply to all contractors or vendors serving the District.

Such a policy will ensure the perpetuation of a high quality educational system in accordance with the tenets on which this country was founded.

2. The Board of Directors of the District has as its goal an affirmative action program of recruiting, hiring, and placing staffs in every department, every school, and at every level of operation with proportions of racial minority to total employees corresponding to the proportion of racial minority students to total students in the entire school system. Priority will be given to the recruitment, hiring and placement of minority personnel who have the appropriate qualifications.

3. In implementing the Affirmative Action Program, the District shall recruit, employ, and assign personnel in conformity with state and federal laws, rules, regulations, and directives.

Seattle School District No. 1 and the Seattle Alliance of Educators.

Anti-discrimination provisions in collective bargaining agreements have resulted in arbitration of such cases. A major concern to arbitrators has been whether or not government agencies and the courts would defer their own involvement in preference to the arbitration process.

In *Alexander v. Gardner-Denver,*[6] the Supreme Court held that an employee is not precluded from asserting his or her claim of employment discrimination under Title VII because he or she had previously submitted the claim to binding arbitration in carrying out the terms of a collective bargaining agreement. In *Rios v. Reynolds Metal Co.,*[7] the Fifth Circuit Court stated that an arbitration award may be deferred to if the contractual rights coincide with rights under Title VII and if there is no violation of private rights occurring under Title VII. In addition, before deferring to arbitration a court must find the following:

1. The factual issues before the court are identical with those decided by the arbitrator.

2. The arbitrator had power under the collective bargaining agreement to decide the ultimate issue of discrimination.

3. The evidence presented at the arbitration hearing dealt adequately with all factual issues.

4. The arbitrator actually decided the factual issues presented to the court.

5. The arbitration proceeding was fair and free of procedural errors.

APPLICATION OF EXTERNAL LAW

Just as a court has a choice when it comes to deciding whether or not it will defer to an arbitrator's decision, the arbitrator has a choice in deciding how much weight to give to external law when interpreting a collective bargaining agreement. Given the decision in *Rios,* unless an arbitrator does give weight to external law, the likelihood of judicial review is increased, and the chances of reversal on judicial review may be increased if the collective bargaining agreement is in opposition to external law. Nevertheless, it has been argued that arbitrators should not give weight to external law unless specifically directed to do so in the collective bargaining agreement or the submission agreement.

At the other end of the continuum of opinion is the position that it is an arbitrator's obligation to interpret the collective bargaining agreement in light of external law unless the parties have specifically directed the arbitrator not to do so. There are various middle-of-the-road views attempting to make the use of external law conditional on the presence of certain factors in the case.

The two ends of the continuum of opinion are occupied by Arbitrators Bernard D. Meltzer and Robert G. Howlett. A middle position has been espoused by Michael I. Sovern. Their arguments are examined here.

Meltzer's position

The court's decision in *Rios* may tend to encourage arbitrators to apply external law to their decisions. Indeed, if the law were not applied, it would be a clear invitation by the arbitrator for a court to review the arbitrator's decision and perhaps set it aside. Nevertheless, some arbitrators have taken the position that their involvement in the application of external law could seriously undermine the stature of arbitration and its place in the administration of organizational justice.

Meltzer has claimed that arbitrators should normally not venture to apply external law for two main reasons.[8] First, he says, arbitrators are not necessarily competent to apply external law. Meltzer's view of arbitral competence goes beyond a knowledge of external law to include the notion of an institutionalized form of competence.[9] Meltzer has asserted that arbitration as a function obtained its present stature by confining its activities to an interpretation of the collective bargaining agreement. Since the landmark "Trilogy" decisions of 1960, the courts have increasingly deferred to arbitral opinions regarding the interpretation of collective bargaining agreements.[10] For example, in one of the "Trilogy" cases, the Supreme Court, through Justice Douglas, stated that as an institution arbitrators were more competent to interpret the language of collective bargaining agreements than were the courts themselves. Douglas's opinion stated, in part:

> The labor arbitrator performs functions which are not normal to the courts; the considerations which help him fashion judgments may indeed be foreign to the competence of courts. The labor arbitrator's source of law is not confined to the express provisions of the contract, as the industrial common law — the practices of industry and the shop — is equally a part of the collective bargaining agreement although not expressed in it. The labor arbitrator is usually chosen because of the parties' confidence in his knowledge of the common law of the shop and their trust in his personal judgment to bring to bear considerations which are not expressed in the contract as criteria for judgment. The parties expect that his judgment of a particular grievance will reflect not only what the contract says but, insofar as the collective bargaining agreement permits, such factors as the effect upon productivity of a particular result, its consequence to the morale of the shop, his judgment whether tensions will be heightened or diminished. For the parties' objective in using the arbitration process is primarily to further their common goal of uninterrupted production under the agreement, to make the agreement serve their specialized needs. The ablest judge cannot be expected to bring the same experience and competence to bear upon the determination of a grievance, because he cannot be similarly informed.[11]

Justice Douglas's remarks assured arbitration of its place in the scheme of organizational justice. Meltzer and others who support his point of view emphasize that, for arbitration to continue to enjoy its stature, the institution of arbitration must exercise self-restraint and confine itself to the interpretation of contract language.

Meltzer's second area of concern is that arbitrators will apply external law without the explicit consent of the parties who employ their services. He has recognized that there will be instances where the parties will clearly invite the arbitrator to apply external law to the interpretation of their agreement. In such instances, Meltzer would have arbitrators search their conscience to ascertain whether or not they are capable of fulfilling the wishes of the parties. If they find themselves wanting, then they should refuse the assignment or state that they do not intend to apply the external law if chosen.

The most difficult situation the arbitrator faces is one where the parties state no clear intention that the arbitrator should apply external law but the arbitrator is aware that if the contract is enforced there will be a violation of the law. How can an arbitrator justify the enforcement of a contract that is in violation of law? Meltzer has made this proposal for handling such a situation:

> The position that I have outlined may be challenged on the following grounds, among others: It is wasteful and misleading for an arbitrator to render an award that is clearly repugnant to a controlling statute. Furthermore, insofar as such an award commands illegal conduct, it makes the arbitrator a party to illegality, requires a judicial proceeding to set things straight, and generally demeans the arbitration process by inviting noncompliance with, and reversal of, awards.
>
> Although those considerations reflect a praiseworthy desire to have arbitrators solve the whole problem in a fashion compatible with the pertinent regulatory framework, they are, in my opinion, not persuasive. Any deception of the parties could be avoided by the arbitrator's noting that he is not passing on the validity of any contractual provision that appears to be questionable or invalid under the law. Similarly, if an award based solely on the agreement would call for illegal action, the arbitrator could make it clear that his mandate is contingent on the legality of the contractual provision involved . . .[12]

Other arbitrators sharing Meltzer's position point out that in many situations the external law itself is ambiguous because of conflicting court opinions. Consequently, the image of numerous arbitrators' inflexibility directing parties to disobey the law in order to uphold the contract may be somewhat overdrawn.

HOWLETT'S POSITION

Meltzer's position grows out of a concern for the long-term implications of applying external law. Perhaps not surprisingly, Howlett's reasons for advocating an active involvement of arbitrators in the application of external law stem from the same concern. Howlett has rejected the view that arbitration is an activity involving private rights that occur in isolation from the social and political processes taking place within the environment of arbitration.[13] He believes that the demise of arbitration will result from its failure to respond to the urgent needs of the times.

Howlett's position is endorsed by arbitrators who see the removal of discrimination in organizations as one of the most pressing needs of modern times. To understand the sense of urgency associated with this view, one should understand that the term "discrimination" has taken on meanings which were not necessarily present in an earlier period of employee relations.

In *Griggs*,[14] the court adopted the view that racial discrimination was embedded in the social and political systems of our society. Discrimination was not limited to the motivation of individuals who, through intention and deed, deliberately deprived racial minorities of their rights. The legal view of discrimination as adopted in *Griggs* was that a whole society of nonminorities had absorbed patterns and practices of discrimination of which they were unaware. If arbitrators were willing to enforce contracts that violated external law, then arbitration as an institution ran the risk of prolonging discriminatory practices.

With regard to the issues of competence and consent, Howlett and his supporters have not seen these issues as significant deterrents to arbitrators' being more actively involved in the application of external law.

The issue of consent can be taken care of by the parties either in the body of their agreement or in their submission agreement. Even in those instances where explicit language is not used, some arbitrators have used a "saving" or "separability" clause to justify the application of external law.[15] It has also been argued that language specifying that arbitration be final and binding can serve as justification for the application of external law in the absence of more explicit language.[16]

The competence issue can be taken care of by the parties at the time of their selection of an arbitrator. It has been pointed out that it is not unusual for parties to agree to select arbitrators having special expertise. If the special expertise needed happens to be in some phase of external law, then qualified arbitrators can be found.[17]

SOVERN'S POSITION

Sovern believes that the central issue is one of finding the best forum for employees, whether it be arbitration or the courts. He acknowledges the persuasiveness of certain arguments from both Meltzer's and Howlett's positions, and has attempted to combine them into a list of four standards; if met, these standards would make arbitration an appropriate forum for consideration of external law.[18]

First, the arbitrator should be qualified to interpret and apply relevant external law.

Second, there should be a question of law implicated in a contract-interpretation dispute. In other words, the primary mission of the arbitrator should be to interpret the contract. The interpretation and application of external law must be a means to achieving the arbitrator's primary mission.

Third, arbitration is a proper forum for consideration of external law if one of the parties claims that the contract "immunizes" or in some way requires a violation of the law.

Fourth, external law may be taken into consideration by an arbitrator if the courts lack primary jurisdiction to adjudicate the question of law.

A would-be follower of Sovern's advice would have the most difficulty with the fourth standard. It applies very well to issues and interpretations of federal labor laws, over which the National Labor Relations Board (NLRB) — and not the courts — has primary jurisdiction. However, with regard to civil rights statutes, primary jurisdiction resides with the courts and not with regulatory agencies.

RACIAL DISCRIMINATION ISSUES

Some school arbitration cases have been reported in which minority employees have brought charges of discrimination against the employer. But such cases have been few compared to instances where nonminority employees have brought charges of contract violations against an employer who was in the process of engaging in some form of affirmative action. Such affirmative action activities have fallen into three general categories. First, there have been situations where school employees have entered into agreements with employee representatives endorsing the goal of staff balance between minority and nonminority employees. Second, employers have engaged in affirmative action activities as part of programs agreed to during the course of negotiations with either federal or state civil rights agencies. Third, school employers have unilaterally undertaken affirmative action activities.

STAFF BALANCE AS A CONTRACTUAL OBLIGATION

In the first of the cases reported here, the school employer failed to implement a standard of minority recruitment that had been agreed to with the teachers' union. In the second case, the employer, who was faced with a layoff situation, retained more minority teachers on the staff than was permissible according to the standard agreed to in the contract with the teachers' union. In both cases, arbitrators were able to resolve the contract-dispute issue by traditional means of contract interpretation.

A case of minority recruitment. The school board had agreed to the following fair employment practice: "The Board of Education shall seek out and hire a certified integrated Staff reflective of all races."

128   *Chapter 7*

At the hearing both parties agreed that they particularly had had black teachers in mind at the time they agreed to the provision. The school district was in a suburb of a major city. It had no black children enrolled in the school and employed one black teacher.

The parties were in dispute over the intent of the recruitment provision. The school board spokesman took the position that the statement was a reaffirmation of an existing school board policy against discrimination in school district recruitment practices. The teachers' union claimed that something more was intended. They asserted that the contract provision called for an "active" recruitment effort on the part of the school board and its agents to employ more racial minorities.

The arbitrator agreed with the union's interpretation of the contract. He pointed out that if the parties had intended merely to endorse the school board's existing policy on nondiscrimination, the contract might have read, "The Board of Education shall *continue* to seek out and hire a certified integrated Staff reflective of all races." The specific inclusion of the phrase "to seek out" had particular significance, because it suggested that the school board was to be more than passive in its efforts to find minorities. The arbitrator characterized the school board's existing posture as one of "passive" nondiscrimination. However, the recruitment provision in the agreement called for an "active" program of minority employment.

During the course of the hearing, it was brought out that the personnel department had not engaged in aggressive measures to contact potential black teachers. By way of a remedy, the arbitrator directed the personnel department to take steps that would actively bring openings to the attention of potential black teachers. These steps were to include the advertising of available positions and the on-campus interviewing of potential minority candidates on a minimum of two college campuses that have large black student bodies.[19]

A case of minority layoffs. A contract between the school board and teachers specified that in the event of staff reductions reasonable effort would be made to maintain among staff a racial balance which was not to be lower than a stated base ratio. During a subsequent reduction in staff, a dispute developed over the administration's application of the contractual agreement regarding the maintenance of a base minority ratio.

The administration interpreted the racial balance provision to mean that it was no longer bound to observe the contractual seniority provision. Consequently, the reduction in staff did not include any minority teachers. However, nonminority teachers with greater seniority were laid off.

The teachers argued that the seniority provision had been incorporated into the affirmative action provision pertaining to staff reductions. The teachers were persuasive in showing that the original intention of the reduction provision had been to constrain reduction procedures within the limits of the seniority provision. They pointed out that it was not necessary to nullify the seniority provision or to abandon the base ratio of minorities if reduction procedures incorporated the concept of grouping teachers into certain designated categories.

The arbitrator held that in nullifying the seniority provision the school board had breached its contract with the teachers.[20]

IMPACT OF AFFIRMATIVE ACTION PROGRAMS

In the preceding two cases, the school employer was committed to affirmative action activities by virtue of contractual agreements with teachers. In the following two cases, the employers' commitment to affirmative action involved an agreement with a federal or state agency. In both cases, the action taken by the school board was motivated by its agreement with the governmental agency and resulted in a detrimental impact upon a nonminority employee.

A case of involuntary transfer. A physical education teacher with seniority was involuntarily transferred to the position of an industrial arts teacher, a position he had previously held. The teacher association claimed that, when consolidation was necessary in the physical education department, involuntary transfers should have been along lines of seniority in the department.

The school board rejected the use of seniority so that it could retain a minority group teacher. The school board claimed, but was unable to prove, that nonretention of the minority teacher would have violated HEW guidelines.

The arbitrator held that the school board's action was proper, given the possibility that a loss of federal funds might have resulted if the school board had not maintained the prescribed guidelines. The needs of the school program took priority and justified the involuntary transfer of the physical education teacher.[21]

A case of position rights. A teacher who had been involuntarily transferred requested return to her former position when it was vacated. The contract between the school board and teachers required that priority for filling positions be given to teachers who had been involuntarily transferred. However, school authorities denied the teacher's request and proceeded to fill the position with a minority group teacher.

The arbitrator held that even though the teacher had contractual rights to return to her former position, those rights could not be interpreted so strictly as to ignore the school district's affirmative action plan, which was part of an agreement with the state's Human Rights Commission. The grievance was denied with the proviso that the grievant was entitled to be reinstated as soon as another vacancy occurred.[22]

STAFF BALANCE AS AN ADMINISTRATIVE GOAL

In the preceding cases, school boards were motivated to achieve staff balance as part of agreements with teacher associations or governmental agencies. There are cases, however, in which school authorities have attempted to achieve staff balance as a unilaterally assumed goal. The general motivation for unilaterally seeking recruitment of minorities appears to be associated with an increase in the number of minority students served by the schools. There has been a corresponding belief that minority staff would be in a position to help school districts understand and meet the needs of minority students.

As a general rule, arbitrators have considered race to be a valid criterion for the selection of staff. In cases where the general qualifications of the grievant and a minority teacher were "relatively equal," it was held valid to consider race as a basis for selecting the minority person over the nonminority person.[23,24] In one case, the arbitrator considered race to be a valid criterion as long as contractual rights of teachers were not violated in achieving staff balance.[25] In a complicated case where a black had been promoted to principal without following contractual procedures for promotion, the arbitrator sustained the teacher association's grievance over the promotion. However, he refused to nullify the promotion as a remedy because no one in the teachers' bargaining unit had suffered any injury as a consequence of the promotion and evasion of contractual procedures.[26]

SEX DISCRIMINATION ISSUES

Sex discrimination cases discussed here fall within three categories: job qualifications, compensation, and teacher pregnancies. Each category contains two basic issues. With regard to job qualifications, the issues pertain to *bona fide* occupational qualifications and the "nondiscriminate" use of job qualifications. Compensation issues concern equality of pay and equity of fringe benefits. Teacher pregnancies result in the issues of granting or requiring maternity leave and granting or denying sick leave pay.

JOB QUALIFICATIONS

Arbitrators have held that under certain circumstances a person's sex may be a *bona fide* occupational qualification. Except in a few situations, however, sex cannot be considered as a valid qualification for a job.

Locker and washroom attendants. Within the setting of schools, sex is a *bona fide* occupational qualification for locker and washroom attendants. An arbitrator determined that there was no violation of the contract when the school board decided that only female applicants would be accepted for certain positions posted in the maintenance department. A *bona fide* job qualification existed where the jobs involved working in girls' locker rooms and lavatories. The school administration was persuasive in claiming that male custodians who had worked on the duties had problems getting into the lavatories on a regular basis and consequently the rooms were so dirty that students complained.[27]

In another case, the union contended that school authorities' insistence that a man serve as an equipment attendant in the men's locker room was arbitrary, since a woman was capable of doing the job. The arbitrator denied the grievance and held that community standards and legal enactments recognized the need for certain restrictions based on sex.[28]

In a case where a male swimming instructor was involuntarily transferred, the arbitrator held the transfer to be valid since, of the three instructors who could have been transferred, two were men and one was a woman. It was necessary to retain the woman instructor even though the male instructor had more seniority because of the need to provide separate supervision in both male and female student locker rooms.[29]

Guidance counselor. In a school where all three guidance counselors were female, the principal expressed the opinion that one of the appointments should be held by a male. The arbitrator agreed that sex could be a *bona fide* occupational qualification in the placement of a guidance counselor.[30]

"Nondiscriminate" use of job qualifications. In selecting for the position of curriculum coordinator a male applicant who was less qualified than a female applicant, school authorities violated the contract provision forbidding discrimination based on sex.[31] In another district, the school board violated the agreement when it refused the request of a female teacher for a transfer to the position of physical education instructor in a middle school. The school board's reason of wanting to improve the male image in the middle school was rejected. [32,33]

COMPENSATION

The term "compensation" as used here refers to an employee's basic salary and fringe benefits. Since most school districts have adopted a single salary schedule for all classroom teachers, the potential for discrimination in the area of basic salaries has been reduced. However, the area of extracurricular activities, particularly the coaching of varsity and intramural teams, has been one in which compensation has not been uniform. Therefore, the potential for sex discrimination has been greater. With regard to fringe benefit disputes, women employees have brought grievances when they have not been given the same options for insurance coverage as men have received.

Pay for coaching positions. In paying male boys' basketball coaches more than female girls' basketball coaches, where the work load for both boys' and girls' coaches was equal, one school board was held to have violated the contract clause and state law.[34] In a similar situation, an arbitrator directed a school board to pay the girls' varsity coach at the same rate as the boys' varsity coaches. The position description posted for the girls' coach indicated that the assignment entailed the same responsibilities as the boys' coaching assignment. The lower rate paid to the girls' coach was unilaterally set by the board, since there had been no female coaches at the time the coaches' pay schedule was negotiated.[35]

In another case, an arbitrator concluded that equal pay was to be given for coaching when assignments were equal in relation to skill, effort, and responsibility. Applying this standard, he found that the school district violated the contract's fair practice clause by paying female coaches who taught girls' tennis and golf less than male coaches who taught boys' tennis and golf. However, no violation occurred in track and field, where female coaches had a lighter work load than male coaches.[36,37]

Fringe benefits. In a school district where the school board picked up the full cost of single coverage while employees who wanted family coverage made up the difference, it was found that the school board had no right to deny married female teachers single coverage. The arbitrator held that not to allow female teachers the same options as male teachers was a violation of the Fourteenth Amendment and the state constitution.[38]

In another school district, the school board had agreed to provide full family coverage but failed to do so in the instances of three female grievants. They alleged that although the board provided them with additional coverage, it charged them additionally for their children and spouses. The board claimed that the grievants were eligible for full family coverage only if they were heads of households. The school board was unable to convince the arbitrator that a head-of-household limitation had been agreed to between the parties. Consequently, the board was directed to furnish full family coverage to the three married female teachers.[39]

In another case, the school board violated its agreement when it refused to pay a married female librarian a dependency allowance for her three dependent children. The agreement contained no exception for married teachers whose spouses worked. Consequently, the grievant was entitled to the allowance.[40,41]

MANDATORY MATERNITY LEAVE

Most arbitrators have not upheld mandatory leave policies. The Civil Rights Act of 1964 or some similar state statute has been the source of authority most frequently cited by arbitrators in upholding grievances that contest mandatory leave policies.[42] Generally, arbitrators have found mandatory leave policies that require a teacher to leave work, frequently without pay, to be a form of sex discrimination not permitted under Title VII of the Civil Rights Act. One of these opinions stated:

> The automatic rule that all teachers must vacate their position at the end of the fifth month of pregnancy irrespective of their ability to perform their work satisfactorily without injury to themselves is arbitrary and results in unnecessary financial loss and hardship. Since the rule, by its nature, applies only to women and to a condition attendant to their sex it results in discrimination in terms of condition of employment on the basis of sex.[43]

One arbitrator upheld a mandatory leave grievance because he found the policy to be a violation of individual constitutional rights. Anticipating a later decision of the United States Supreme Court, his findings concluded:

> In any event the parties have adopted constitutional rights as a portion of their collective bargaining agreement. Continued employment while pregnant is evolving in a most compelling manner as just such a right. It is therefore a violation of this agreement for grievant not to have been permitted the right of continued employment which she gave every indication of being fully capable to perform.[44]

The reasons given by arbitrators for denying grievances where mandatory leaves have been imposed were

1. that a search of external law did not uncover any rule which prohibited the use of mandatory leave policies[45]
2. that external law was in a state of conflict which the arbitrator did not have the authority under the agreement to resolve.[46]

In *Cleveland Board of Education v. LaFleur,* the Supreme Court resolved the conflict among lower court opinions by ruling that mandatory maternity leave policies were unconstitutional.[47] As a result of a policy adopted by her employers, Mrs. LaFleur was required to take a maternity leave without pay, beginning five months before the expected birth of her child. Mrs. LaFleur wanted to continue teaching until the end of the school year. However, because of her employer's policy, she was required to leave three months before the end of the school year. Mrs. LaFleur was not permitted to return to work until the beginning of the next regular school semester following the date when her child attained the age of three months. A doctor's certificate attesting to her health was a prerequisite to her return; an additional physical examination could be required.

Mrs. LaFleur's employer gave two main arguments for a mandatory leave:

1. that firm cutoff dates were necessary to maintain continuity of instruction
2. that at least some teachers become physically incapable of adequately performing certain duties in the latter period of their pregnancy.

The court examined both the arguments.

The court found the first argument to be a valid concern, but did not see how the school board's rules fulfilled the objective of continuity of instruction. Advance-notice provisions are rational, but the absolute requirement of termination at the end of the fourth or fifth month is not. If continuity were the only objective, later cutoff dates would serve as well as earlier ones. The court asserted that continuity might be best served by allowing the teacher herself to choose the date upon which to commence her leave, as long as due notice was given. The court concluded that arbitrary cutoff dates as contained in the mandatory leave rules in the *LaFleur* case had no rational relationship to valid state interest in preserving continuity of instruction.

With regard to the school board's second argument for mandatory leaves, the court found it to be a legitimate one both on educational and on safety grounds. The question was whether mandatory rules were unnecessarily broad in achieving their goal. The mandatory leave rule created an "irrebuttable presumption" of physical incompetence. The court pointed out that historically it had been suspicious of the creation of irrebuttable presumptions when the state had other means of making determinations necessary to the achievement of its legitimate objectives. In the instance of a pregnant teacher, an irrebuttable presumption of physical incompetence was applied even when medical evidence as to a woman's physical status was wholly to the contrary. Such irrebuttable presumptions unnecessarily interfered with an individual's rights under the Fifth and Fourteenth Amendments, according to the court.

The court also concerned itself with the rules governing eligibility to return to work after giving birth. Under the Cleveland rule, Mrs. LaFleur was not eligible to return to work until the beginning of the next regular school semester after her child had attained the age of three months. In addition, she was required to have a doctor's certificate attesting to her health. The court found no objection to the medical or the next-semester eligibility provisions. The medical provision was sufficiently narrow to provide an individualized decision as to the teacher's condition and avoid the pitfalls of presumptions. The next-semester provision was also narrowly drawn and was consistent with the legitimate goal of providing instructional continuity.

The court took exception to the provision requiring Mrs. LaFleur to wait until her child was three months of age before returning to work. The court could not find any legitimate state interest to be served by the three-month provision. As such it unnecessarily penalized a female teacher for asserting her right to bear children.

SICK LEAVE PAY FOR PREGNANT TEACHERS

A number of arbitration cases reported involve the granting of sick leave pay during the period of pregnancy and recovery from giving birth. An implicit issue in each case has been the unwillingness of school boards to consider pregnancy and recovery as disabilities related to being sick. As one arbitrator phrased the school board's position:

> The basic problem is that the grievant was not "sick" and sick leave was inappropriate to the circumstances. Maternity is a natural function and one within the control of husband and wife. It is defined as "the character, relation, state, or condition of a mother." Sickness means "affected with disease, ill . . ."[48]

The distinction is important, since payment for circumstances associated with pregnancy need not be made if pregnancy is something other than "sickness."

Probably the single most important challenge to the position taken by school boards has been EEOC guidelines stating that pregnancy and recovery from pregnancy are to be regarded as temporary disabilities and are to be compensated under sick leave plans in the same manner as are other disabilities.[49] State law prohibiting sex discrimination and court rulings supporting the lawfulness of state and federal sex discrimination guidelines also have been used as rebuttals to school board arguments.

A major difference between an arbitration case in which the grievance of a pregnant teacher was denied and one in which the grievance was sustained has been the arbitrator's view of applying external law to resolve the contract dispute. Arbitrators who have denied the validity of applying sex discrimination guidelines have done so in some instances by pointing out the existence of conflicting rulings in the courts over the lawfulness of guidelines in sick leave cases.[50,51] Other arbitrators have found the language of the contract and the intent of the parties to be controlling in the face of external law. For example, the existence of separate clauses for maternity leave and sick leave has been taken as evidence that pregnancy-related disabilities were not intended to be compensated as sick leave.[52]

In one instance, the teacher association requested that the arbitrator enforce a provision of the agreement which would have required the school board to renegotiate the existing unpaid maternity leave provision to bring the provision in line with a decision of the state supreme court. The association contended that the court decision required payment for maternity leaves. The arbitrator refused the teacher association's request and pointed out that to require the school board to renegotiate the existing contract provision would be to presume that the contract provision was in violation of the state supreme court ruling. The arbitrator stated that such a decision was ultimately a matter for the courts to determine.[53]

Arbitrators who believe the application of sex discrimination guidelines to be appropriate to their role have frequently found justification for their decisions in a separability or savings clause.[54] The following is typical of such a clause:

> If any provision of this Agreement, or any application of the Agreement to any employee or group of employees, shall be found to be contrary to law, then such provision or application shall not be deemed valid and subsisting except to the extent permitted by law, but all other provisions or applications shall continue in full force and effect for the duration of this Agreement.

In other cases, arbitrators have justified the application of external law through other contractual language, such as provisions that assure teachers of their rights under state law or other statutes.[55,56]

SUMMARY

Two basic types of discrimination cases have been reported most frequently: racial discrimination and sex discrimination. The primary issues in most reported racial discrimination cases have grown out of employers' attempts to implement affirmative action programs. In most cases the impetus for school boards to engage in such programs has been agreements made between school boards and teacher representatives, or agreements between school boards and government agencies. In some instances school boards have unilaterally initiated affirmative action programs in response to an increase in the number of minority children in the school district.

Most reported grievances, but not all, occur when a nonminority staff member has been detrimentally affected by the implementation of an affirmative action program. The primary goal of an affirmative action program is usually to increase the number of minority staff. Recruitment and employment of minority staff has involved departures from contractual promotion procedures, suspension of seniority rules, suspension of position rights, and involuntary transfers.

Arbitrators have determined that race is a valid criterion to be considered in the employment of staff. However, arbitrators have also voiced concern that contractual procedures, rules, and rights of nonminority staff should not be nullified by affirmative action programs. Consequently, an arbitral task inherent in cases involving nonminority and contractual rights is to balance management's interests in an affirmative action program against the grievant's interests.

Sex discrimination cases have for the most part involved grievances by female employees alleging lack of equity in compensation or discrimination in maternity policies. Inequities in compensation have occurred when school employers have failed to give women the same insurance options that they offer men. Inequities also have occurred when women, particularly women coaches, have been paid less than men for positions involving the same work load. Discrimination in maternity policies has occurred in connection with school board policies which create an irrebuttable presumption that a pregnant teacher is physically incapable of performing her duties after the fourth or fifth month of pregnancy.

The United States Supreme Court made it clear in the *LaFleur* case that a teacher's incapacity due to pregnancy must be individually determined by her doctor, the school board, and the teacher. In addition, the court has held that the time for a teacher's resumption of her duties cannot be tied to the age of her newborn child. Less well settled has been the issue of receiving sick leave pay for maternity-related disabilities.

The major challenge to a school board's claim that disabilities due to pregnancy are not sickness comes in the form of federal and state guidelines which assert that, for purposes of sick leave pay, pregnancy-related disabilities are to be considered in the same way as any other temporary disability. Arbitrators have differed in their opinions over the appropriateness of applying sex discrimination guidelines.

Arbitrators have taken a number of positions on the issue of applying external law to the resolution of contractual disputes. At one end of the opinion spectrum is the view that arbitrators are not necessarily competent to apply external law nor is it always explicitly clear in the agreement that the parties intended to have the arbitrator apply external law. At the other end of the continuum is the position that arbitrators have an obligation to apply external law because the distinction between private law and public law is an unreal distinction. The private law of labor-management agreements is not intended to be isolated from the public law within which it transpires.

Prior to 1972, federal sex discrimination laws did not apply to school districts. If school districts were affected by federal rules, it usually was because of their status as federal contractors. Following the passage of the Equal Opportunity Act of 1972, educational institutions were brought within the purview of the Act. Like the Civil Rights Act of 1964, the Equal Opportunity Act made it unlawful to fail or refuse to hire or to discharge or discriminate against any individual with respect to compensation, terms, conditions, or privileges of employment because of the individual's race, color, sex, or national origin.

There are some important exemptions to the 1972 Act. Religious institutions may discriminate on religious grounds but not on grounds of race, color, sex, or national origin. In addition, the 1972 Act recognizes that under certain circumstances sex, but not race or color, may be a *bona fide* occupational qualification.

There are some court cases that may have an effect on arbitrators' behavior. Historically, the institution of arbitration has earned the high respect of the courts. After the "Trilogy" cases, arbitration became an integral part of the system of organizational justice which rested on collective bargaining and grievance procedures.

In the *Gardner-Denver* case, the United States Supreme Court held that, in cases of discrimination coming under the 1964 Cvil Rights Act, an employee did not waive his right to a hearing in the courts if he initially submitted his case to arbitration. In effect this meant that in discrimination cases the courts need not follow the tradition of deferring to an arbitrator's interpretation of a contract dispute.

In the *Rios* case, the court clarified its position on deferral to arbitration by setting forth standards that would identify circumstances under which lower courts could consider deferral. One of the preconditions for deferral was the requirement that the arbitrator must have given consideration to the grievant's statutory rights. The court's cautious attitude with regard to deferring to arbitral opinion in discrimination cases was partly explained by its decision in the *Griggs* case. In *Griggs,* the court defined discrimination not only in terms of the actions of individuals who seek to discriminate against minorities, but also in terms of a social system which fosters patterns and practices of discrimination that go beyond the motivation of individuals.

Implicit in the court's view of discrimination is the possibility that the labor-management system of bargaining, including arbitration, could at times be party to institutionalized forms of discrimination. The force of the various court decisions on arbitration's role in discrimination cases may cause some arbitrators to consider and apply external law as it pertains to discrimination in employment situations.

NOTES

1. For a discussion and comparison of the Civil Rights Act of 1964 and the Equal Opportunity Act of 1972, see *The Equal Employment Opportunity Act of 1972* (Washington: The Bureau of National Affairs, 1973) prepared by the editorial staff of BNA.
2. Ibid., pp. 55–65.
3. See also Russell L. Greenman and Eric J. Schmertz, *Personnel Administration and the Law* (Washington: The Bureau of National Affairs, 1972), pp. 70–100.
4. Affirmative action strategies have been traced to the implementation of President Kennedy's Executive Order 10925. In implementing Executive Order 10925, the President's Committee on Equal Employment Opportunity required government contractors to set up effective recruiting programs to give members of minority groups equal opportunity for employment. The recruitment programs were labeled "plans for progress." This strategy for increasing employment opportunities for minorites was later adopted by the Office of Federal Contract Compliance. See Greenman and Schmertz, *Personnel Administration and the Law,* p. 18.
5. Ibid., p. 6.
6. *Alexander v. Gardner-Denver,* 415 U.S. 36 (1974).
7. *Rios v. Reynolds Metal Co.,* 5 FEP I (5th Cir. 1972).
8. Bernard D. Meltzer, "Ruminations About Ideology, Law, and Labor Arbitration," *The Arbitrator, the NLRB, and the Courts,* Proceedings of the Twentieth Annual Meeting, National Academy of Arbitrators (Washington: BNA Incorporated, 1967), pp. 1–20.
9. Bernard D. Meltzer, "Labor Arbitration and Conflicting Remedies for Employment Discrimination," 39 *University of Chicago Law Review* 30, 34 (1972).

10. *United Steelworkers of America v. American Manufacturing Company,* 363 U.S. 564, 46 LRRM 2414 (1960); *United Steelworkers of America v. Warrior and Gulf Navigation Co.,* 363 U.S. 574, 46 LRRM 2416 (1960); and *United Steelworkers of America v. Enterprise Wheel and Car Corporation,* 363 U.S. 593, 46 LRRM 2423 (1960).
11. *United Steelworkers of America v. Warrior and Gulf Navigation Co.,* 363 U.S. 574, 80 S. Ct. 1347, 4 L. Ed. 2d 1409.
12. Meltzer "Ruminations," p. 17.
13. Robert G. Howlett, "The Role of Law in Arbitration—A Reprise," *Developments in American and Foreign Arbitration,* Proceedings of the Twenty-First Annual Meeting, National Academy of Arbitrators (Washington: BNA Incorporated, 1968), pp. 64–75. See also Robert G. Howlett, "The Arbitrator, the NLRB, and the Courts," *The Arbitrator, the NLRB, and the Courts,* Proceedings of the Twentieth Annual Meeting, National Academy of Arbitrators (Washington: BNA Incorporated, 1967), pp. 67–110.
14. *Griggs v. Duke Power Company,* 401 U.S. 424 (1971).
15. Richard Mittenthal, "The Role of Law in Arbitration," *Developments in American and Foreign Arbitration,* Proceedings of the Twenty-First Annual Meeting, National Academy of Arbitrators (Washington: BNA Incorporated, 1968), pp. 42–58.
16. Ibid., p. 50.
17. Ibid., p. 48.
18. Michael I. Sovern, "When Should Arbitrators Follow Federal Law," *Arbitration and the Expanding Role of Neutrals,* Proceedings of the Twenty-Third Annual Meeting, National Academy of Arbitrators (Washington: BNA Incorporated, 1970), pp. 29–47.
19. *East Detroit (Michigan) Board of Education,* 54 LA 530, Robert G. Howlett, Arbitrator.
20. *Ann Arbor (Michigan) Board of Education,* 46 AIS 13, Richard I. Bloch, Arbitrator.
21. *San Francisco (California) Unified School District,* 70 AIS 10, La Verda O. Allen, Arbitrator.
22. *Seattle (Washington) School District,* 70 AIS 5, J. B. Gillingham, Arbitrator.
23. *Ann Arbor (Michigan) Public Schools,* 41 AIS 10, William P. Daniel, Arbitrator.
24. See also *Board of Trustees, Genesee (Michigan) Community College,* 31 AIS 21, George T. Roumell, Jr., Arbitrator.
25. *Board of Education, Colorado Springs (Colorado) School District No., 11,* 23 AIS 10, William E. Rentfro, Arbitrator.
26. *Jersey City (New Jersey) Board of Education,* 31 AIS 9, Daniel G. Collins, Arbitrator.
27. *Bloomfield Hills (Michigan) Schools,* 67 AIS 1, Jerome Gross, Arbitrator.
28. *Wayne State University (Detroit, Michigan),* 38 AIS 1, Alan Walt, Arbitrator.
29. *Centennial (Pennsylvania) School District,* 52 AIS 6, J. Charles Short, Arbitrator.

30. *Billerica (Massachusetts) School Committee,* 94 AIS 8, Joseph P. O'Donnell, Arbitrator.

31. *Alum Rock (California) Union Elementary School District,* 91 AIS 9, William B. Gould, Arbitrator.

32. *Community Unit School District, No. 205 (Galesburg, Illinois),* 55 LA 895, Reynold C. Seitz, Arbitrator.

33. See also *Gloversville (New York) Central School District,* 92 AIS 15, Daniel C. Williams, Arbitrator; *The Hoboken (New Jersey) Board of Education,* 58 AIS 15, S. Herbert Unterberger, Arbitrator.

34. *Garfield (New Jersey) Board of Education,* 90 AIS 8, Gladys Gershenfeld, Arbitrator.

35. *Providence (Rhode Island) School Committee,* 61 AIS 11, Marcia L. Greenbaum, Arbitrator.

36. *Washoe County (Nevada) School District,* 67 AIS 12, Arnold O. Anderson, Arbitrator.

37. *Camden County (New Jersey) College,* 71 AIS 1, Jonas Aarons, Arbitrator.

38. *Springfield (Ohio) Board of Education,* 17 AIS 17, Robert G. Howlett, Arbitrator.

39. *Board of Education of Comstock Park Public Schools,* 57 LA 279, Alan Walt, Arbitrator.

40. *Longmeadow (Massachusetts) School Committee,* 60 AIS 19, Stanley M. Jacks, Arbitrator.

41. *Roseville (Michigan) Board of Education,* 46 AIS 11, Leon J. Herman, Arbitrator.

42. *Clio (Michigan) Area School District,* 61 LA 37, James R. McCormick, Arbitrator; *Manasquan (New Jersey) Board of Education,* 46 AIS 15, John M. Malkin, Arbitrator; *Middletown (Connecticut) Board of Education,* 56 LA 830, John A. Hogan, Arbitrator.

43. *Middletown (Connecticut) Board of Education,* 56 LA 830, 832, John A. Hogan, Arbitrator.

44. *Board of Education of Southgate (Michigan) Community School District,* 57 LA 476, 478, David G. Heilbrun, Arbitator.

45. *School District No. 7 (Depew, New York),* 58 LA 1329, Frederic Freilicher, Arbitrator.

46. *Milwaukee (Wisconsin) Area Technical College,* 60 LA 302, Reynolds C. Seitz, Arbitrator.

47. 414 U.S. 632 (1974).

48. *East Hartford (Connecticut) Board of Education,* 57 LA 831, David C. Altrock, Arbitrator.

49. See *Federal Guidelines of Discrimination,* Title 29, Labor, Chapter XIV, Part 1604.10.

50. *Wausau (Wisconsin) District Public Schools,* 64 LA 187, Philip G. Marshall, Arbitrator; *Merrill Area Joint School District No. 1 (Wisconsin),* 63 LA 1106, Marvin L. Schurke, Arbitrator.

51. The conflict in court opinion has been disclosed in *Wetzel v. Liberty Mutual Insurance Co.,* 7 FEP Cases 34 (U.S. Dist. Ct. WD Pa. 1973). The court relied on EEOC guidelines to rule that the company's insurance plan was

unlawful because it provided for all disabilities except pregnancy. In *Newman v. Delta Air Lines,* 7 FEP Cases 27 (U.S. Dist. Ct. ND Ga. 1973), the court concluded that pregnancy was neither a sickness nor a disability and refused to apply EEOC guidelines.

52. *Madison (Wisconsin) Area Board of Vocational, Technical and Adult Education,* District 4, 56 LA 316, Donald B. Lee, Arbitrator.

53. *Hartford (Wisconsin) Common School Joint District No. 1,* 68 LA 608, H. Herman Rauch, Arbitrator.

54. *Clio (Michigan) Area School District,* 61 LA 37, James R. McCormick, Arbitrator; *Thornapple-Kellog School District (Michigan),* 60 LA 549, M. David Keefe, Arbitrator.

55. *Leland (Michigan) Board of Education,* 66 LA 975, A. Dale Allen, Jr., Arbitrator; *Walled Lake (Michigan) Consolidated Schools,* 64 LA 239, James R. McCormick, Arbitrator.

56. See also *Apollo-Ridge School District (Pennsylvania),* 68 LA 1235, William J. LeWinter, Arbitrator; *Andover (Massachusetts) School Committee,* 86 AIS 6, David R. Bloodsworth, Arbitrator.

8

Conditions of Work

Many states have defined the scope of negotiations between school boards and teacher representatives as being limited to "wages, hours, terms, and conditions of work."[1] However, states still differ on whether or not a specific topic is negotiable.

This chapter covers arbitration cases on four conditions: hours of work, class size, workload, and work assignments. The selection of topics does not imply that these topics are regarded as negotiable in all states having collective bargaining laws permitting negotiations on conditions of work.[2] Rather, these topics have been chosen because arbitration cases on these and related subjects have been reported frequently.[3]

Ambiguity of contractual terms is the most common characteristic of arbitration disputes involving conditions of work. A phrase or term is said to be ambiguous if the words suggest more than one meaning. Contractual terms are not ambiguous in any absolute sense; a term may be ambiguous to one person and not to another. General semanticists have noted that meanings are related to an individual's or group's underlying needs and self-interests.[4] The task of the arbitrator who is attempting to resolve a dispute over the meaning of contractual terms is a difficult one. Various principles of contract interpretation are employed by arbitrators to accomplish this task.[5] The cases reported in this chapter will touch on some of the principles of contract interpretation.

The main objective of the chapter, however, is to identify contractual language that has resulted in arbitration disputes. Knowledge of such arbitration disputes could assist educators in wording or rewording contract language so as to avoid needless controversies.

HOURS OF WORK

The following is an illustration of a collective bargaining agreement covering hours of work:

> The arrival and departure time for each employee shall be determined at the sole and exclusive discretion of the Employer.
>
> The total of which shall consist of not more than 7¾ hours which shall include a scheduled duty-free lunch period of at least 30 uninterrupted minutes. The employees shall not be required to be available during this scheduled lunch period for conferences with students or parents or for supervision unless an emergency situation arises involving the safety of students. Employees may leave their assignment during the time encompassed by the employee's work day upon receipt of permission from their principal, their supervisor, or the employer's appointed designee.
>
> No employee shall be required to remain in attendance at a faculty meeting more than 1¼ hours beyond their pupils' dismissal time the day of a faculty meeting.
>
> No employee shall be required to attend more than two (2) evening assignments or meetings outside their regular school day each semester. Attendance at additional meetings shall be at the professional discretion of the employee.
>
> No employee shall be required to remain in the building after students have vacated the building on days preceding a vacation.[6]

The illustration just cited contains four topics that have appeared as issues in arbitration disputes. These topics are the determination of who is covered by the work hours provision, whether lunch time is excluded from or included in the defined hours of work, how evening activities are affected by the definition of working hours, and the school board's authority to establish the beginning and ending of the school day.

TO WHOM DO HOURS OF WORK APPLY?

The three cases reported here involve three separate agreements. In each case the arbitrator had to determine if negotiated hours of work applied to teachers in nontypical situations. In the first case, it was the arbitrator's task to determine if a contract clause that set the work day at "no more than seven hours and thirty minutes" gave the school board the right to require special education teachers who had worked shorter hours to work the seven and a half hours mentioned in the contract.[7] In the second case, teacher representatives had negotiated the terms of a "normal teaching day." The arbitrator's task was to determine if the contractual definition of a "normal teaching day" applied to music and physical education teachers as well as classroom teachers. In the past, music and physical education teachers had been required to report earlier or stay later than the contractually defined "normal teaching day."[8] In the third case, a school nurse grieved the requirement that she work beyond the contractual maximum for a school day. The arbitrator's task was to determine if the contract prevented the school board from requiring her to do so.[9]

"No meeting of minds." Testimony in the case of the special education teacher made it clear to the arbitrator that at the time of negotiations the two parties had something different in mind when they adopted the phrase setting the work day at "no more than seven hours and thirty minutes." The teacher representatives claimed the phrase was used to permit an in-school work day of less than seven hours and thirty minutes. The school board took the position that the phrase applied equally to all teachers in the same building, but that within the system there could be different total working hours from one building to another.

Since there had been no common intention at the time of negotiations, the arbitrator concluded:

> ... the Board cannot now properly interpret the language of this article in a manner not contemplated by the parties . . . . Equity suggests that, given the facts in the case, redress of the grievance be limited to a restoration of the status quo as to the in-school workday of the Special Education teachers for the remainder of the contract term.[10]

Evidence of Exclusion. In the case pertaining to music and physical education teachers, the arbitrator acquired evidence in the form of a fact-finder's report stating that certain groups, including physical education teachers and music teachers, had been required to report early or stay late. In reflecting on whether it had been the intention of the parties to include music and physical education teachers in the recently negotiated normal school day, the arbitrator made the following statement:

It is not always easy to determine what was the intention and understanding of the parties at the time that they negotiated their agreement. Nor can we always depend upon their testimony as to what their intention was. Sometimes what may have been in the thoughts of one of the negotiators may not have been given the slightest thought in the mind of the negotiator on the other side.

For the agreement to be deemed to have modified existing practices we must look beyond the naked words of the agreement and see whether the other evidence available confirms this intent.[11]

In looking beyond the "naked words of the agreement," the arbitrator drew on a fact-finder's report which stated that some groups of teachers were required to report earlier (music, science) and others to stay later (physical education). The fact-finder noted that the teacher association had asked for a uniform policy. In the fact-finder's report it was obvious that he intended to let the status quo remain. When the fact-finder's report was added to the contractual statement regarding the "normal working day," it was clear to the arbitrator that music and physical education teachers had not been covered by the contractual statement.

Evidence of inclusion. In the case of the school nurse who grieved a requirement that she work beyond the negotiated maximum working day for classroom teachers, the arbitrator could find no evidence why she should be treated differently. The fact that she did not have any classroom duties was not a controlling factor in the situation. More to the point was the fact that she was a tenured teacher and was being paid according to the teachers' salary scale.

IS THE LUNCH PERIOD EXCLUDED OR INCLUDED?

In the following case description, one can sense the difficulty faced by an arbitrator trying to resolve an ambiguous contract phrase when he is restricted to the semantic arguments of the disputing parties.

The contract stated that teachers will be present for a school day of seven hours and forty-five minutes except for their thirty-minute duty-free lunch. The school administration interpreted the word "except" to mean exclude; therefore, it scheduled a school day of eight hours and fifteen minutes. In defending a teacher's grievance over the administration's schedule, the teacher's representatives claimed that the phrase introduced by the term "except" actually modified the terms "will be present." Thus, from the teacher's point of view, one should be present for seven hours and forty-five minutes per school day except when at the duty-free lunch.

The arbitrator was reluctant to grant an award on the basis of such narrow interpretations and lack of supporting evidence; nevertheless he supported the teacher's interpretation of the contract.[12]

ARE EVENING ACTIVITIES EXCLUDED?

A collective bargaining agreement contained the following provision:

> The working day for teachers shall not exceed seven hours and twenty minutes, including a half hour lunch period. Teachers will indicate their attendance by initialing a check-in sheet at the opening of the school day.[13]

A grievance arose over the interpretation of the provision when a school administration announcement directed teachers to attend an evening concert and included specific assignments for some of the teachers. The teacher association claimed that the contract provision describing the working day was inclusive and any activities which fell outside of the contractual definition of their working day were to be regarded as voluntary. The school board asserted that the definition of the working day as it appeared in the collective bargaining agreement placed no limitation on time required for teachers to attend meetings or assist in cocurricular or extracurricular activities.

The arbitrator resolved the differences in favor of the school administration's point of view. First, he noted that in the paragraph defining the working day and in the section of the agreement of which the paragraph was part, there was no mention of meetings and activities outside the school day. All references were limited to teaching and instructional preparation activities. He concluded from this that the hours mentioned pertaining to the work day were meant to define the day as it pertained to teaching activities.

Second, the arbitrator noted that in a previous negotiation session the teachers' representatives had proposed that ten dollars an hour be paid to any teacher who was required to extend his service beyond the normal work day; the demand had been withdrawn during the course of negotiations. The arbitrator thought it reasonable to assume that the limitations on the working day remained applicable following the negotiations. Finally, the arbitrator also noted the existence of administrative regulations pertaining to teachers' obligations to attend various activities following the working day, and the accepted practice of teacher attendance at the activities.[14]

UNDER WHAT CIRCUMSTANCES WILL CHANGES IN
HOURS OF WORK BE CHALLENGED?

A collective bargaining agreement provided the following:

> The workday of classroom teachers will begin no earlier than 30 minutes
> before the student starting time and end no later than 30 minutes after the
> student dismissal time.[15]

In this case, the administration made a change in the students'
school day which affected the teachers' working hours. Because 90
percent of the student population was transported by bus and the school
district was short of buses, the school board found it necessary to
lengthen the students' school day. The teachers' work day was corre-
spondingly lengthened in order to accommodate the revised student
schedules. The teachers grieved the action under the contractual provision for maintenance of standards, which read as follows:

> All conditions of employment, including teaching hours, extra compen-
> sation for duties outside regular teaching hours, relief periods, leaves, and
> general teaching conditions, shall be maintained . . . . [16]

The arbitrator took the point of view that even if it were conceded
that the maintenance of standards provision applied to past practice,
it would have to give way to the more specific provisions defining the
teachers' work day. The general wording of the maintenance of standards provision was judged to be less revealing of the parties' intentions
regarding the length of the teachers' work day than the specific provisions for the work day.[17]

There have been a number of grievance cases in which teachers
have used the language of a maintenance of standards provision to
restrict a school board's attempt to change hours of work. A critical
feature of the cases in which teachers have been successful is the fact
that the maintenance of standards provisions incorporated consultation
rights as well. Thus, before the school board or one of its agents could
modify any of the items mentioned in the maintenance of standards
provision, there was the requirement to "negotiate" or at a minimum
"discuss" pending changes with the teachers' representatives.[18,19]

CLASS SIZE

The principal issues associated with arbitration disputes over class size
raise such basic questions as: Was the contractual figure set for class

size a guideline or an absolute maximum? Where management has obligated itself to make "sufficient effort" to reduce class sizes, what is "sufficient effort"? Are there situational factors that could be used to rescind management's contractual obligation to reduce class loads? What compensation should be granted to teachers whose classes exceed contractual limits?

ARE CLASS SIZE NUMBERS GUIDELINES OR ABSOLUTE
MAXIMUMS?

Three grievants alleged that the school board had violated the collective bargaining agreement regarding class size. All three had classes that exceeded the figures mentioned in the agreement. In addition, the grievants brought out the fact that they were engaged in an experimental program which would greatly benefit from smaller class sizes. They presented evidence pointing out the deficiencies in attempting to contend with the larger class sizes. In their view, the school board should have met its contractual obligation regarding class size by hiring an additional teacher to instruct in the experimental program. The principal of the school in which the grievants taught supported their position.

The arbitrator declined to uphold the grievance and called attention to the fact that she had not been called on to judge the educational policies of the school district, but rather to judge whether the terms of the collective bargaining agreement had been violated. She found that, although the class sizes in the grievants' situation exceeded the class sizes in the agreement, the average class size in the school district as a whole conformed with those in the agreement. In addition, she pointed out that class size figures in the agreement were guidelines established as class load objectives and were not to be interpreted as maximum limits for specific classes.[20,21]

In another case, the language establishing class size guidelines used three different standards, one for elementary classes, one for secondary classes, and one for special classes. With regard to elementary classes, the contract language stated that the school board would keep the class size "as close to 25–30 as possible: except in the case of emergencies." The secondary standard expressed class sizes as "maximum" pupil load per teacher. In the case of special classes such as typing, industrial arts, and physical education, "the number of students in the . . . classes [would] be governed by the physical facilities present . . . ."

The grievants taught elementary classes. In expressing his opinion in the case, the arbitrator stressed three points. First, he pointed out that contractual standards for class sizes differed within the school system. In the grievants' case, the standard was expressed as a guideline and not as a maximum. Therefore, the fact that the grievants' elementary classes exceeded contractual figures was not in itself an indication of a contractual violation. Second, he stated that the words "as close as possible" meant that the school board could not let elementary classes exceed the contractual figure and do nothing about it. Third, it was the union's burden to show that the school board had not attempted to keep classes "as close as possible" to the figure mentioned in the contract, a task that the union failed to carry out persuasively.[22,23]

An illustration of contractual language that clearly establishes maximums for regular classes and special education classes is offered for purposes of comparison:

> No regular class shall have more than thirty (30) pupils (excluding classes such as physical education, band, team teaching, etc., where a larger class is necessary or desirable) and no special education class shall have more than fifteen (15) pupils . . . .

> Any planned departure from the above ratios shall be discussed with the Union and the reason given for such departures.[24]

WHAT OBLIGATIONS ARE IMPLIED BY THE NEED TO MAKE "REASONABLE EFFORT"?

In a number of collective bargaining agreements pertaining to class size, school managements have agreed to make "sufficient effort" or "reasonable effort" to achieve the class size ratios indicated in negotiated agreements. Although the specific language may vary, the essential idea is that management will actively seek out ways to reduce class size if they exceed contractual ratios or are expected to exceed contractual ratios. The concept of "reasonable effort" also includes the idea that management will not knowingly take any action that would increase class size above contractual ratios.

Arbitrators have sustained teachers in their grievances that management did not exhibit "reasonable effort" under the following circumstances:

1. It was held that a school board erred in leasing classrooms to outside groups during school hours instead of using the classrooms to ease an overcrowding problem.[25]
2. A school board violated a "reasonable effort" clause when it refused to employ qualified substitute teachers to replace team teachers who were absent.[26]
3. When a dean of instruction did not take into consideration the recommendation of the chairman of the Department of Humanities that class size of English composition classes be main-

tained at twenty-two students, the arbitrator held the dean's action to be in violation of the agreement.[27]

4. When a school board adopted the superintendent's budget calling for reduction in faculty, it violated the class size goal of the collective bargaining agreement. The arbitrator rejected the board's defense of budgetary restrictions.[28,29]

In the opinion of at least one arbitrator, the obligation to raise "concrete alternatives" that can be examined in an effort to reduce or maintain class sizes does not rest exclusively with school management. In one arbitration case, the teachers' union was held to have a share of the burden for coming up with feasible alternatives to problems involving class size.[30]

WHAT FACTORS HAVE BEEN USED TO RESCIND MANAGEMENT'S OBLIGATION TO REDUCE CLASS SIZE?

Given a pattern of facts which supported school management's contention that it could not reduce class size, the following factors have been cited by arbitrators as valid reasons for rescinding management's contractual obligation:

1. financial circumstances[31]
2. unanticipated enrollment increases[32]
3. lack of adequate facilities[33]
4. emergency situations[34]
5. educational innovations[35]
6. conflict with other legitimate goals.[36]

WHAT REMEDIES HAVE BEEN GRANTED TO TEACHERS WHOSE CLASSES EXCEED CONTRACTUAL LIMITS?

Arbitrators have devised a variety of remedies to rectify situations in which school management did not live up to its class size agreements. One arbitrator issued an order for management to "cease and desist" in the future from making the assignments that brought about the grievance.[37] Arbitrators have not always been specific about when management must change practices that increase class size standards. Some have recognized that immediate compliance with the contract is not always in the interest of the educational process and have given management until the following year to make corrections.[38] However, in those cases where an immediate, specific solution to the grievance is apparent from evidence offered during the hearing, arbitrators have directed school boards to take immediate action.[39]

In some situations, arbitrators have devised monetary remedies as compensation for work overloads where the number of students has exceeded the contractual maximum.[40] Punitive monetary awards have been made to impress upon a school board the need to comply with contract requirements.[41] But arbitrators have been reluctant to grant punitive awards in the absence of evidence that management was completely insensitive to its contractual obligations.[42]

WORKLOAD

Under the topic of workload, teachers have negotiated the type and amount of activity that they engage in while on duty. The fact that teachers' workloads were defined through negotiations has become a major element in arbitration cases when school management has sought to increase teacher workloads.

HOW HAS THE TERM "WORKLOAD" BEEN DEFINED?

The term "workload" as used in school arbitration cases refers to periods or segments of a teacher's day. There are instructional or teaching periods, and noninstructional periods. Nonteaching periods may be related to the instructional program, as in the case of teacher preparation time, time spent in supervision of study hall, or time spent as an activity sponsor. Not all supervision duties are considered to be instructional in nature. Hall duty, lavatory duty, and detention duty are forms of supervision considered to be primarily noninstructional. Noninstructional duties also may be administrative or clerical in nature.

Through collective bargaining, teachers have attempted to influence both the amount and the content of their workload. Table 8-1 is an example of various teachers' schedules. It is apparent from this example that equity is a problem inherent in the process of determining teachers' workloads. Even though teachers' schedules may vary, an attempt must be made to equalize the demands on their time and effort.

Two approaches to the problem of achieving equity among teacher workloads are used most frequently. One approach is to develop contractual concepts that attempt to embrace the essential elements of a teacher's work activity. For example, one essential element, "contact time," would be the amount of time that a teacher spends in contact with pupils. Presumably it would be possible to achieve a degree of equity by standardizing the amount of contact time each teacher has. The problem with such a generic approach to workload analysis is that terms such as "contact time" tend to be less precise than a term such

TABLE 8-1. *Example of Senior High School Teachers' Schedules in Periods/Week*

Daily Schedule	Teaching	Duty	Preparation	Duty-Free Lunch	Total
a. 5 classes 1 duty	25	5	10	5	45
b. 4 science classes plus labs	28	0	12	5	45
c. 3 double classes 1 duty	30	5	5	5	45
d. 2 double classes 1 single class 1 duty	25	5	10	5	45
e. 1 double class 3 single classes 1 duty	25	5	10	5	45

From *Government Employee Relations Report,* Reference File 81, RF-116 (Washington: Bureau of National Affairs, 1976) p. 1007.

as "teaching period." The lack of precision in the use of terms leads to ambiguity, which may in turn result in more contract disputes over workloads.[43]

The other basic alternative to equalizing workloads is to identify in detail the various programs in which certificated personnel are employed, in regard to both level of schooling (elementary, junior high, or high school) and type of workload (counseling, vocational instruction, librarianship, special education, etc.). Once major program categories have been identified, an analysis of work activities within program areas usually will result in expressions of workload equity that are satisfying to the parties and relatively easy to administer.

There is of course, less precision across program areas and between types of activities such as elementary counseling and science teaching. However, when the approach to workload analysis is detailed and specific, many of the equity problems that could arise as a result of comparisons between program levels and types of activities can instead be worked out by teacher representatives in the process of making contract proposals. Although the end result should be a contract that has less ambiguity regarding workloads, it is a time-consuming approach. In addition, the amount of contractual detail regarding workloads is extensive.[44]

WHAT RESTRICTIONS HAVE BEEN PLACED ON INCREASES IN WORKLOADS?

Teachers are protected from increases in workloads by a variety of restrictions. Sources of these restrictions include contractual language, past practice, maintenance of standards, teachers' consent, and state regulations.

Contractual language. Within specified work hours, management has the right to arrange the number of work assignments unless management has contractually limited its right or unless that right has been limited by state law.[45] Where the contractual limitations are clearly expressed, an arbitrator will normally enforce the contract. For example, when a school board directed homeroom teachers to give instruction on the United States Constitution, a grievance brought by homeroom teachers was upheld because the contract forbid the assignment of teaching subjects in areas outside a teacher's certification. In addition, the school board's directive resulted in certain teachers' having more teaching periods than were allowed under the contract.[46]

In another case, where the contract clearly limited a teacher's instructional time to twenty-two periods per week, the arbitrator rejected the school board's claim that as long as teachers were given their five preparation periods, they could be scheduled for twenty-five teaching periods. The school board did not have the discretion to schedule more than twenty-two instructional periods each week to its teachers. They could schedule less than twenty-two periods, or they could give noninstructional duty assignments to teachers who had been given the maximum of twenty-two instructional periods. The total number of periods allowable under the contract was thirty per week.[47,48]

Past practice. The source of workload standards is at times the past practices of the school district.[49] In fact, some school boards and teacher associations have expressly written into their agreements that class assignments are to be maintained in accordance with past practice.[50] Even when past practice is not expressly mentioned in an agreement, it can be used to limit a school board's right to increase workloads. For example, an arbitrator determined that a teacher was unfairly treated when he was assigned six teaching periods, when all other teachers had four or five teaching periods. The arbitrator found that by past practice five periods had been the maximum teaching load.[51]

In another situation, some teachers who had volunteered for extracurricular assignments filed grievances when they were given a maximum teaching load. The arbitrator upheld the grievance after finding that it had been the past practice of the school district to consider extracurricular assignments a teaching duty. The fact that the teachers had volunteered for the extracurricular assignments did not give school management the right to exceed the contractual teaching load.[52] By way of contrast, in a situation where management had not assigned teachers the maximum workload permissible under the contract, the arbitrator held that management's past practice of not assigning the maximum workload did not restrict it from increasing workloads in the future.[53]

Maintenance of standards. In agreeing to a maintenance of standards provision, a school board may be limiting its right to increase workloads. In one contract the school board agreed that it would not require teachers in the English Department to teach more than twenty periods per week without making "every effort" to maintain the practice of assigning only twenty classes per week. When evidence presented at the hearing persuaded the arbitrator that every effort had not been made, he held that the contract had been violated.[54] In another case, the contract stated that "whenever possible" teachers' workloads would be maintained. A teacher who had one of the heaviest workloads in the school won her grievance when an arbitrator was persuaded that management had other alternatives than to increase her workload.[55]

Teachers' consent. Under certain circumstances, a school board and the teachers' representative will agree to maximum workload specifications. Part of the agreement also includes the provision that before the specified workloads can be exceeded, the teachers' consent must be obtained. For example, an arbitrator held that "clear and unambiguous" language provided that not more than twenty-five teaching periods would be assigned per week unless additional periods were agreed to by the teachers.[56] In another case, the arbitrator enforced an agreement stating that a teacher would have no more than three separate preparations per week unless the teacher's consent for additional preparations was received.[57]

State regulations. In some states there are statutes that regulate specific work conditions of teachers. These statutes may exist in addition to collective bargaining laws. In one arbitration case, the arbitrator upheld a teacher's grievance over an increase in the number of teaching periods by referring to a state statute that called for a maximum of five teaching periods a day.[58]

WORK ASSIGNMENTS

There are direct and indirect sources of limitations on management's right to make work assignments. A limitation is direct when management has agreed to specific contractual language restricting the right to make certain work assignments — for example, routine assignments to noninstructional duties, assignments to clerical duties, or assignments during duty-free lunch periods. The limitation is indirect when contractual language does not pertain directly to the assignment grieved, but nevertheless curtails management's flexibility in making work assignments. Illustrations of both direct and indirect limitations on work assignments are provided in this section.

WHAT LIMITATIONS ON WORK ASSIGNMENTS HAVE
BEEN SUBJECT TO ARBITRATION DISPUTES?

Disputed limitations fall into three primary categories, explained here in detail.

No routine assignments to noninstructional duties. A major topic of negotiations between school boards and teachers has been the elimination of noninstructional duties as routine assignments. One school board and teacher association agreed to the following provision regarding nonteaching duties:

> The Superintendent and the Association acknowledged that a teacher's primary responsibility is to teach and that his energies, to the extent possible, should be utilized to this end. Therefore, the Superintendent and Association agree that professional staff members will not be routinely asked or assigned to do non-professional duties except in unusual circumstances.
>
> 1. Non-professional duties shall be defined as: any job assignment that should normally be carried out by a non-professional employee, or any job assignment that should normally be carried out by the maintenance, clerical or janitorial staff.
> 2. Any professional staff member who is given any assignment or duty he deems unprofessional shall report this to the Educational Policy Committee.[59]

A group grievance was brought by teachers who regularly were assigned to cafeteria duty, bus duty, playground duty, hall and corridor duty. The school board argued that such duties were professional in nature because they were directly or indirectly of an instructional nature. The school board further argued that the provision about nonteaching duties was not intended to relieve teachers of all nonteaching duties. Finally, the school board asserted that the primary intention of the provision was to provide assurance to teachers that they would maintain the ratio of teacher aides to teachers.

The arbitrator learned that the parties had primarily agreed to relieve teachers of cafeteria duty, bus duty, and playground duty. The arbitrator concluded that the provision on nonteaching duties was not intended to relieve teachers completely of all such duties, just as the school board had contended. However, the arbitrator rejected the school board's other assumption that the duties being grieved were professional in nature. And in a separate provision in the same agreement pertaining to teacher aides, it was stated that teacher aides would be employed to relieve teachers of nonteaching duties.

Among the suggested activities listed as being suitable for teacher aides were cafeteria supervision, bus duty, playground supervision, clerical work, inventory of books and supplies, and corridor supervision. The arbitrator held that the school board had violated the agreement by routinely assigning teachers to cafeteria, playground, and bus duty.[60,61]

No clerical assignments. In the preceding case, the provision limiting work assignments pertained to all nonteaching duties. In the case reported here, the agreement referred to the limitation of the school board's right to assign clerical duties *per se*. The relevant contractual agreement read as follows:

> No teacher shall be assigned duties that are principally clerical in nature, such as the collection of monies, book fees, insurance, PTA collections, running off and typing of dittos, and the compilation of monthly and yearly attendance records, provided that reasonable notice of clerical assistance requirements is given by the teacher to the Building Principal or his designee.[62]

The grievance that gave rise to the arbitration case was brought by teachers in three out of the eleven elementary schools in the district whose principals required them to enter the names of their students in the student attendance rosters. The grievants believed that the students' names should be entered in the attendance rosters by clerical help, since this was a duty that was primarily clerical in nature.

The school board took the position that state law required teachers to take daily attendance. According to the school board, the law requiring teachers to take attendance could also be construed to require teachers to enter the names of students in the rosters. In the language of the law cited by the school board, the arbitrator could find no support for the school board's interpretation. The teacher association did not contest the fact that teachers were responsible by law for taking daily attendance. The law, however, specified that attendance registers would be furnished by school directors and "shall be in a form prescribed by the Superintendent of Public Instruction."[63]

The arbitrator concluded, "If the school administration is the agency to furnish the forms to the teachers, it is proper to assume that the forms will be furnished so designed and prepared as to permit the teachers to commence immediately the attendance-taking task."[64] The arbitrator also held that the writing of names in the attendance register was a task "principally clerical in nature," and the principals in eight of the eleven elementary schools had taken the proper action of relieving teachers of the task. The principals in the three schools in which the grievants worked were directed to cease requiring teachers to write the names of students in the attendance register.

Given the complex problems faced by schools, the elimination of clerical tasks may seem minor. Writing names in an attendance register might not strike everyone as deserving the amount of concern that such an assignment is capable of generating. Nevertheless, one is forced to face the reality that such problems do absorb the attention of administrators and teachers. Teachers in one school district grieved the task of computing and analyzing the raw scores of a standardized test. Their grievance was upheld because the assignment was in violation of the contract, which specifically stated the work was to be done by data processing.[65] In another school district, the school board was found to have violated its agreement with teachers when school administrators in the district required teachers to calculate monthly and year-end attendance figures on their students.[66] Finally, a school board violated its agreement with the teachers when it required them to complete an additional attendance form.[67]

Duty-free lunch period. The collective bargaining agreement between a school board and teachers provided elementary teachers a one-hour duty-free lunch period; however, when it was in the best interests of students, the teachers' duty-free lunch hour could be shortened. The relevant provision in the agreement read as follows:

1. Secondary school teachers shall have a duty-free lunch period with a minimum time equivalent to the length of the student's lunch period in conformance to state law. All teachers in the elementary schools shall have a duty-free lunch period of one (1) hour. Elementary teachers may be required to supervise lunch programs on a rotating basis where the best interest of the pupil is served.
2. Teachers may leave the building without permission during their duty-free lunch period.[68]

A grievance came about when school administrators, in cooperation with parents and teachers, developed the concept of a systemwide school lunch program. When the administration implemented the concept, all elementary teachers found that they were required to supervise the lunch program on a rotating basis. Before implementation of the systemwide program, some elementary teachers had had their duty-free lunch hour reduced in order to supervise certain handicapped students who needed the help and attention of their regular teachers during the noon hour. Most elementary teachers were able to have a duty-free lunch period as called for in the agreement.

The administration defended the implementation of the new lunch program on the grounds that it was in the best interests of students. Furthermore, the administration claimed that teachers had forfeited their rights to grieve the new program's implementation when they withheld their criticisms during the joint discussion meetings between parents, administrators, and teachers prior to implementation of the program.

The teachers countered that they were not opposed to the implementation of a new lunch program. They were opposed to the unilateral change in the duty-free lunch hour for elementary teachers, who had enjoyed that benefit in the past and who had also enjoyed the benefit of being able to leave the building, a benefit that was curtailed by the shortening of the teachers' lunch period.

The arbitrator claimed that it was not within his jurisdiction to determine what was or was not in the benefit of pupils, nor was it in his jurisdiction to change the terms of the contract. The contract clearly stated that elementary teachers were to receive a duty-free lunch period of one hour's duration. The school board could not unilaterally change the terms of the contract. The meetings between parents, administrators, and teachers could not be substituted for direct negotiations between the school board and representatives of teachers. Although there was a historical precedent of rotating the lunch period of some elementary teachers, the precedent did not give the school board the right to institute unilaterally a systemwide change. The grievance was upheld.[69,70]

HOW HAVE AGREEMENTS ON WORKING CONDITIONS BEEN INTERPRETED AS LIMITATIONS ON ASSIGNMENT RIGHTS OF MANAGEMENT?

A review of arbitral determinations reveals a broad range of limitations on assignment rights of management. Some of the interpretations are exemplified in the cases reported next.

1. Where agreements have been reached containing specific statements about teachers' hours of work, management has been

limited in assignment of bus duty,[71] assignment of after-school study hall,[72] and assignment of detention hall supervision.[73,74]

2. A school board erred when it required those teachers who had earned compensatory time to use such time for assignment to noninstructional duties.[75]

3. A contract, that limited teachers' assignments to five classroom periods plus one instructionally related period and one preparation period prevented a principal from assigning a teacher to a "time-out" room where pupils who could not be managed by their classroom teachers were sent.[76]

4. A teacher was improperly denied his request to be relieved from homeroom assignment under a contract which stated that equitable standards would be applied within each school to determine exemptions from homeroom assignments.[77,78]

5. Where an agreement limited the assignment of extra duty such as lunchroom or study hall supervision to *one* period, the school administration violated the agreement when it gave a gym teacher *two* extra duty assignments even though the teacher had only four classes to teach.[79]

SUMMARY

Four broad topics typically fall within the scope of negotiations between school boards and teachers. They are wages, hours, terms, and conditions of work. This chapter has been limited to a consideration of arbitration disputes involving hours of work and other terms and conditions such as class size, workload, and work assignments. The main reason for arbitration disputes over conditions of work can usually be traced to differences over interpretation of contract language.

With regard to hours of work, a task faced by arbitrators has been to determine if the contractual definition of working hours was intended to apply to all members of the bargaining group alike. Since the meaning of contractual language is conditioned by the intentions of the parties, an arbitrator may try to determine to what extent there was a meeting of minds at the time of negotiations. Arbitrators have tended to look for evidence that some element of the bargaining unit has been specifically excluded.

Other issues involving hours of work have resulted in arbitration disputes. A number of disputes have pertained to the inclusion or exclusion of lunch period. Another issue over which parties have differed has been the intention to include or exclude evening activities. Questions about the beginning and ending of the work day have also contributed to disagreements resulting in arbitration disputes.

As an aspect of conditions of work, class size has generated a number of arbitration disputes. One element of ambiguity has been whether class size figures represent statements of maximum classload or are merely guidelines for the distribution of class loads. It is not uncommon for a class size provision to contain the expression that management will make "reasonable effort" to maintain stated class sizes. It has been the task of some arbitrators to establish a standard of "reasonable effort."

Not infrequently, management has insisted on the inclusion of language with regard to class size which would rescind its obligation to reduce or maintain stated class sizes under certain conditions. When such language has existed, it has been the arbitrator's task to determine whether or not conditions actually existed which relieved management of its contractual obligations regarding class size.

Finally, when it has been shown that management violated the contract by giving the grievant more students than called for by the contract, grievants have asked the arbitrator to grant a remedy. Where a remedy was not specified in the contract, arbitrators have improvised a number of remedies to adjust for a finding of a class overload.

Workload is a term used to refer to the number of teaching, preparation, and/or duty periods assigned to a teacher in a given amount of time. Teachers have used negotiations to define their workload. Arbitration has been used to resolve disputes over management's attempts to increase a teacher's workload. In such cases, the arbitrator's task has been to determine if management's right to define a teacher's workload was restricted by contractual agreement and whether management's actions were within the confines of the agreement.

The final condition examined was the area of work assignments. Various limitations have been placed on management's right to make work assignments. Some of these limitations have involved the elimination of routine assignments to noninstructional duties, the elimination of clerical assignments, and the elimination of assignments during the lunch period.

NOTES

1. For examples see *Government Employee Relations Report,* Reference File 51, RF-112 (Washington: Bureau of National Affairs, 1975), p. 1411, Sec. 3500; *Government Employee Relations Report,* Reference File 51, RF-141 (Washington: Bureau of National Affairs, 1977), p. 2812, Sec. 965; *Government Employee Relations Report,* Reference File 51, RF-157 (Washington: Bureau of National Affairs, 1978), p. 5818, Sec. 111.70(d).

2. For a discussion of practices in education regarding the scope of negotiations, see Donald H. Wollett and Robert H. Chanin, *The Law and Practice of Teacher Negotiations* (Washington: The Bureau of National Affairs, 1974), p. 6:43.

3. See *Arbitration in the Schools* (New York: American Arbitration Association), Vols. 1–96.

4. For a discussion of general semantics and its application to arbitration, see Paul Prasow and Edward Peters, *Arbitration and Collective Bargaining: Conflict Resolution in Labor Relations* (New York: McGraw-Hill Book Company, 1970), pp. 44–77.

5. See Frank Elkouri and Edna Asper Elkouri, *How Arbitration Works* (Washington: The Bureau of National Affairs, 1973), pp. 296–320.

6. Government Employee Relations Report, No. 653 (Washington: Bureau of National Affairs, 1976), p. X-5.

7. *Board of Education of the Township of Ewing (New Jersey)*, 33 AIS 21, Allan Weisenfeld, Arbitrator.

8. *Board of Education, Union Free School District 31 (New York)*, 2 AIS 4, Bernard P. Lampert, Arbitrator.

9. *Depew (New York) Board of Education*, 9 AIS 10, Thomas G. Dignan, Arbitrator.

10. *Board of Education of the Township of Ewing (New Jersey)*, 33 AIS 21, Allan Weisenfeld, Arbitrator, pp. 6–7.

11. *Board of Education, Union Free School District 31 (New York)*, 2 AIS 4, Bernard P. Lampert, Arbitrator, p. 4.

12. *Chippewa Falls (Wisconsin) Joint School District No. 1*, 3 AIS 21, Howard S. Bellman, Arbitrator.

13. *Newburgh (New York) City School District*, 12 AIS 2, Jonas Silver, Arbitrator, p. 2.

14. See also *Dundee (New York) Central School District*, 78 AIS 10, Max M. Doner, Arbitrator.

15. *Carroll County Board of Education (Maryland)*, 33 AIS 31, Jacob Seidenberg, Arbitrator, p. 2.

16. Ibid, p. 1.

17. See also *East Islip (New York) Board of Education*, 15 AIS 8, Daniel G. Collins, Arbitrator.

18. *Great Neck (New York) Board of Education*, 56 AIS 3, Edward Levin, Arbitrator; *Board of Junior College, District No. 508 (Illinois)*, 33 AIS 1, John W. Noble, Jr., Arbitrator; *Lakeland (New York) School District, Board of Education*, 29 AIS 9, Josef Sirefman, Arbitrator.

19. For other negotiation strategies used by teachers to prevent unilateral changes in their hours of work, see *School Committee of the Town of Billerica (Massachusetts)*, 33 AIS 25, Mark Santer, Arbitrator; *Georgetown (Massachusetts) School Committee*, 2 AIS 11, Joseph M. Cronin, Arbitrator.

20. *Webster Central School District No. 1 (New York)*, 13 AIS 22, Alice B. Grant, Arbitrator.

21. See also *Board of Education of Ridgefield (Connecticut)*, 94 AIS 14, James V. Altieri, Arbitrator; *Board of Education, Union Free School District No. 1 (Huntington, New York)*, 2 AIS 38, Joseph P. Doyle, Arbitrator.

22. *Chesaning (Michigan) Union Schools Board of Education,* 19 AIS 19, George T. Roumell, Jr., Arbitrator.

23. For another case of mixed standards, see *Lincoln Park (Michigan) Board of Education,* 19 AIS 1, George T. Roumell, Jr., Arbitrator.

24. *Oak Park (Michigan) Board of Education,* 17 AIS 18, George T. Roumell, Jr., Arbitrator.

25. *Liberty Central School Board (New York),* 32 AIS 23, Milton Friedman, Arbitrator.

26. *Connetquot (New York) School District No. 7,* 26 AIS 11, Milton Friedman, Arbitrator.

27. *Genesee (New York) Community College,* 73 AIS 11, Louis Yagoda, Arbitrator.

28. *Trumbull (Connecticut) Board of Education,* 76 AIS 23, Alfred B. Clark, Arbitrator.

29. See also *Watervliet (New York) Enlarged School District,* 92 AIS 8, Elizabeth B. Croft, Arbitrator.

30. *Waterbury (Connecticut) Board of Education,* 31 AIS 20, Archibald Cox, Arbitrator.

31. See *Roosevelt (New York) Board of Education,* 59 AIS 18, Josef Sirefman, Arbitrator.

32. See *Bolivar (New York) Board of Education,* 77 AIS 18, John E. Drotning, Arbitrator; *Gloverville (New York) School District,* 74 AIS 1, John E. Drotning, Arbitrator; *North Colonie (New York) Central School District,* 54 AIS 5, Eva Robins, Arbitrator.

33. See *Pleasantville (New York) Union Free School District,* 96 AIS 6, Max M. Doner, Arbitrator; *Madison (Wisconsin) Joint School District No. 8,* 47 AIS 14, J. L. Stern, Arbitrator.

34. See *Warren Woods (Michigan) Public Schools,* 52 AIS 2, C. Keith Groty, Arbitrator.

35. See *Gloucester County (New Jersey) College,* 74 AIS 14, John M. Malkin, Arbitrator.

36. See *Rush-Henrietta (New York) Central School District,* 63 AIS 2, Byron Yaffe, Arbitrator.

37. *Board of Education of Clarkstown (New York),* 83 AIS 21, Nicholas S. Falcone, Arbitrator.

38. *Trumbull (Connecticut) Board of Education,* 76 AIS 23, Alfred B. Clark, Arbitrator; *Oakfield-Alabama (New York) Central School District,* 74 AIS 4, Margery Gootnick, Arbitrator.

39. *Liberty Central School Board (New York),* 32 AIS 23, Milton Friedman, Arbitrator; *Lincoln Park (Michigan) Board of Education,* 19 AIS 1, George T. Roumell, Jr., Arbitrator.

40. *Roseville ((Michigan) Board of Education,* 45 AIS 4, Leon J. Herman, Arbitrator.

41. *Coventry (Rhode Island) School Committee,* 94 AIS 13, Peter R. Blum, Arbitrator.

42. *Trenton (New Jersey) Board of Education,* 32 AIS 50, Irving R. Shapiro, Arbitrator; *Oak Park (Michigan) Board of Education,* 17 AIS 18, George T. Roumell, Jr., Arbitrator.

43. *Indianapolis (Indiana) Board of School Commissioners,* 76 AIS 9, Raymond L. Scheib, Arbitrator.
44. See *Government Employee Relations Report,* Reference File 81, RF-150 (Washington: Bureau of National Affairs, 1977), pp. 1581–1632.
45. *Nashua (New Hampshire) Board of Education,* 76 AIS 20, Milton J. Nadworny, Arbitrators.
46. *Jersey City (New Jersey) Board of Education,* 83 AIS 11, John J. Saracino, Arbitrator.
47. *Smithfield (Rhode Island) School Committee,* 78 AIS 7, Robert M. O'Brien, Arbitrator.
48. See also *Syracuse (New York) City School District,* 39 AIS 10, Alice B. Grant, Arbitrator; *Boston (Massachusetts) School Committee,* 28 AIS 2, Thomas Kennedy, Arbitrator.
49. See Chapter 1 of this book.
50. *Ardsley (New York) Union Free School District,* 51 AIS 8, Max M. Doner, Arbitrator.
51. *Lee (Massachusetts) School Committee,* 63 AIS 14, Craig E. Overton, Arbitrator.
52. *New Haven (Connecticut) Board of Education,* 57 AIS 5, William J. Fallon, Arbitrator.
53. *Orange County (New York) Community College,* 75 AIS 22, Jonathan S. Liebowitz, Arbitrator.
54. *Falconer (New York) Board of Education,* 43 AIS 4, Fred L. Denson, Arbitrator.
55. *Central High School, District 3, Board of Education, (Nassau County, New York;),* 2 AIS 29, Louis Yagoda, Arbitrator.
56. *City School District of Buffalo (New York),* 17 AIS 6, Irving R. Markowitz, Arbitrator.
57. *Waverly Schools (Lansing, Michigan),* 18 AIS 6, George T. Roumell, Jr., Arbitrator.
58. *Putnam Valley Board of Education (New York),* 32 AIS 43, John M. Stochaj, Arbitrator.
59. *Rome (New York) School District,* 22 AIS 1, Byron Yaffe, Arbitrator.
60. Ibid.
61. See also *Maine School Administrative District No. 1, Board of Directors,* 77 AIS 20, Alexander Macmillan, Arbitrator; *Canton (Massachusetts) School Committee,* 61 AIS 21, Clyde W. Summers, Arbitrator; *The Board of Education of the School District of Philadelphia (Pennsylvania),* 50 AIS 15, Thomas Kennedy, Arbitrator; *Board of Education U.F.S.D. No. 3 Town of Huntington (New York),* 1 AIS 6, Peter Seitz, Arbitrator.
62. *South Stickney School District (Illinois),* 35 AIS 9, Pearce Davis, Arbitrator, p. 2.
63. Ibid., at 3.
64. Ibid.
65. *Waterbury (Connecticut) Board of Education,* 96 AIS 11, Edward C. Pinkus, Arbitrator.
66. *East Providence (Rhode Island) School Committee,* 85 AIS 21, Earl Eddy Greene, Jr., Arbitrator.

67. *The Board of School Trustees (Gary, Indiana)*, 82 AIS 20, Irwin M. Lieberman, Arbitrator.
68. *Trenton (New Jersey) Board of Education*, 26 AIS 2, G. Allan Dash, Jr., Arbitrator, pp. 1–2.
69. Ibid.
70. See also *Independent School District No. 621 (Minnesota)*, 84 AIS 15, Arnold A. Karlins, Arbitrator; *Joint School District No. 8 (Madison, Wisconsin)*, 44 AIS 5, Reynolds C. Seitz, Arbitrator; *Port Jefferson Station (New York) Union Free School District No. 3*, 15 AIS 14, Daniel G. Collins, Arbitrator.
71. *Nassau County (Florida) School Board*, 71 AIS 6, Julius E. Kuczma, Arbitrator.
72. *Township of Ocean (New Jersey) Board of Education*, 33 AIS 4, Joseph F. Wildebush, Arbitrator.
73. *School Committee of the Town of Bellerica (Massachusetts)*, 33 AIS 25, Mark Santer, Arbitrator.
74. See also *Newburgh (New York) City School District*, 12 AIS 2, Jonas Silver, Arbitrator.
75. *Providence (Rhode Island) School Committee*, 77 AIS 3, William Croasdale, Arbitrator.
76. *Montgomery (Maryland) Public Schools*, 68 AIS 6, Howard W. Kleeb, Arbitrator.
77. *Providence (Rhode Island) School Committee*, 63 AIS 19, Edward C. Pinkus, Arbitrator.
78. See also *New York Mills (New York) Union Free School*, 75 AIS 13, Rodney E. Dennis, Arbitrator; *School District No. 86 (Will County, Illinois)*, 62 AIS 11, Martin A. Cohen, Arbitrator.
79. *Waldwick (New Jersey) Board of Education*, 68 AIS 7, Meyer Drucker, Arbitrator.

9

Employee Benefits

Collective bargaining has been justified on the assumption that both management and labor are free agents. They have entered into an agreement whereby employees exchange services for considerations and benefits that are of value to them. Each member of a work force has some image of his or her personal worth as an individual and as an employee. Other things being equal, a bargain is struck when a majority of employees are willing to ratify an agreement with management which reflects their conception of their own worth.

The single most important index of worth to most employees is probably salary. However, salary alone is not sufficient compensation for most employees. There is in most work forces, both public and private, the expectation that fair compensation will also include fringe benefits.

With regard to public schools, personal leave, sabbatical leave, insurance coverage, and tuition reimbursement are four areas of fringe benefits that have generated a substantial number of arbitration cases. They are covered in this chapter.

PERSONAL LEAVE

There are three types of grievance disputes associated with negotiated personal leave clauses. First, there have been disputes over the nature of a valid personal leave. For example, is attendance at a public rally related to an important personal conviction a valid reason for taking personal leave? Second, there have been disputes concerned with the latitude management can take in administering personal leave agreements. For example, can the superintendent of a school district require teachers to put their leave requests in writing when the agreement is silent on such a procedure? Third, there have been disputes over the restrictions placed on the use of personal leaves. For instance, can extenuating circumstances exist that would permit personal leaves on the day before or the day following a holiday?

DISPUTES OVER THE NATURE OF A VALID PERSONAL
LEAVE

When an employee requests permission to take personal leave, the employee's supervisor can determine if the request falls within an acceptable category for granting personal leave by considering the language of the contractual provision for personal leave. In this section, examples are given of contractual language on the subject of personal leave. In addition, a review is made of disputed terms that have been and are part of personal leave provisions. Finally, the specific issue of taking personal leave for reasons of personal convictions is covered.

Personal leave provisions. Three formats for writing personal leave provisions are in common use. One format provides only a statement of general purpose. The second attempts to combine a statement of both general purpose and specific purposes for personal leave. The third expresses the purposes for personal leave in specific terms alone.

Illustration of First Format:
A Statement of General Purpose Only

Two days of personal leave with full pay can be used for personal business.[1]

Illustration of Second Format:
A Statement of Both General and Specific Purposes

Personal business shall mean any situation of urgency requiring the teacher's attention during the school day and impossible to transact during off-work hours. Certain types of family commitments, legal obligations, special religious ceremonies, and emergencies are considered to be valid reasons for using provisions of the personal leave policy.[2]

Illustration of Third Format:
A Statement of Specific Purposes Only

A teacher is credited with three days each school year for personal business purposes without loss of pay when taken for any one or a combination of the following reasons:

1. grave illness or death in the immediate family
2. religious occasion requiring personal observance
3. attendance at court proceedings which is required of the teacher
4. graduation ceremony of a family member
5. appointment for college enrollment of a family member
6. special school or college honor for a family member
7. getting married
8. attending wedding as a participant
9. attending to legal matters involved in buying or selling of a home
10. having emergency repairs made to a home.[3]

To some extent, the more specific the agreement provision, the easier it is for an arbitrator to discover the original intentions of two parties in the midst of a dispute over the application of the agreement. However, it would be inaccurate to suppose that the parties themselves can eliminate all grievance disputes merely by expressing their agreements in comprehensive terms. Still, when two parties have managed to identify thoroughly their intentions and incorporate them into a contracted agreement, the arbitrator's task of not adding to or subtracting from their intentions is easier.

Basic definitions. Personal leave provisions incorporate such basic terms as "personal business," "commercial transaction," "personal," and "emergency." Various arbitrators have attempted to define these terms. Arbitrator Leon J. Herman has stated that the term "personal business" must "relate to a personal need, duty or obligation in which economic gain or risk" is ordinarily involved.[4] Arbitrator Walter E. Oberer has construed the term "commercial transaction" to mean an exchange of values. Therefore, a teacher on personal business leave for commercial purposes would be engaged in a transaction with a second party wherein each would be giving something of value in return for something of value.[5]

Arbitrator Jean T. McKelvey saw the term "personal leave" as referring to some isolated or sporadic incident that was unique in a person's life.[6] In the opinion of arbitrator Howard A. Cole, the purposes for a "personal leave" must bear on self-oriented needs.[7] Arbitrator Richard H. Siegel viewed an "emergency" as an event over which the individual has no control and which requires the individual's immediate attention.[8]

Personal convictions. Arbitration cases have been reported in which teachers and other school employees have attempted to use personal leave provisions to attend events related to their political beliefs and causes. Employers have denied personal leaves based on political convictions and other statements of personal advocacy. Arbitrators have upheld employers in denying personal leave to attend a peace rally,[9] to participate in a sympathy strike,[10] to protest the building of a nuclear power plant,[11] and to attend a hearing of a state legislature.[12]

DISPUTES RELATED TO THE LATITUDE OF
MANAGEMENT'S DISCRETION WHEN ADMINISTERING
PERSONAL LEAVE AGREEMENTS

Of 254 selected leave agreements involved in one examination, 73 percent made an administrator responsible for final approval and/or processing of leave requests.[13] The superintendent was most frequently designated responsible, followed by the principal.

Approximately 72 percent of negotiated leave procedures examined specified some aspect of the request and approval procedure. Forty percent specified that prior notification was required. Twenty percent indicated that written notification was required. Thirteen percent specifically mentioned that a statement of reasons was required.

When an agreement does not make specific statements regarding management's discretion, a number of questions can arise. Some of the questions arbitrators have dealt with in the past are as follows:

1. Can management require teachers to give them specific information when requesting personal leave?
2. Can a manager take corrective action if he or she knew a teacher was taking an inappropriate personal leave, but did nothing at the time?
3. What effect does past practice have on managerial latitude?
4. Can a manager use his or her own standards in determining the appropriateness of the reasons given for personal leave?
5. Can permission for personal leave be withdrawn once given?

Requiring specific information. Arbitrators have generally agreed that management can require teachers to provide specific information in requesting leaves even when contract language does not mention it. Arbitrators have held that in those cases where permission for personal leaves is not automatic, managers need to base their judgments on information.[14] It has not been considered arbitrary to require specific information in conjunction with personal leaves in order to administer provisions of leave agreements.[15] In addition, some arbitrators have indicated that the burden of proof for adequacy of reasons for personal leave may rest with the teacher.[16] Exceptions to the general tendency to permit the requirement of providing specific information have occurred when the arbitrator viewed the exclusion of such requirements from the agreement language as controlling.[17]

Corrective action. Where management knew that a teacher's purpose for personal leave was not in compliance with contractual requirements but failed to act until after the leave had been taken, arbitrators have not been inclined to support management in a belated effort to enforce contractual requirements.[18]

Effect of past practices. Managerial discretion has been limited by established past practice. Where it can be shown that a grievant has been granted personal leave under identical circumstances in the past, it is likely that an arbitrator will uphold a grievant's request for the same personal leave at a later time.[19] A grievant is also likely to be upheld if he or she can show that the circumstances surrounding the request are the same as the circumstances leading to the granting of personal leave to other employees.[20] The burden of proof of showing that a practice has been established in the past rests upon the grievant.[21,22]

Past practices have been used by arbitrators to clarify contractual ambiguity or silence on particular leave issues in question.[23] Of course, it is possible for an arbitrator to interpret the absence of explicit contract language pertaining to a particular issue as evidence that no right exists in relation to that issue. But, where relevant past practices have taken place, they may be taken as tangible evidence that a mutual understanding was in force between the parties that went beyond the limited language of the contract. The total agreement between the parties is thus taken to include the written agreement plus valid past practices.

Arbitrators cannot easily ignore evidence of a valid past practice. For example, if it can be shown that management has granted personal leave in the past under a given set of circumstances, failure to grant leave at a later time is inconsistent and thus suspect of being arbitrary action on management's part.[24] Arbitrators can hardly support arbitrary action and still maintain their own credibility; thus, they are mindful of giving due weight to evidence of a valid past practice.

Use of personal standards. The question has arisen, Should a manager use his or her personal standards in administering provisions of a personal leave agreement? For example, where a contract specifies that personal leaves are to be of an urgent or emergency nature, whose sense of urgency is to be used, the grievant's or the manager's? The fact that the contract may call for the use of judgment on management's part does not invalidate the question of whose point of view is to be used in making an estimate of the urgency of a situation. Arbitrators have established no firm guidelines; they examine the particular facts in each situation.[25]

Withdrawal of permission. In a number of cases where teachers have requested permission to take personal leaves, responses by their immediate supervisors suggested approval of their requests. Grievances occurred when the final approving authorities denied the requests for personal leave and took administrative action by deducting pay in cases where leaves were taken without final approval. Arbitrators have tended to uphold the grievants. Although their specific reasons for upholding the grievants have varied, it would appear that employees have a right to be able to order their lives in some predictable fashion based on the decisions of their superiors.[26,27]

DISPUTES OVER RESTRICTIONS PLACED ON PERSONAL LEAVE

There are two types of restrictions placed on personal leaves. The first type to be discussed is the denial of personal leave for the purpose of observing a holiday or extending a vacation. A second type of restriction on the use of personal leave is encountered in cases concerned with the definition of the phrase "immediate family." The phrase "immediate family" is associated with attendance at such events as weddings, funerals, and occasions bestowing honors on the immediate family.

Extending vacations and observing holidays. Teachers who attempt to use personal leave to observe a nonscheduled religious holiday may claim religious discrimination if their request is denied. The issue of discrimination has been handled by arbitrators through an inspection of contract language and/or past practices of the parties. Where it has been shown that there had been a consistent practice of treating religious and nonreligious recesses the same, arbitrators have not upheld a claim of religious discrimination.[28] Arbitrators have also dismissed the issue of religious discrimination where the language of the contract explicitly stated that personal leaves could not be taken for religious holidays.[29] In one instance, the arbitrator deferred the issue of religious discrimination to the courts.[30]

When contract language has clearly forbidden the use of personal leave time to extend vacation periods, arbitrators have enforced the contract. The fact that unforeseen events have occurred, such as problems with scheduling return airplane flights[31] or the onset of inclement weather,[32] has not been deemed by arbitrators to be sufficiently compelling to override the explicit intent of a contract unless the contract itself made allowances for such unpredictable events.[33]

Enforcement of personal leave provisions may present difficulties for management. Arbitrators are mindful that a consistent interpretation of personal leave provisions is necessary to the efficient operation of an organization.[34] However, in situations where management suspects that employees are abusing personal leave provisions, the burden for proving an alleged abuse rests with management.[35] If management has relinquished its discretionary authority over the granting of personal leave, when an employee asserts certain contractually approved reasons for requesting leave, the only recourse management has left is to obtain information regarding abuses after permission for taking leave has been granted.[36]

Definition of immediate family. Not infrequently employees request personal leave to attend family events such as weddings, funerals, and occasions when honors are bestowed on individual members of the teacher's family. Disputes have developed over how closely related the family member must be in order to warrant a personal leave.

A typical dispute involving the definition of immediate family concerns a request to attend a family event involving relatives related to the grievant by marriage. Most agreements that attempt to define the phrase "immediate" include only blood relatives and/or relatives and other persons who are residing in the same household as the employee.[37] If the contractual agreement does not attempt to define the phrase "immediate family," the outcome of the grievance is likely to rest on the past practices of the parties involved.[38,39]

SABBATICAL LEAVE

A primary source of grievances has been questions over employees' receipt of fringe benefits while on sabbatical leave. Another frequent issue has centered on the extent to which management's discretion was curtailed by the sabbatical leave provision. The application of contractual qualifications for determining an employee's eligibility for sabbatical leave has been a third major source of grievances. This section also discusses several other grievances which are less frequently reported but which are worthy of consideration nevertheless.

RECEIPT OF FRINGE BENEFITS

When a teacher is granted a salary while on leave, shall the amount of that salary be determined by the policies in force when the initial permission for leave is granted, or shall the policies in force during the period of the leave be controlling? In two separate grievances, arbitrators held that teachers should receive the salaries in force during the period of the leave. In both situations, the change in policies between initial permission for leave and the period of time on leave involved an increase in salary benefits.[40]

In a different situation, the contractual agreement stated that teachers on sabbatical leave would not lose any "emoluments of value." The arbitrator ruled that the provision was not intended to apply to salary credit which a teacher would have received for an extracurricular assignment she would have held if she had not taken a sabbatical leave. The application of the provision was limited to salaries received by individuals in their regular teaching appointments alone.[41] In another case, the language of the contract stated that individuals on sabbatical leave were to "receive all benefits as if [they] were actually teaching." Testimony at the arbitration hearing also showed that it was the intention of the parties to protect a teacher's earnings. In light of the evidence, the arbitrator held that a department chairman who had been granted sabbatical leave should be paid on the basis of the salary index for department chairpeople and not some lower index.[42,43]

However, in a different case the arbitrator was persuaded that a teacher was not entitled to have sick leave accumulate while on sabbatical leave; the contract was silent on the issue and past practice had been that of not accumulating sick leave.[44] In a case where the contractual provision clearly stated that teachers were to be reimbursed for valid conference expenses while in the employ of the district, a teacher on leave was awarded expenses for attending an educational conference. It was determined that teachers on sabbatical leave were still in the employ of the district and should receive full salary and fringe benefits.[45] In the last case, an arbitrator held that contractual language stating that teachers employed for the full school year were to receive insurance benefits for a full twelve-month period applied to two teachers who had been given a year's sabbatical.[46]

EXTENT OF CURTAILMENT ON MANAGERIAL
DISCRETION

When a school board enters into a contractual agreement that establishes a minimum quota of teachers to be granted sabbatical leaves, providing there are qualified applicants, a school board is contractually bound to budget funds for those sabbatical leaves.[47] Under the conditions just stated, sabbatical leave is not an "illusory benefit." The school board has a definite responsibility to set aside funds for leave requests that meet contractual requirements.[48]

An arbitrator refused to honor a school board's claim of budgetary shortages as a valid reason for denying sabbatical leaves. He pointed out that the school board could evade any economic commitment agreed to in negotiations merely by stating no funds were available.[49,50] Attempts on the part of a school board to unilaterally lower contractually established quotas have not been upheld by arbitrators.[51] The burden of proof that a valid reason exists for not honoring a sabbatical leave provision containing firm quotas rests with the school board.[52]

Under any of the following conditions, a school board retains its discretion to grant or not to grant sabbatical leaves:

1. where the mention of quotas is absent from the contractual agreement[53]
2. where the agreement uses specific discretionary language when referring to the granting of leaves[54]
3. where contractual language requires only that school boards give "consideration" to granting sabbaticals[55]
4. where contractual language explicitly permits the school board to reject any and all applications.[56]

THE FUNCTION OF CONTRACTUAL QUALIFICATIONS

Qualifications for sabbatical leave which are incorporated into the language of the leave provision serve three valid functions. First, qualifications may be used by the school board to deny an application for sabbatical leave.[57] Second, the presence of specifically stated qualifications in the leave provision may serve to assure an applicant of his or her right to a sabbatical leave when an application meets the qualifications specified.[58] Third, when qualifications are included in a leave provision, generally neither party is able to add to or subtract from the qualifications mentioned.[59]

SECONDARY ISSUES

The following issues have been reported with less frequency than those previously covered in this section.

Identification of the authorizing agent. Where a contract recognized the superintendent to be the *authorizing* agent for sabbatical leaves, the school board could not overrule his decisions.[60] In a case where the contract recognized the superintendent to be the *recommending* agent, the school board was free to follow or reject the superintendent's recommendations.[61]

Effect of state laws. An arbitrator determined that a school board did not have legal jurisdiction to grant sabbatical leave in view of a state law suspending all leaves of absence for one year.[62] Another arbitrator held that whether or not a state law suspending sabbatical leaves is controlling depends on the presence of permissive or mandatory language in the contractual agreement.[63]

Effect of bargaining unit membership. Where eligibility for sabbatical leave was defined in terms of membership in the bargaining unit, a school board could not grant leave to a nonunit member and then decrease the bargaining unit quota.[64] When eligibility was inclusive of all bargaining unit members, noncertificated members could not be excluded from taking sabbatical leaves.[65]

Expiration of the contractual agreement. Expiration of a contractual agreement was not a valid reason for refusing to grant sabbatical leaves.[66]

INSURANCE COVERAGE

One significant issue on the subject of insurance coverage has been related to increases in insurance rates and whether or not the employer is obligated to increase the school district's contribution. In addition, there has been the issue of whether coverage began with the signing of the collective bargaining agreement or with some other date such as the beginning of the school year. Another area of contention involves the employer's right to unilaterally make changes in insurance coverage so as to decrease or reduce the quality of coverage. Arbitration disputes have occurred with regard to the consequence that employment status (such as full-time or part-time) has on eligibility. In addition, arbitrators have dealt with the issue of determining management's right to limit an employee's choice of insurance plans.

EMPLOYER CONTRIBUTIONS

Most arbitration cases concerned with employer contributions have occurred when the insurance carrier increased the premium cost. Some contracts provide that in the event of a change in insurance rates, management is obligated to notify employee representatives of the change. Failure to give notification has been viewed as a violation of the contract.[67] Another issue has been the question of whether or not management is obligated to renegotiate its share of the insurance premium. In a case where the collective bargaining agreement was silent, management was not required by the arbitrator to reopen negotiations when the carrier increased the premium.[68] Where contract language used phrases such as the school district will "pay in full" or where the contract has called for "100 percent" coverage, it has been held that the school district must absorb an increase in insurance premiums.[69,70] In a school district where the contract called for 100 percent coverage, the school board was unable to present persuasive evidence of a past practice of paying the full premium only on the least expensive of three medical plan options. The board was obligated to pay the full premium including increases on whichever option the employee had chosen.[71] When contract language specifies the employer's obligation in terms of a monthly contribution toward the cost of insurance, the school district is not likely to be required to pick up the increase.[72,73]

BEGINNING OF POLICY COVERAGE

The issue most commonly contested with regard to the beginning of insurance coverage is whether coverage will commence when the insurance policy is signed or when the collective bargaining agreement begins. In a case where the contract language was ambiguous with regard to the beginning date of policy coverage, an arbitrator was persuaded that coverage began from the date of the contract. His decision was based on evidence that during negotiations the superintendent had committed the school board to making coverage coincide with the onset of the contract. The school board had argued that coverage began when the insurance policy was signed with a carrier.[74]

In another case, the arbitrator held that the contract clearly stated that insurance coverage was to begin with the onset of the new contract period, which was July 1, and not October 1, as had been the situation under the old contract.[75] However, in yet another case, an arbitrator ruled that the coverage began in October rather than in June, when the collective bargaining agreement began. Testimony established evidence of a past practice of beginning coverage with the beginning of payment of the insurance premium. In addition, it was shown that teachers and union representatives were annually notified when insurance coverage would begin.[76,77]

CHANGES IN COVERAGE

Generally speaking, a school board cannot unilaterally change employees' insurance coverage so as to reduce the amount or quality of coverage employees enjoyed at the beginning of a contract period.[78] For example, an arbitrator did not uphold a school board's unilateral action in changing insurance carriers where a specific carrier had been named in the contractual agreement.[79] In another example, the arbitrator held that the school board violated the disability benefit provision when it unilaterally sought coverage that reduced disability benefits when the employee received other payments such as social security or pension payments.[80] In addition, a school board was determined to have no right to unilaterally withhold disability benefits from employees because they were receiving sick leave benefits.[81] Even when unilateral action is permitted, it is not unusual for the school board to be required to notify the union before a new policy changing insurance coverage can take effect.[82]

EFFECT OF EMPLOYEE STATUS

When an employee's employment status has changed — as when an employee is laid off, released, or retired — the question of entitlement to continued insurance coverage sometimes comes up. Part-time employment is another status category that has raised questions for arbitration.

Change in status. It has been a common practice to permit retired employees to continue their participation in insurance programs. However, in a case where the employee had not previously participated in the employer's retirement program, there was debate over whether the employee was entitled to be covered by the employer's life insurance coverage after retirement. The arbitrator ruled in favor of the employee, stating that if previous participation had been intended to be a condition of post-retirement benefits, the contract would have expressed such an intent.[83]

Most teacher contracts are for a nine-month period. However, insurance coverage is typically granted for a twelve-month period so as to give teachers continuous coverage during the summer months. When a teacher's contract is terminated at the end of a nine-month period, the issue may arise as to whether the teacher is still entitled to the additional three-month coverage normally granted to returning teachers. In one arbitration case where a teacher had been laid off at the end of nine months, the arbitrator held that the teacher was entitled to coverage for an additional three months. He noted that the collective agreement called for insurance premiums to be paid in their entirety and made no provision for exceptions.[84]

In another case, an arbitrator determined that a nonreturning teacher was entitled to insurance coverage since the collective agreement specifically stated that insurance benefits would be for twelve months for each teacher and dependents, without provision for exceptions.[85] However, in a case where the collective agreement specifically stated that insurance coverage was limited to the "current school year," the arbitrator held that a teacher who was released and later rehired was not entitled to continuous coverage during the summer months.[86]

Part-time employment. The question of the eligibility of part-time employees has been raised in arbitration cases. In a number of instances, not all members of the bargaining unit were presumed to be covered by insurance benefits. For example, in a school district where full-time employment had been a "historic" qualification for insurance coverage, an arbitrator held that part-time employees were not eligible for coverage; in that case the qualification of full-time employment was not specifically included in the coverage.[87] In another case, an arbitrator came to a different conclusion regarding the eligibility of part-time employees; he based his ruling on language in the preamble of the collective bargaining agreement which stated that the agreement covered all professional employees represented by the bargaining agent. No exclusions were mentioned in the contract.[88] In a case where substitute teachers were specifically excluded from insurance benefits but no mention was made of part-time employees, it was held that part-time employees were eligible.[89]

CHOICE OF COVERAGE

It has not been unusual for more than one insurance option to be available to employees. For example, individual and family medical options have been offered. In addition, certain types of insurance benefits have been provided with a choice of insurance carriers. Arbitration issues have developed when management has attempted to restrict an employee's benefit options.

For example, single teachers in one school district were denied the choice of having family coverage. An arbitrator held that the school administration could not go beyond the qualification criteria stated in the collective bargaining agreement. The agreement mentioned only two limitations: (1) coverage was limited to professional teaching personnel, and (2) an employee contribution of $3.90 per month would be assessed. The arbitrator directed the school administration to grant family coverage to all single teachers who wanted it and were willing to pay the specified amount. He was not persuaded that only single teachers with dependents or family should be eligible.[90,91]

In some situations, insurance options have not been identical in their coverage. Where school managers have attempted to "equalize" coverage by reducing benefits of one of the options, arbitrators have tended not to support management's actions. In one school district, teachers had a choice of two medical plans as agreed to in the collective bargaining agreement. One of the plans included life insurance coverage. Management attempted to "equalize" the plans by deducting the cost of life insurance from the pay of those who chose the medical plan with the life insurance coverage. The arbitrator held that management did not have the right to make the deductions.[92,93]

TUITION REIMBURSEMENT

Most arbitration issues arising from a tuition reimbursement provision have been related to the need to get prior administrative approval before a teacher is eligible for reimbursement. One set of issues has involved the use of contractually stated criteria for determining eligibility. The other set of issues has developed when no contractual criteria were provided.

In the absence of contractual criteria, one arbitrator held that the authorizing administrator had authority to use his own judgment.[94] In another case, the arbitrator noted the absence of contractually stated criteria, but also held that where a party has power it must exercise its power reasonably and in good faith.[95]

In a case where contractual criteria for determining reimbursement did exist, an arbitrator noted that the criteria must be applied consistently.[96] Contractually stated criteria function so as to restrict administrative discretion. Thus, in a case where the contract stated that courses approved for tuition reimbursement must be related to the teacher's field, the authorizing administrator was not free to reimburse teachers for courses not related to their field.[97]

Another set of issues growing out of the need to obtain prior approval for reimbursement has involved the presumption of obligations on the part of both the requesting teacher and the authorizing administrator. An arbitrator has held that a teacher who requests course approval must give the authorizing administrator complete and accurate information about courses.[98] Another arbitrator has held that the authorizing administrator is obligated to give timely notice of approval or disapproval so that a teacher has the information prior to registering for a course.[99] Even though a teacher has a right to know the authorizing agent's decisions prior to registering for courses, it has been held that registration prior to receiving authorization is not valid grounds for withholding authorization of course approval.[100]

SECONDARY ISSUES

The following issues have been reported with less frequency than those previously covered:

Courses required to hold positions. A New Jersey school district had established a policy that incumbent department heads were required to hold a state certificate qualifying them to supervise and evaluate certified personnel. An arbitrator held that the board was obligated by existing contractual language to pay tuition and other expenses of incumbent department heads. However, the board was not obligated to pay expenses of individuals who were applying to become department heads.[101]

In another school district, the contractual language between the school board and the teacher association obligated the board to pay for expenses of any teacher who was required by the school board of the state to take courses beyond the initial certificate. An arbitrator interpreted the language as requiring the board to pay for the courses a teacher needed to renew her standard five-year certificate.[102]

In a third case, contractual language stated that the school board was obligated to pay tuition expenses only when the board specifically requested an employee to take designated courses. An arbitrator interpreted the provision as relieving the board from paying for courses taken by an incumbent department head in order to meet certification requirements of the position. The arbitrator was not persuaded by the union's argument that the certification requirement for holding the position was tantamount to the school board's having made a request. The arbitrator gave the contract language its literal meaning, a specific request to a specific individual to take specific courses. In spite of his incumbent status, the grievant was not eligible for tuition reimbursement since he had not received a specific request from the school board.[103]

Effect of sabbatical leave. A school board was successful in persuading an arbitrator that it was under no obligation to pay a teacher tuition for a course taken while on sabbatical leave. Central to the school board's argument was the fact that the contract made no mention of payment of tuition during sabbatical leave. The board also persuasively argued that the section of the contract pertaining to tuition reimbursement applied only to teachers in full-time employment. The sabbatical leave clause and the provision for tuition reimbursement were held to be mutually exclusive sections of the contract.[104]

Advance payment for tuition. Under contractual language which stated that advances for tuition "may" be made to employees, an arbitrator upheld management's right to discontinue a practice of making advance payments. The fact that the practice of granting advance payments predated the existence of contractual language did not diminish management's right to unilaterally terminate the practice.[105]

SUMMARY

Running throughout this chapter on fringe benefits has been the issue of administrative discretion. The initial approach to answering questions about managerial discretion has been to examine the contractual language concerning fringe benefits. If an arbitrator could reach a decision through an examination of contractual language alone, there usually has been no need for other evidence regarding the extent of managerial discretion intended. However, if the contractual language was ambiguous or silent on the issue, other evidence has been taken into account. The past practices of the parties have often been cited by arbitrators to clarify the parties' intentions. Other forms of evidence used to indicate the intentions of the agreement include comparison of changes in contract language and testimony about discussions during bargaining sessions.

Generally speaking, with regard to the fringe benefits covered in this chapter, no employee has had an unqualified claim to a fringe benefit. Each benefit presumes a set of qualifications or criteria that has to be met by the employee before a benefit can be granted. For example, insurance benefits usually presume full-time employment; tuition reimbursement benefits typically presume that courses taken would be of benefit to the school district; and personal leave benefits frequently presume qualified emergency needs.

The existence of qualifications in contractual language gives an administrator a basis for granting or denying benefits. Contractual qualifications condition managerial discretion to some degree. The extent to which management's discretion is conditioned depends on the specific nature of qualifications listed in an agreement. For example, under personal leave provisions, employees have been granted leave to attend the funeral of a relative. If the provision is stated in general terms, management usually has more discretion in granting the benefit than if the provision specifically lists the relatives covered by the provision.

Beyond the specific qualifications and criteria that have been found in conjunction with benefits covered in this chapter, definitions of managerial discretion have been written in board terms. For example, a tuition reimbursement provision usually states that courses taken must be of benefit to the school district. However, even if a teacher wants to take courses that are of potential benefit to the school district, he or she can be refused the benefit if contractual language or past practice gives management the discretionary authority to do so. For example, contractual language which states that tuition reimbursement "may" be granted has been used by arbitrators to support greater administrative discretion than contract language stating that tuition reimbursement "shall" be granted when specific qualifications are met by the employee.

Whether or not specific contractual qualifications have been present or absent, the "common law" of contract administration has required that administrators apply qualifications for benefits in a nonarbitrary, noncapricious, and nondiscriminatory way. Even when an administrator has been permitted by contractual language to use his or her own standards, the "common law" expectations of contract interpretation have been applied by arbitrators in reviewing administrative actions.

NOTES

1. See *Government Employee Relations Report*, No. 574 (Washington: Bureau of National Affairs, 1974), p. X-9; *Government Employee Relations Report*, No. 631 (Washington: Bureau of National Affairs, 1975), p. X-11; *Government Employee Relations Report*, No. 653 (Washington: Bureau of National Affairs, 1976), p. X-5; *Government Employee Relations Report*, Reference File 81, RF-157 (Washington: Bureau of National Affairs, 1978), p. 1017.
2. See *Government Employee Relations Report*, No. 596 (Washington: Bureau of National Affairs, 1975), p. X-3; *Government Employee Relations Report*, No. 622 (Washington: Bureau of National Affairs, 1975), p. X-7.
3. See *Government Employee Relations Report*, No. 593 (Washington: Bureau of National Affairs, 1975), p. X-7.
4. *Highland Park (Michigan) Board of Education*, 14 AIS 7, Leon J. Herman, Arbitrator.
5. *Vestal (New York) Central Schools*, 18 AIS 10, Walter E. Oberer, Arbitrator.
6. *Rush-Henrietta (New York) Central School District*, 53 AIS 11, Jean T. McKelvey, Arbitrator.
7. *Board of Education of the Grandville (Michigan) Public Schools*, 3 AIS 9, Howard A. Cole, Arbitrator.
8. *Wadsworth (Ohio) Board of Education*, 87 AIS 1, Richard H. Siegal, Arbitrator.
9. *Highland Park (Michigan) Board of Education*, 14 AIS 7, Leon J. Herman, Arbitrator.
10. *Board of Trustees of the Community College District of the County of Macomb (Michigan)*, 33 AIS 32, Leon J. Herman, Arbitrator.
11. *City of Midland (Michigan) School District*, 35 AIS 20, Charles A. Rogers, Arbitrator.

12. *Milwaukee (Wisconsin) Area District Board of Vocational, Technical and Adult Education,* 61 AIS 16, Reynolds C. Seitz, Arbitrator.
13. *Negotiation Research Digest,* February 1972, p. 15.
14. See *Forest Hills (Michigan) Public Schools,* 24 AIS 8, Robert G. Howlett, Arbitrator; *Carrollton (Michigan) Board of Education,* 29 AIS 6, George T. Roumell, Jr., Arbitrator; *Springfield (Ohio) Public Schools,* 59 AIS 12, Wayne T. Geissinger, Arbitrator; *Norton (Massachusetts) School Committee,* 75 AIS 21, Edward C. Pinkus, Arbitrator; *Hillsboro (Oregon) Elementary School District No. 7,* 80 AIS 17, Carlton J. Snow, Arbitrator.
15. *Oscoda (Michigan) School District,* 37 AIS 19, E. J. Forsythe, Arbitrator.
16. *Town of Hempstead, Uniondale (New York), U.F.S.D. No. 2,* 22 AIS 23, Sidney L. Cahn, Arbitrator.
17. *Board of Education, School District 149 (Illinois),* 19 AIS 20, Martin A. Cohen, Arbitrator; *Norwell (Massachusetts) School Committee,* 2 AIS 18, Stanley Jacks, Arbitrator.
18. See *Vestal (New York) Central Schools,* 18 AIS 10, Walter E. Oberer, Arbitrator; *Unified School District No. 12 (Islip, New York),* 45 AIS 11, Josef P. Sirefman, Arbitrator; *Board of School Commissioners (Burlington, Vermont),* 60 AIS 16, Albert J. Hoban, Arbitrator.
19. *South Colonie (New York) Central School District,* 91 AIS 8, Elizabeth B. Croft, Arbitrator.
20. *Westwood Community Board of Education (Dearborn Heights, Michigan),* 19 AIS 7, George T. Roumell, Jr., Arbitrator; *Rush-Henrietta (New York) Central School District Board,* 36 AIS 12, Byron Yaffe, Arbitrator; *Shenendehowa (New York) School District,* 88 AIS 8, Rodney E. Dennis, Arbitrator.
21. *Bay Shore (New York) Union Free School District No. 1,* 75 AIS 19, Josef P. Sirefman, Arbitrator.
22. See also *Barnstable (Massachusetts) School Committee,* 65 AIS 19, Jerome S. Rubenstein, Arbitrator.
23. For a general discussion of the application of past practice, see Paul Prasow and Edward Peters, *Arbitration and Collective Bargaining: Conflict Resolution in Labor Relations* (New York: McGraw-Hill Book Company, 1970), pp. 78–121.
24. *South Colonie (New York) Central School District,* 91 AIS 8, Elizabeth B. Croft, Arbitrator.
25. See *Toms River (New Jersey) Board of Education,* 17 AIS 19, Benjamin H. Wolf, Arbitrator; *Reynolds (Pennsylvania) School District,* 48 AIS 6, Clair V. Duff, Arbitrator; *Bay Shore (New York) Union Free District No. 1,* 75 AIS 19, Josef P. Sirefman, Arbitrator; *M.S.A.D. No. 32 (Maine),* 78 AIS 21, Robert M. O'Brien, Arbitrator; *Wabash County (Indiana) School District,* 66 AIS 4, Robert E. Dunham, Arbitrator.
26. See *Clarkstown Central School District No. 1 (New York) Board of Education,* 17 AIS 2, Irving R. Markowitz, Arbitrator; *Washingtonville (New York) Central School, Board of Education,* 18 AIS 16, Max M. Doner, Arbitrator; *Clinton (Connecticut) Board of Education,* 27 AIS 16, John A. Hogan, Arbitrator; *Napoleon (Michigan) Board of Education,* 73 AIS 18, Harry N. Casselman, Arbitrator.

27. See also *Board of Education of the City of Flint (Michigan)*, 12 AIS 1, David G. Heilbrun, Arbitrator.
28. See *Syracuse (New York) Board of Education*, 48 AIS 5, Robert F. Koretz, Arbitrator.
29. See *Board of Education of the City of Grand Rapids (Michigan)*, 11 AIS 17, Alan Walt, Arbitrator.
30. *Madison (Connecticut) Boad of Education*, 55 AIS 5, Peter L. Adomeit, Arbitrator.
31. See *Algonac (Michigan) Community Schools, Board of Education*, 36 AIS 8, Ronald W. Haughton, Arbitrator.
32. See *Northport Board of Education, Union Free School District No. 4 (Nassau County, New York)*, 2 AIS 24, Milton Friedman, Arbitrator.
33. See *Marion (Indiana) Community Schools*, 80 AIS 19, George Jacobs, Arbitrator.
34. See *Red Bank (New Jersey) Board of Education*, 11 AIS 22, Irving Halevy, Arbitrator.
35. See *Stratford (Connecticut) Board of Education*, 71 AIS 12, James V. Altieri, Arbitrator.
36. See *South Colonie (New York) Central School District*, 91 AIS 8, Elizabeth B. Croft, Arbitrator.
37. See *Montgomery Township (New Jersey) Board of Education*, 65 AIS 9, Stanley L. Aiges, Arbitrator; *West Haven (Connecticut) Board of Education*, 48 AIS 11, Connecticut State Board of Mediation and Arbitration; *Illinois State University (Normal, Illinois)* 39 AIS 8, Neil M. Gundermann, Arbitrator.
38. See *Orion (Illinois) School District No. 223*, 80 AIS 10, Albert A. Epstein, Arbitrator.
39. See also *Wabash County (Indiana) School District*, 66 AIS 4, Robert E. Dunham, Arbitrator.
40. *Central School District No. 1, Harrison (New York)*, 9 AIS 4, Byron Yaffe, Arbitrator; *Bedford (New York) Public Schools, Central School District No. 2*, 39 AIS 5, George Nicolau, Arbitrator.
41. *Mohonasen (New York) Central School District No. 3*, 45 AIS 12, Sumner Shapiro, Arbitrator.
42. *Bellmore-Merrick (New York) Board of Education*, 51 AIS 3, Alfred H. Brent, Arbitrator.
43. See also *Trotwood-Madison (Ohio) Board of Education*, 62 AIS 4, Marian K. Warns, Arbitrator.
44. *Seaford (New York) Board of Education*, 57 AIS 2, James C. Hill, Arbitrator.
45. *Morris (New York) Central School Board of Education*, 58 AIS 12, James R. Markowitz, Arbitrator.
46. *Hopatcong (New Jersey) Board of Education*, 69 AIS 13, Robert L. Mitrani, Arbitrator.
47. See *Scotch Plains-Fanwood (New Jersey) Board of Education*, 73 AIS 24, Joseph P. Doyle, Arbitrator.
48. See *Belvidere (New Jersey) Board of Education*, 94 AIS 6, Stanley L. Aiges, Arbitrator.

49. *South Amboy (New Jersey) Board of Education,* 34 AIS 7, Jonas Aarons, Arbitrator.
50. See also *Board of Education U.F.S.D. No. 4 (New York),* 32 AIS 49, George S. Roukis, Arbitrator; *Tarrytown (New York) Board of Education,* 39 AIS 3, Eva Robins, Arbitrator; *Portland (Maine) School Committee,* 82 AIS 19, Herman Gadon, Arbitrator.
51. See *North Salem (New York) Board of Education,* 9 AIS 3, Milton Ruben, Arbitrator; *Westchester (New York) Community College,* 79 AIS 9, Sidney Sugerman, Arbitrator; *Putman Valley (New York) Central School District,* 79 AIS 11, Paul G. Kell, Arbitrator; *Delaware Valley (New York) Central School District,* 94 AIS 15, Daniel G. Collins, Arbitrator; *Kelso (Washington) School District,* 96 AIS 12, Michael H. Beck, Arbitrator.
52. See *Middletown (Connecticut) Board of Education,* 21 AIS 21, Harry B. Purcell, Arbitrator; *Board of Education of the Kent Intermediate School District (Michigan),* 33 AIS 27, David G. Heilbrun, Arbitrator.
53. See *Board of Education of the City of New York (New York),* 91 AIS 12, Monroe Berkowitz, Arbitrator.
54. See *Washingtonville (New York) Central School District,* 85 AIS 5, Woodrow J. Sandler, Arbitrator.
55. See *Malden (Massachusetts) School Committee,* 79 AIS 17, William J. Fallon, Arbitrator.
56. See *Grosse Pointe (Michigan) Public School System,* 46 AIS 1, George T. Roumell, Jr., Arbitrator.
57. See *Central Islip (New York) Board of Education,* 9 AIS 5, Daniel G. Collins, Arbitrator; *Seneca Falls (New York) Central School District No. 1,* 43 AIS 12, Irving R. Markowitz, Arbitrator; *Hempstead (New York) Board of Education,* 68 AIS 4, Bertram T. Kupsinel, Arbitrator.
58. See *Fairport (New York) Central School District,* 10 AIS 4, Irving R. Markowitz, Arbitrator; *Bridgewater-Raritan (New Jersey) Board of Education,* 91 AIS 23, Robert L. Mitrani, Arbitrator.
59. See *Board of Education of the City School District of North Tonawanda (New York),* 13 AIS 3, Irving R. Markowitz, Arbitrator; *Marcus Whitman Central School District (New York)* 13 AIS 8, J. D. Hyman, Arbitrator; *Bridgeport (Connecticut) Board of Education,* 70 AIS 13, Archibald Cox, Arbitrator.
60. *Bethpage (New York) Schools, U.F.S.D. No. 21,* 36 AIS 20, George Marlin, Arbitrator.
61. *The Warwick (Rhode Island) School Committee,* 53 AIS 4, Harry B. Purcell, Arbitrator.
62. *Hudson Valley Community College (New York),* 32 AIS 37, Robert G. Bowling, Arbitrator.
63. *Board of Education, Central School District No. 2, Bedford Public Schools (New York),* 32 AIS 25, Joel M. Douglas, Arbitrator.
64. *Middle Island (New York) School District No. 12,* 64 AIS 6, Daniel Kornblum, Arbitrator.
65. *Flint (Michigan) Board of Education,* 37 AIS 8, Alan Walt, Arbitrator.
66. *Board of Education, Port Washington (New York) School District,* 49 AIS 15, Jonas Silver, Arbitrator; *Central School District No. 1 of the Towns*

of Orangetown and Clarkstown (New Jersey), 67 AIS 11, Daniel G. Collins, Arbitrator.

67. *Seattle Community College Board of Trustees (Washington)*, 32 AIS 35, Robert A. Sutermeister, Arbitrator.

68. *Taylor (Michigan) School District*, 78 AIS 26, Richard L. Kanner, Arbitrator.

69. *Cupertino (California) Unified School District*, 78 AIS 11, Emily Maloney, Arbitrator.

70. *Pullman (Washington) School District No. 267*, 80 AIS 16, Richard B. Peterson, Arbitrator.

71. *Carle Place (New York) Board of Education*, 4 AIS 21, Eric J. Schmertz, Arbitrator.

72. See *Davison (Michigan) Community Schools*, 29 AIS 10, Harry N. Casselman, Arbitrator.

73. See also *Lafayette (Indiana) School Corporation Board of Trustees*, 71 AIS 23, Duane L. Traynor, Arbitrator.

74. *Board of Education, City of Chicago (Illinois)*, 12 AIS 7, Joel Seidman, Arbitrator.

75. *High Point (New Jersey) Board of Education*, 31 AIS 43, Robert L. Mitrani, Arbitrator.

76. *Board of Junior College District No. 515 (Illinois)*, 66 AIS 15, Herbert M. Berman, Arbitrator.

77. See also *Amity (Connecticut) Board of Education*, 46 AIS 2, James V. Altieri, Arbitrator.

78. See *Riverside (California) Unified School District*, 61 AIS 17, Orrin B. Evans, Arbitrator.

79. *Arlington County (Virginia) School Board*, 41 AIS 6, John N. Gentry, Arbitrator.

80. *Bloomfield Hills (Michigan) School District*, 51 AIS 15 James T. Dunn, Arbitrator.

81. *Monticello (New York) Board of Education*, 58 AIS 7, George Nicolau, Arbitrator.

82. See *Ballston Spa (New York) Central Schools*, 85 AIS 13, Thomas N. Rinaldo, Arbitrator.

83. *Wayne State University (Michigan)*, 33 AIS 24, Alan Walt, Arbitrator.

84. *Scranton (Pennsylvania) School District*, 75 AIS 5, Morrison Handsaker, Arbitrator.

85. *Mona Shores (Michigan) Board of Education*, 40 AIS 1, Harry N. Casselman, Arbitrator.

86. *Beecher (Michigan) Board of Education*, 11 AIS 15, E. J. Forsythe, Arbitrator.

87. *Midland (Michigan) City School District*, 26 AIS 7, James R. McCormick, Arbitrator.

88. *Marcus Whitman Central School District (Rushville, New York)*, 48 AIS 1, Carr W. Magel, Arbitrator.

89. *Fort Madison (Iowa) Community School District*, 86 AIS 7, Thomas P. Gilroy, Arbitrator.

90. *Providence (Rhode Island) School Committee,* 80 AIS 20, William B. Post, Arbitrator.

91. See also *Hainesport (New Jersey) Board of Education,* 77 AIS 14, Maurice C. Benewitz, Arbitrator.

92. *School District of the City of Ferndale (Michigan),* 21 AIS 20, Robert G. Howlett, Arbitrator.

93. *Swartz Creek (Michigan) Community School District,* 29 AIS 1, David G. Heilbrun, Arbitrator.

94. *Manchester (New Hampshire) Board of Education,* 75 AIS 7, Abraham J. Siegel, Arbitrator.

95. *Mountainside (New Jersey) Board of Education,* 39 AIS 1, Jonas Aarons, Arbitrator.

96. *Bloomfield (Connecticut) Board of Education,* 76 AIS 17, Alfred B. Clark, Arbitrator.

97. *Morris Hills Regional District (New Jersey),* 48 AIS 9, Daniel House, Arbitrator.

98. *Spencer-East Brookfield (Massachusetts) Regional School Committee,* 51 AIS 7, Lawrence T. Holden, Jr., Arbitrator.

99. *Frankford (New Jersey) Township Board of Education,* 74 AIS 23, Daniel G. Collins, Arbitrator.

100. *Howell Township (New Jersey) Board of Education,* 37 AIS 20, Jonas Aarons, Arbitrator.

101. *Willingboro (New Jersey) Board of Education,* 91 AIS 5 Samuel Ranhand, Arbitrator.

102. *Madison (Wisconsin) Area Board of Education No. 4,* 80 AIS 3, Thomas L. Yaeger, Arbitrator.

103. *East Brunswick (New Jersey) Board of Education,* 71 AIS 4, Meyer Drucker, Arbitrator.

104. *Lower Camden County (New Jersey Regional High School District No. 1,* 77 AIS 7, Max M. Doner, Arbitrator.

105. *School District of Cheltenham Township (Pennsylvania),* 83 AIS 20 J. Joseph Loewenberg, Arbitrator.

Index